RAQUETTE LAKE

A Time to Remember

Ruth Timm

North Country Books, Inc.
18 Irving Place
Utica, New York 13501-5618

Raquette Lake
A Time to Remember

ISBN 0-932052-63-0

Library of Congress Cataloging-in-Publication Data

Timm, Ruth, 1925-
Raquette Lake.

Bibliography: p.
Includes index.
1. Raquette Lake Region (N.Y.)—History. 2.
Raquette Lake Region (N.Y.)—Biography. I. Title.
F127.H2T56 1989 974.7'52 89-12306
ISBN 0-932052-81-9

Published by
North Country Books, Inc.
Publisher—Distributor
18 Irving Place
Utica, New York 13051-5618

Dedicated
to
Cathy

TABLE OF CONTENTS

ACKNOWLEDGEMENTS

To write a book of this nature entails many years of research. It also requires a love of the area and a sense of belonging. For these emotions I am deeply indebted to my family. My husband Al, introduced me to Raquette Lake, and brought me here to reside; my sons, Greg and Rich, who taught me to love Raquette, and my native-born grandchildren, Tina, Bob and Heather, who have helped make me a part of this hamlet's history.

In addition to numerous manuscripts, maps, pamphlets, magazine and newspaper articles listed elsewhere, data on people and events of the early years has been obtained from persons living then or from their descendants.

As with any information depending upon one's memory, individuals are prone to remember similar events and people in different ways. I have taken precautions to avoid myths or incorrect information by attempting to verify facts whenever possible. Unfortunately there may be some who will view parts of these writings as false or incorrect. There may also be omissions of names or events some would deem essential to this volume. Because of limited space or lack of information, this was unavoidable.

I am indebted to many erstwhile strangers, as well as neighbors and friends for valuable information and help in making this book possible. Effort has been made to acknowledge such assistance in the proper place. Any omission to do so is an unintentional oversight.

Special recognition must be given to Charles Henry Carlin who urged me to write Raquette Lake's history. His contributions of the diary and notes of his father, Frank Carlin, as well as his own memoirs were invaluable. It is with deep regret he did not survive to view the fruition of this endeavor.

Appreciation is extended to Jim Bird for his "above and beyond" prompt attention to the author's numerous requests to seek out and provide accurate information.

Edna Lanphear Colligan* and Rowena Roblee Bird have been consultants from the beginning, verifying facts throughout the two years of writing and rewriting of the manuscript. Their assistance is gratefully acknowledged.

Gratitude is also extended to those whose names follow, some of whom are deceased (*). Without their source of data, this publication would have been impossible. Ted Aber, Libby Adelman, Cleo Aldous, Bertha Baltz, Horace Bartow, Richard and Jean Beckingham, Helen Bird, Marion Bird, Norton Bird, Jr., Herbert and Margaret Birrell, Jim and Mary Blanchard, John Paul Blanchard, Betsy Booth, Fred Burke,* Tom Callahan,* Frank Carlin,* Rev. Ralph M. Carmichael, Madeline Fallon Case, Dayt and Theresa Cleaveland, Helen Collins, Janet Collins, Bertha Conley,* Eunice and Jay Cummings, Margaret Collins Cunningham, Freda and Walter Czarniawski, Carol and Gene Darling, Mary* and Bruce Darling, Mary Dillon,* Dennis Dillon, Jr.,* Mildred Dillon, James Dillon, Jan and Bob Egenhofer, Robert Morley Evans, Constance Finnegan, Shirley and Kurt Forsell, George and Marguerite Fuge, Deborah Fuge, Frances Fulton, Katherine Beals Garlipp, Mabel B. Garvin,* Patricia Gauthier, Tev Goldman, Gerald Halsband, Rosemary and George Hardin, Francis Clough Havinga, Marion Holmes, Father Kirk Howland, OFM, Lee G. Irving, David Inman, Roy Irving, Father Marcian Kandrac, OFM,* Father Paul Knapp, OFM, Dr. H. Kirschenbaum, Doris and Frank Lamphear, Edgar and Anne Lamphear, Donald and Betty Langham, Gerald and Mary Lanphear, Richard Lauterbach, John Leach, Jr., Father Robert Leahy, OFM, Naomi Levine, Walter W. Linck, George and Lucille* Loriot, Karen Lux, Doris and Glenn Martin, Nancy Madden, J.A. Mallenckrodt, Reuben Mick,* Jennifer Markworth, Gary McChesney, Doreen Pelletier Murphy, Margaret Norris, Thomas Norris, Phyllis Parsons, Ellen Lewis Parisot, Joseph Payne, Louise Porter Payne, Joseph Pelletier,* Gerald

Pepper, Rachel and Roderick Phinney, Donna and Dean Pohl, Bruce Risley, William Rivet, Morgan Roderick, Dr. Mira Rothenberg, Betty Dillon Schaufler, Francis Seaman, Dr. Zev Spanier, Robert and Betty* Tyler, Ethel Tripp, Beatrice and Harry Waldron, Emma Lou and Howard Waldron, Maurice and Betty Waldron, Freda Becker Westfall, Helen and Edwin Wires, Ernest Wood, Prentice Wood and Isabella Worthen.

PREFACE

The Adirondacks have been the subject of many books. Authors who have included the Raquette Lake area wrote of Durant and his Great Camps, of colorful men such as Alvah Dunning and Rev. Murray, and almost always of the railroad and steamboat era. Few, if any, have written of the pioneers who settled Raquette Lake before Durant chose the area as his retreat for the "rich and famous."

Little mention has been made of the men and women who built and served the camps, ran the railroad and steamboats, remaining after the "Golden Age" to maintain the area so rich in history and so in much demand for recreation.

This volume is a continuation of the early history of the region following that written by past historians whom I have taken the liberty of quoting throughout the book. History is an unending chain of time and events. What is written here covers the changing times of Raquette Lake. Each section covers the subject matter from inception to the year 1986.

The intent is to introduce newcomers to the area's history and to reopen an interest in the past to all who have been a part of it. When the last page is read, it will not be the end of the story - for today's events will remain as the history of tomorrow.

CHAPTER I

EARLY HISTORY

TOTTEN AND CROSSFIELD PURCHASE

In the 1760's, land speculators from New England and New York had great plans for making a fortune from huge land purchases in the Adirondacks. At that time unclaimed lands in the state belonged to the Indians and the white man had to purchase from them. The Crown, however, saw to it that Indian title had to pass through it first, then to the white man, allowing the Crown to collect large fees for its service.

Early in 1771, Joseph Totten and Stephen Crossfield arrived in Albany to purchase a triangle of land in the Central Adirondack region, sight unseen. They estimated the tract to contain 800,000 acres. In fact, it actually contained 1,115,000 acres. Its northern line ran from Keene Valley to the west, and to the south of Cranberry Lake including Raquette, Blue Mountain and Indian Lakes, Lake Pleasant and others. History relates that, although their names were written into every deed issued for land in the years to come, the responsible parties were not Totten and Crossfield. It was believed Totten and Crossfield were front men for other New York entrepreneurs including Alexander Macomb, who later became one of the largest purchasers of lands in the Crossfield grant.

Macomb, son of an Irish emigrant, had grown rich in the fur trade in Detroit. Much of his knowledge of northern New York was gained while traveling back and forth along the Saint Lawrence River pursuing his occupation. Being more knowledgeable than others who had never been in the area, he was in a position to influence some men to purchase land for speculation. Six months after the first patent was issued in 1792, Macomb found himself in great trouble and almost bankrupt. He was forced to sell some of his acquisitions. However, the entire area of more than 5,000 square miles conveyed by patent between 1792 and 1798 issued by New York State to Alexander Macomb was and is still known as "Macomb's Purchase."

On April 10, 1771, Joseph Totten and Stephen Crossfield "petitioned" His Excellency, the Right Honorable John, Earl of Dunmore, Captain-General and Governor-in-Chief of the Province of New York for "a certain tract of land" (referring to the aforementioned tract containing an estimated 800,000 acres).

That same year, on June 7, the petition was read at a council meeting held at Fort George in the City of New York and permission was granted to purchase the land from the Indians, as required by law. That same day, Totten and Crossfield met with the Indians at Johnson Hall in Johnstown. In the presence of Governor Tryon and interpreter John Butler, the purchase was consummated for the sum of 1,135 pounds.

On April 21, 1775, a request was submitted by letter from Governor Tryon to the Crown for a patent for the same acreage. Although the land had been sold by the Mohawks for 1,135 pounds, about four acres for a penny, the Crown asked 8,774 pounds for acting as intermediary in the transfer of title.

The Totten and Crossfield purchase set a pattern for later land deals. The new purchasers planned to subdivide the land into fifty townships and to sell at a profit. They ordered an immediate survey which is said to be the first survey of the area and the first exploration of a large part of it.

With the beginning of the Revolutionary War, all land in New York reverted to the state and, by the end of the war, the impoverished State of New York (with a debt of $1,675,575) was anxious to sell land to raise money. When Totten and Crossfield repetitioned the state on May 9, 1785 asserting claim to the patent, the state readily granted the petition.

Among the subsequent patentees of the Totten and Crossfield Purchase was Robert G. Livingston who acquired Township 40 in 1786.

Professor Farrand N. Benedict, a teacher of math at the University of Vermont, first visited the Adirondacks in 1834.

Encouraged by William Coventry H. Waddell, a New York businessman who suggested that scientific exploration of the wilderness had never been made, Benedict (also an engineer and surveyor) made calculations of the altitudes of the mountains and mapped possible dams and canals to drain water of the upper Raquette River into the Hudson River instead of the St. Lawrence. This would have allowed lumber companies to float logs from Blue Mountain Lake, Raquette Lake and Long Lake to sawmills on the Hudson and assure the loggers that there would always be a reserve of water to drive their logs when the waters of the Hudson were at a low level during certain times of the year.

During this period Benedict gained large parcels of land throughout the Adirondacks and by 1845 owned all of Township 40, including Raquette Lake. Eventually, property was allowed to revert to the state by tax default. Later it was acquired from the state by such men as the Bennetts, Durant and others who settled Raquette Lake.

ORIGIN OF THE NAME "RAQUETTE LAKE"

Sir William Johnson arrived in America from Ireland in 1738. He came to manage his uncle's property in the Mohawk Valley, twenty-five miles west of Schenectady on the south bank of the Mohawk River. Eventually, Johnson was able to purchase 4,000 acres west of Fort Amsterdam where he built Fort Johnson, and erected a store and a mill on the premises.

He set up a trading post for his few white neighbors and the Indians. Through the years he became a very powerful man having great influence over the Indians, thereby gaining prestige with the Crown.

A son, John, was born to Sir William and his wife Catherine (Weissenberg). The boy was sent to study in England and, upon his return to Fort Johnson, became almost as influential as his father. Sir William died in 1774.

During the American Revolution, Sir John persuaded the Mohawks and Senecas to side with the English. In May 1776 he fled to Canada from Johnson Hall with a few of his followers. The route they chose took them through Raquette Lake (then unnamed) north to Canada.

As the story goes, when they started their trip there was snow in the woods necessitating the use of snowshoes. However, upon reaching the lake, they were overtaken by the spring thaw forcing them to abandon their snowshoes. They piled them together, leaving them on the shore of South Inlet where they had set up camp. Traces of the snowshoes were found years later. Thus came the name *Raquet* (French for snowshoes) Lake.

Although this has been the accepted legend, there have been several other interesting theories.

In *The Hudson*, speaking of Raquette Lake, author Lossing says: "Around it the Indians, in the ancient days, gathered on snowshoes, in winter, to hunt the moose then found in large droves; and from the circumstances they named it *Raquet*, the equivalent in French for snowshoe in English. This is the account of the origin of its name given by the French Jesuits who first explored the region."

Referring to the above theories, Donaldson, in his *History of the Adirondacks* states, "Setting aside all minor objections to this general theory of origin it assumes that the lake was named before the river. This assumption not only violates the natural and usual course of geographical events but is documentarily contradicted by the evidence of early maps and gazetteers, which indicate they named the Raquet River long before they did the lake."

Another theory mentioned by Donaldson is ". . . the Indian name for river was Ta-Na-Wa-deh, meaning 'swift water.' Easily extended to mean 'noisy water,' with an explanation following that the river was called *Raquet* because of the noise it made. . ."

Donaldson further states, "The most authentic and plausible solution of the problem is given by Dr. Hough in his *History of St. Lawrence and Franklin Counties*. He says the name was suggested by the shape of a morass or wild meadow at the mouth of the river, and was applied to it by a Frenchman named Parisein, in the early days of French occupancy. Later the lake was named after the river."

Spellings in various books and documents have been Raquet, Racket and Racquette Lake. An accurate date or reason for the permanent change to Raquette Lake has not been discovered. However, on February 2, 1889, an official application was made to the Postmaster General requesting a Post Office in the area, the proposed office was to be called "Raquette Lake."

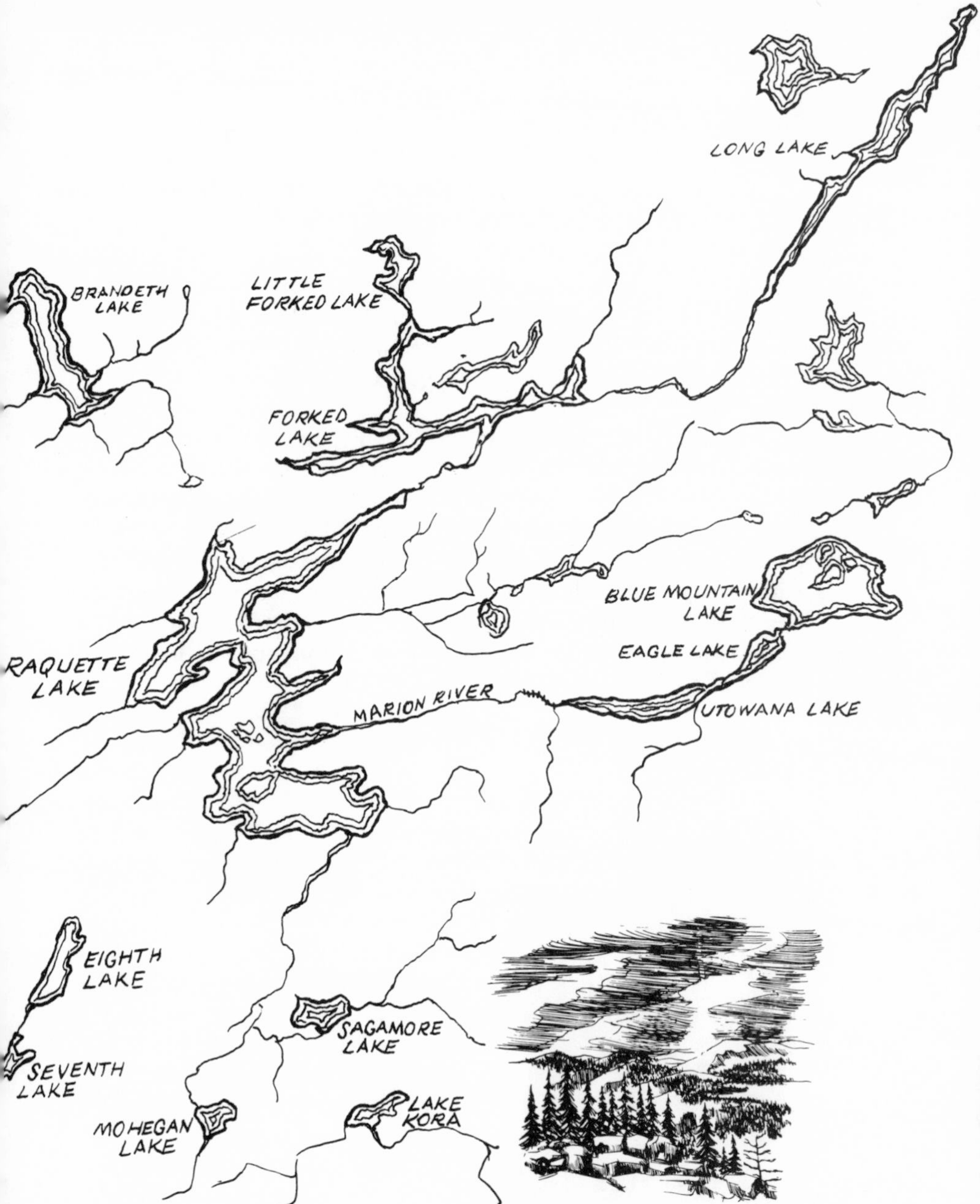

RAQUETTE LAKE

In the Adirondacks

GEOGRAPHICAL DESCRIPTION

Seventy miles northwest of Lake George and seventy-five miles northeast of Utica lies Raquette Lake, the largest lake in the Central Adirondacks. It is also the fourth largest of all Adirondack Lakes, following Lake George, Great Sacandaga and Cranberry.

The particular charm of Raquette Lake lies in the varied scenery due to the irregular shoreline, 99 miles in extent (although the lake's approximate length in five miles and width is three) and in the number of wooded islands which dot its surface. The shoreline is mostly bold and rocky, with forest extending down to the water's edge throughout much of its length. Here and there are some fine stretches of sandy beaches including Golden Beach, which is probably the most outstanding beach in the Adirondacks.

CHAPTER II

EARLY INHABITANTS AND THEIR DESCENDANTS

BEFORE THE INDIANS

One may assume from Donaldson's *The History of the Adirondacks* that Raquette Lake was inhabited long before the Indians. Referring to Alvah Dunning's camp, he wrote, "This second home on Osprey Island was built at the foot of a big cedar, three feet in diameter. Once during a severe storm Alvah noticed that the side of his shanty was lifted several inches every time the big tree swayed in the gale. When the wind subsided, he cut down the dangerous tree and dug up the roots. Under them he found a bed of coals, which seemed to indicated an ancient focus or hearth. He discovered the shards of three earthen pots, which must have been of great antiquity, because the tree proved to be between four and five hundred years old. Alvah gave these interesting relics to Dr. Arpad G. Gerster of New York . . . to whom I am indebted for the facts concerning them." Continuing, Donaldson states Dr. Gerster also informed him that, near the Brown's Tract Inlet shanty, Alvah found other "finely decorated bits of pottery, and a very beautiful ax of greenish stone. All of which tends to confirm the theory, advanced by some historians . . . that these woods once housed a prehistoric race whose skill in the rude arts exceeded that of the Indians."

Other varied accounts indicate Indians did in fact visit and reside at Raquette Lake before and after the white man came.

William L. Wessels in his *Adirondack Profiles* wrote, "Mohawk Indians claimed and used areas of the Adirondacks covering in 'a large measure' areas of Wells, Lake Pleasant, Long Lake, Blue Mountain, the Fulton Chain and Raquette Lake. They used the areas as private hunting grounds, labeling the area 'Couchsachrage' meaning Beaver Hunting Grounds."

History relates that Indians often left their homes to go forth in the wilderness searching for game and good fishing. The town of Long Lake, of which Raquette Lake is a part, takes credit for having an Indian, Mitchell Sabattis, as its first settler.

Joel T. Headley describes Indian Point on Raquette Lake in his book, *In the Adirondacks*, "so called because there was once an Indian settlement upon it."

Ernest Wood of Eagle Bay (grandson of Jerome Wood, the first white child born on Raquette Lake) tells of Indians being on Indian Point in the early 1850's.

In a letter from Constance Finnegan of Esperance, New York (a granddaughter of Jerome Wood) she mentions Jerome's Uncle William being with Chief Uncas (the Indian Chief written about in *The Last of the Mohicans*) when the chief was ambushed and killed. The two were canoeing near the banks of the narrows at First Lake, "when a man stepped out of the woods and fired a gun, shooting the chief in the back, killing him."

Another verification of Indians frequenting Raquette Lake stems from the existence of two candleholders made by Indians after 1879, while they were staying at Sucker Brook Bay. The candleholders are owned by Rosemary (Payne) Hardin and her brother, Sid Payne, who still maintain camps in Sucker Brook Bay on land once owned by their ancestor, "Old Billy" Payne. The holders were given to them by their mother, Louise Payne, who was born in Raquette Lake.

One candleholder is made from a small log that appears to have been slightly burned in a fire; a face is carved on both sides. Wooden beads are nailed around what appears to be the neck, and the top of an old kerosene lamp (the part that holds the wick) is nailed in place to hold a candle.

The other, a little taller, is also carved on both sides of a piece of wood with beads nailed around the neck. A square wooden base is nailed onto the bottom for a stand. Unlike the other holder, this one shows signs of being decorated with red, blue and white paint. The section that holds the candle appears to be made with one can placed inside another. The workmanship is extremely crude.

Rosemary Hardin relates a story of a time when some Indians were staying at the Payne Camp. Hannah, wife of Old Billy, never approved of the Indians trapping during their visits at Sucker Brook Bay. "One night when they were asleep, Hannah gathered all the trapping gear and disposed of it down the hole in the outhouse." It is unknown if the Indians ever returned to the Paynes or Raquette Lake after that.

THE FIRST WHITE SETTLERS

"Men have come to the Adirondack country with varied motives—for wealth, a career, a refuge, health, or inspiration. Some have just come for the summer."

"Some appeared mysteriously and left nothing but legends or old wives' tales. Others stood like one of the great white pines; when they left a place not easily filled. Many who have come stayed only a short time and left little or no impression."

"Most of these Adirondack visitors were transients and in time went their way. There were others who stayed on for years or for a lifetime."

Raquette Lake has been inhabited by men and women representative of all the above as described by William Chapman White in his *Adirondack Country*.

Because of the lack of roads in the area near Raquette Lake, the water provided the primary means of transport.

Traveling from Long Lake by old Indian trails until they reached Raquette Lake, two men became the lake's first white settlers. They were William Wood and Matthew Beach.

WILLIAM WOOD AND MATTHEW BEACH

William Wood, when about twenty-nine years of age, came to the area in or about 1830. He purchased 208 acres of land for $44 on May 11, 1833 from James Sergeant of Duchess County in Lot 38 between Nehasne and Lake Lila. Information has not been found as to the disposal of this property.

In 1837, Matthew Beach, a man of about fifty years of age, met

Wood, who was said to be suffering from "affairs of the heart" at that time. Beach's business had collapsed and he wanted to escape his creditors. The two decided to seek refuge at Raquette Lake, choosing a site on the west side of the lake known as Indian Point where they built a log cabin.

Beach and Wood temporarily left their seclusion to become politically involved. In 1839, they were elected assessors and inspectors of common schools in the town of Long Lake serving terms of one year each. Wood was also elected justice of the peace.

In *The Adirondacks*, Joel Headley wrote, "Indian Point, so called because there was once an Indian settlement upon it. Now two huts are standing there, looking like oases in the desert, occupied by two men, who dwell thus shut out from the civilized life."

As for Woods and Beach, he states, "Their leisure hours they spend in preparing the furs they have taken, and in tanning the deer skins, of which they make mittens. When the snow is five feet deep on the level, and the ice three and four feet thick on the lake, and not the sign of a human footstep anywhere to be seen, the smoke of their cabin rises in the frosty air like a column in the desert. . . . When a quantity of these mittens are made up, Beach straps on his snow shoes, and with his trusty rifle in hand, carries them out to the settlements, where they meet with ready sale."

In 1846, William Wood invited his brother, Josiah, known as "Si," and his wife, Martha (Alvert) to join him. The couple and their six children, traveled through the wilderness from Essex County to Raquette Lake.

Si elected to build his log cabin on the east side of the lake on the point to be known as Woods Point. On July 21, 1849 a son named Jerome was born with the distinction of being the first white child to be born at Raquette Lake.

The Wood brothers each had about forty acres, on which they raised not only berries and vegetables for themselves but enough to supply visiting sportsmen. Potatoes became their main crop and they were able to raise enough hay to winter their cattle.

The *Tupper Lake Free Press and Herald* published an account in the magazine *Spirit of the Times* in the fall of 1849. It was written of an Adirondack outing enjoyed by an Albany man identified only as the "sporting naturalist." During a trip from Long Lake through Forked to Raquette Lake, he and his guide,

Mitchell Sabattis, headed for the "hut of Old Beach, the hunter and trapper," to stay overnight. His description of Beach and his surroundings is as follows:

> Securing our boat, we walked to the hut, but a few rods from the edge of the lake and of such peculiar and original construction that few would imagine it at first sight a human habitation. On reaching the door we were met by the old man and his dog. The old white-haired veteran, stalwart and hearty whose step is still elastic and eyes bright as ever, was coarsely dressed, with true hunter-like air, and he advanced to welcome us, appeared indeed, no ordinary woodsman.
>
> Beach seated his guests at a crude table and plied them with fried lake trout, raspberries and maple sugar, coarse bread and tea, - all tasty to the hungry wayfarers except the tea, which the author excused on the ground that 'it could hardly be expected to be of superior quality in so remote a part of the backwoods.'
>
> Living with Beach was a hunter of some 38 years, whose name has escaped me, of tall and rather thin figure and not altogether prepossessing but who, in fact, is one of the best-hearted men to be met with - a real son of Nimrod and a fit companion for his elderly friend.

Logically, this friend had to be William Wood.
The article continued:

> A glance at the arrangements of our quarters would not here be amiss. The hut was scarcely more than a hunter's bark shanty of large size, excepting there was a huge fireplace at one end, and the roof was formed of three different thicknesses of spruce board - besides there being a rough floor to the 'building' - if indeed, I may use the term here. Two or three large chests were placed against the walls and from the rafter poles depended no small collection of odds and ends. A large ship glass was stuck between two pieces of bark overhead, and four rifles and a shotgun stood in a corner. A rudely constructed door with a large bolt attached to it served as protection against midnight intruders, and more than anything else, gave something of an air of semi-civilization to the whole. Imagine, then, a low wide bedstead covered with blankets of different hues and you then have all before you, as it was with us on the night of July 28th, 1849.

In addition, the naturalist elaborated on the external surroundings.

> I amused myself in looking about the 'grounds' in the immediate vicinity. I observed quite a respectable garden on the west side of the hut, in which were some 18 or 20 currant bushes, laden with ripened fruit, interspersed with red raspberry bushes and wild cherry trees - besides cabbages and potatoes in flourishing condition. On the other side of the hut, toward the lake, was a little patch containing pea vines, then in blossom. A shed connected with the hut presented within a goodly array of deer skins, barrels of salted 'lakers' and strings of the same kind of trout, smoked, while lying around were traps of all sizes, from such as were capable of holding a bear, to mink traps. In the neighborhood of the hut were about six acres in all, given to him many years ago - shortly after his removal from the waters of the Saranac, where he spent his earlier days.

William Wood suffered a serious injury in about 1850. While trapping on a bitter cold winter day, his legs suffered severe frostbite necessitating amputation. This was done by Indians who also nursed him back to health. They later made pads and snowshoes for his stumps and Wood continued to hunt, fish and trap.

Of Wood, Headley wrote, "The case of Mr. Wood should not pass unnoticed; as it furnishes an instance of man's capacity to overcome the serious deprivations rarely to be found . . . he has used his knees as a substitute for feet; and, strange as it may seem, he follows his line of traps for miles through the wilderness, or with rifle in hand, hops through the woods in pursuit of deer. He may be seen plying his oars, and driving his little bark over the lakes and along the streams; and when he comes to a portage, the upturned boat will surmount his head and take its course to the adjacent waters. His is a case that proves that there are instances in reality, "where truth is stranger than fiction."

Shortly after the accident, Wood and Beach had a disagreement, resulting in Wood moving to a hut a short distance from the original cabin. After residing at Raquette Lake for twenty years, William moved to Elizabethtown where he died in 1868.

About 1852 Beach gave his property to Amos Hough of Long Lake when Hough and his married son moved in with him. The arrangement was made with the condition the Houghs would maintain Beach for the rest of his life. A chain of title for the twenty-five acres on the end of Indian Point that Beach occupied is noted on an old abstract as follows:

Farrand Benedict and David Reed conveyed to Matthew Beach on September 31, 1849; Matthew Beach to Amos Hough on April 15, 1852; Amos Hough to Marshall Shedd on January 4, 1876 and Marshall Shedd to John B. Thacher on August 15, 1876. With the exception of several parcels sold by Ken Thacher in recent years, the property remains in possession of members of the Thacher family.

In *Lake George, Schroon Lake and the Adirondacks*, published in 1868, B.F. DeCosta notes that "about four miles of Raquette Lake and accessible by the Carthage Road lies Beach Lake, noted not only for its beauty, but for preserving the name of the first hunter and trapper who made his home on Raquette Lake at Indian Point . . ."

"In the autumn of 1861," he writes, "while endeavoring, after a visit to his relatives, to return to the forest home that he loved so well, Mr. Beach was overcome by the infirmities of age and finally died in the month of March, 1862, at the 'Lower Works' having arrived at the advanced age of more than 80 years . . . Beach's Lake was subsequently renamed Brandreth Lake."

THE JOSIAH WOOD FAMILY

In the census of 1850, Josiah (Si) Wood and his wife, Martha, were residing in Raquette Lake with their children: Martha 18, William 15, Alonzo 14, Cynthia 11, Harriet 10, Sophrona 7, Samantha 5, and Jerome 11 months. Another child, Amy, age 2, was listed.

Another son, Franklin, is listed as having been born in 1854. On an old map, he is listed as occupying property on Outlet Bay in the 1870's. The only other record of his presence in the area are two gravestones for his wife, Caroline, and daughter, Amy. They record the two died the same month in the year 1881 during the diptheia epidemic.

Samantha remained in the area for a period, guiding parties in the Blue Mountain region. William was one of the first men from

Hamilton County killed in the Civil War. With the exception of Alonzo and Jerome, no record has been found as to the activities of other members of the Wood family, leading to the assumption they may have left the area at an early date.

Alonzo Wood remained on Raquette Lake as a guide, residing on property previously occupied by Franklin Wood. He later moved to Inlet. While guiding a party down the Fulton Chain to "Arnold Clearing," he met his future wife, Ophelia, one of ten daughters born to Otis and Amy Barber Arnold. The couple were married in 1857 in Boonville.

Alonzo and Ophelia Wood are credited with building and owning the first authentic hotel on Fourth Lake, near the old Kenmore Hotel which is now a cottage colony.

The Woods offered kennels for their guests' pets as well as Quoits, Whist (a card game, forerunner to Bridge), bean bags and picnics as the camp activities and as a diversion for the ladies. Other hostelries in the North Country followed suit.

"Lon Wood's Camp" immediately attracted the more prosperous clientele of sportsmen. Alonzo was sought after for his expert knowledge of the woods and his ability to guide. Ophelia, later known as "Grandma Wood," gained affection and admiration from the increasing number of vacationers visiting the area.

The couple had five children: Alfred, Oscar, Josiah, Cornelia and Millie. The boys, following in their father's footsteps, grew to be excellent woodsmen and guides. The daughters assisted their mother tending to the needs of the guests. One daughter, Millie, married Milo Bull who owned and occupied a summer camp on the north shore of Fourth Lake now occupied by Fairview Lodge.

Mrs. Leo (Freda) Westfall of Old Forge remembers "Grandma Wood." As a child, her mother, Ida Becker, who with her husband, Fred, operated the Becker Camps, was friendly with Wood's daughter, Millie Bull.

"When visiting the Wood family," said Freda, "Grandma Wood always had some of her famous molasses cookies on hand. They were large and round with three raisins in the middle."

When Ophelia Wood died in 1912, her cookbook which included the recipe for the molasses cookies was inherited by her daughter, Millie Bull. Millie gave the recipe to her friend, Ida Becker, whose daughter, Freda Westfall, has consented to share it with the readers. The following is the recipe as recorded in the

Wood cookbook:

Molasses Cookies

> Mix and bake a few at a time as you want fresh ones. 1 cup molasses, 1 cup shortening, 1 cup brown sugar, 7/8 cup hot water with 1 scant teaspoon baking soda in it, 1 tablespoon ginger, 1 egg, salt and 4 cups flour. Mix very soft and place 3 raisins in the middle. (Mrs. Westfall said bake at 325° until done.)

Jerome Wood remained in Raquette Lake. Long Lake records indicate he married Rosellen Keller, daughter of David and Sarah (Dornberg) Keller of Long Lake on January 24, 1875. Rosellen, born November of 1851, was the niece of Betsy Dornberg who married Mitchell Sabattis (Indian guide and first settler of Long Lake).

Records further show Rosellen died at age 25, January 16, 1876, a year after their marriage. Wood is listed in the 1880 census as a boat builder living with a son, Edward J., age 4. It was later recorded the child died at age 6, September 4, 1881. Both mother and child are buried in the Wood plot in the Long Lake cemetery.

One day while shopping for supplies in Long Lake, Jerome purchased an umbrella on which he later found the name Hannah Hodgson, with an address in England. On a whim he wrote to her and she responded. He learned she worked in the umbrella factory and wrote her name on the handle of the umbrella that found its way into his hands. Subsequently they decided she should come to the North Country. In 1887 Hannah, a widow, left her daughter, Mary, with relatives in England and journeyed to America joining her brother who was living in Troy, New York. The next two years found her in Warrensburg and then at Raquette Lake where she was employed at the Antlers. On April 15, 1890 Hannah and Jerome were married in Luzerne, New York with the Reverend Father Brady officiating. A year later, a son, William,was born.

Jerome became interested in property on Big Island owned by Tom Bennett. Bennett had been trying, unsuccessfully, to grow strawberries which he intended to sell commercially. When it proved too difficult to transport the berries to distant clients without spoilage, he abandonded the idea. Records show that the property was sold by Bennett's heirs to Wood on October 23,

1896. The Woods settled on the island, starting "Island Camp." Jerome also served as caretaker and guide for North Point during Carnegie's ownership from 1902 until about 1913.

The February 21, 1901 edition of the *Warrensburg News* printed the following notice: "Mrs. Jerome Wood of Raquette Lake went to New York last week to meet her daughter, Mary Hodgson, who arrived from England on Friday on the steamer service. Miss Hodgson comes to this country to reside permanently with her mother at Raquette Lake."

On March 15, 1902, Mary married Freeland Jones of Raquette Lake.

William Wood grew up on Big Island. As a young man he married Alice Chubb from Lead, South Dakota who worked as a waitress for his mother at Island Camp. The couple continued to live on the island helping to run the establishment. Seven children were born to William and Alice Wood, all being raised on Big Island. They attended Raquette Lake School, traveling by boat when the water was free of ice. When the lake was beginning to freeze or ready to thaw, the family remained on the island since the lake was unsafe. When the lake was frozen they traveled by snowshoes or skates.

Helen Wood was the couple's first born in 1915. She grew to marry Donald Haischer, son of Florence and Francis Haischer, a school teacher at Raquette Lake School for a number of years.

Prentice (Print) Wood was born in 1917 and, after graduating from Raquette Lake High School, moved to Jericho, Long Island. He was employed as a cook in the "Maine Maid Tea Room" where he met his future wife who worked as a waitress. Alveida Kofoed of Seacliff, Long Island and Print Wood were married in 1939.

Print served in the Marines from 1943 to 1946 after which he returned to Raquette Lake for a short period, then moved back to Long Island. In 1948 the Woods returned to Inlet where they purchased and ran "Tobaggan Inn." In 1975 they sold the Inn moving to Marco Island, Florida where Print worked at the Country Club. Alvieda died August of 1984 and Print has "retired again" living in his home in Goodland, Florida.

Gertrude Wood, born in 1919, worked at Hunters Rest until about 1938 when she left Raquette Lake.

Ernest (Ernie) Wood was born in 1921. After graduating from high school he went to live with his brother, Print, in Long

EARLY CAMPS ON RAQUETTE LAKE

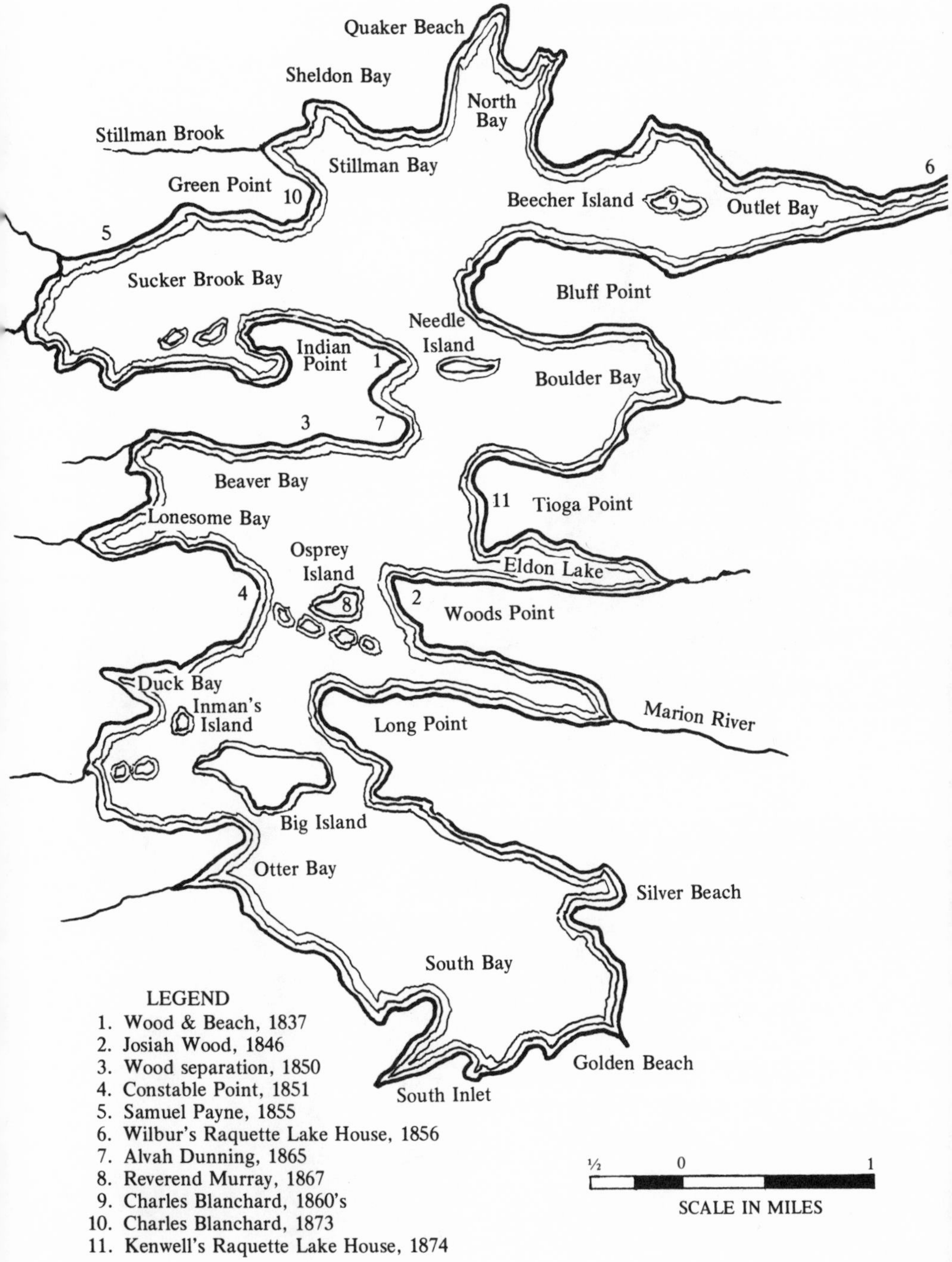

Quaker Beach
Sheldon Bay
North Bay
Stillman Brook
Stillman Bay
Green Point
10
6
Beecher Island
9
Outlet Bay
5
Sucker Brook Bay
Bluff Point
Needle Island
Indian Point
1
Boulder Bay
3
7
Beaver Bay
11
Tioga Point
Lonesome Bay
Osprey Island
Eldon Lake
4
8
2
Woods Point
Duck Bay
Inman's Island
Long Point
Marion River
Big Island
Otter Bay
Silver Beach
South Bay
Golden Beach
South Inlet
LEGEND
1. Wood & Beach, 1837
2. Josiah Wood, 1846
3. Wood separation, 1850
4. Constable Point, 1851
5. Samuel Payne, 1855
6. Wilbur's Raquette Lake House, 1856
7. Alvah Dunning, 1865
8. Reverend Murray, 1867
9. Charles Blanchard, 1860's
10. Charles Blanchard, 1873
11. Kenwell's Raquette Lake House, 1874
½
0
1
SCALE IN MILES

Author's Collection

Indians made these candle-holders while staying at Old Billy Payne's camp in Sucker Brook Bay on a hunting expedition. Circa 1880

Courtesy Frances Seaman
Jerome Wood, credited with being the first white child born on Raquette Lake, with his first wife, Rosellen Keller. Circa 1875.

Courtesy Ernie Wood
Jerome Wood's wife Hannah doing laundry for Island Camp. Circa 1900.

Courtesy Ernie Wood
Villiam Wood and guests at Island Camp 'ith their catch. Circa 1920's.

Courtesy Ernest Wood

Potatoes were one of the main crops grown on Island Camp. Here William Wood and his son Ernest harvest the yield. Circa 1939.

Courtesy Ernie Wood

Ernie Wood and friends portaging guide boat. Circa 1940's.

Uncle Alvah Dunning, his 84th year. 1899.

Author's Collection

When Charles Durant acquired Osprey Island from Dunning, he built Camp Fairview, shown here, on the western tip of the island. Circa 1885.

Island. In 1942 he joined the Marines, serving in Saipan, Tinian, and the Marshall Islands. Although Ernie is known as a hero, when asked about it he replies, "It was just a rotten job that had to be done!" After his discharge in November 1945, he stayed at Raquette Lake and worked as a caretaker at Eighth Lake campsite for one season. He later moved to Eagle Bay working as a plumber.

Ernie's son, Ernest, died in 1978 while attending Syracuse University. His daughters, Tammy and Bonnie have both been exchange students in various countries. Ernie resides in Eagle Bay.

Josiah Alonzo Wood, born in 1924, left the area at age seventeen when he joined the Marines.

Dorothy, born in 1931, went to school in Old Forge while living with her brother, Print. Later she married Walter Wharram. Both were killed in a motorcycle accident about 1982.

Gerald Edward, born 1935, served on submarine duty during the Korean War.

Ernie Wood remembers his grandmother "falling in love" with a floating "Japanese Tea House" owned by Horace Inman, a neighbor. "He used to rent it sometimes in the summer. It was shaped like a pagoda with a curved roof; the walls were made of bamboo and Japanese silk. Surprisingly it weathered real well. She paid $500 for it, a lot of money in those days. It was moved across the ice to the camp by a team of oxen - probably Asa Payne's."

Jerome Wood died April 4, 1928 and was buried in the Wood plot at the Long Lake cemetery. Hannah died about 1933; it is unknown if she is buried there. Among the marked graves lies one unmarked which could possibly be Hannah's resting place, but the fact has not been verified.

In 1940, Island Camp was recorded as Hannah Wood's Estate. The property went to the County Treasurer for non-payment of taxes, then was sold to Hamilton County by auction in 1941.

Lt. Donald Haischer, son-in-law of William and Alice Wood, purchased it in 1944. Two years later it was sold to Edward W. Fitzpatrick. Under a new deed it was assigned in 1950 to Dorothy V. Russell and E. W. Fitzpatrick. A deed of the same description of the aforementioned camp was also recorded in 1951 as being assigned solely to Dorothy Bess.

Ernie Wood believes his mother moved to Buffalo the early

part of World War II, returning to sell the homestead property to Roscoe Carlin. For about a year or so she lived on a houseboat near Carlin's Marina. In about 1945 or 1946 she moved to California where she died in 1950. Dorothy Bess eventually acquired that parcel also.

Sometime in 1957, Mira Rothenberg, a certified psychologist, and Dr. Zev Spanier, also a psychologist, along with Tev Goldsman, a mental health planner, contacted Bess about renting Island Camp. They were involved with The League School in Brooklyn, a day school for emotionally disturbed children. Their plan was to develop a summer camp on Big Island where the students could be exposed to the advantages of camp life. They rented Island Camp in the summer of 1958, renaming it "Pine Hill." The name met with resistance from associates and it was renamed "Camp Scenic." The program was run on an experimental basis with twelve students. With the exception of two students from The League School, the children were drawn from referrals or from patients of Spanier and Rothenberg. During this period the camp included the Japanese Tea House, five cabins, a two-story dormitory and a small house used by the "Russian Cossack" caretaker, "Ino."

The camp was held on Raquette Lake only one season. However, it was the beginning of the Blueberry Treatment Center in Brooklyn with summer programs conducted in Burlingham, New York.

In late 1966, George W. Linck, employed since 1947 as Associate Professor of Special Physical Education at West Point, purchased the two twelve-acre parcels of land from Dorothy V. Russell Fitzpatrick Bess. Upon purchase of the property, he transferred operation of his summer "Canoe Trip Camp," from an island on Little Sacandaga Lake, to Raquette Lake. The Raquette Lake camp was advertised as "Wilderness Canoe Trip Camp" opening its first session in 1967. It remained in operation until the end of the summer of 1978.

When purchased, the original homestead was partially caved in. The building "Ranger Cabin" at Island Camp, occupied by Bess, plus one large cabin and a smaller one were usable. The floating pagoda purchased by Hannah Wood was in bad shape and was renamed the "Wreck Hall." Used occasionally as a recreation building, the Lincks tried to have it restored, but raccoons had destroyed the curved eaves irreparably and in 1976 the building was demolished. A two-story log cabin was built by the Lincks which they used during summer sessions and hunting season.

Walter Wayne Linck, the fifth of six sons resided on the island from spring through the fall of 1978 before leaving for graduate school. He returned the spring of 1986 planning to occupy the island year 'round.

ADIRONDACK MURRAY

The person deserving credit more than anyone else in awakening an interest in tourism in the Adirondack Mountains is Reverend William Henry Harrison Murray, often referred to as "Adirondack Murray."

In the early 1860's, Murray, a young Connecticut clergyman, visited the Adirondacks on a fishing trip. While passing through Long Lake on the trip, Murray and his companions engaged the services of guide John Plumley, who accompanied them to Raquette Lake. Finding shelter and a spring on Constable Point, (purchased by William Constable from Farrand Benedict in 1851) they set up camp on the sandy beach. Plumley became Murray's regular guide as evidenced by this description by Wallace in his 1894 *Descriptive Guide of the Adirondacks*:

> Murray's favorite guide was 'Honest John Plumley' who he referred to as the prince of guides, patient as a hound and as faithful . . .

Wallace also states that Plumley had a deep affection for Murray as well:

> Mr. Murray is tall and athletic, being six feet, two and finely proportioned. And he is noble at heart and he is manly in form. No guides in his employ are ever ill-used or over-taxed; on the contrary, he never fails to consider their wants and comfort. If a hard days work is to be performed, he insists on taking the burden of it upon his shoulders. He invariably carries his own boat - a light, unique piece of workmanship, manufactured out of Spanish cedar, imported expressly for him. Many a time have I returned to camp, late in the evening, after a difficult trip, to find that

> Mr. Murray had, with his own hands, prepared for me a warm supper. God bless the man who is kind to guides!

In an introductory note by Warder H. Cadbury in a reprint of Murray's *Adventures in the Wilderness*, Cadbury suggests that when the group camped on Constable Point they stayed in a shanty which "may have been the one occupied in earlier summers by the celebrated artist, Arthur Fitzwilliam Tait and his friends. In 1862, Tait had done a painting of a group of sportsmen at Constable Point. The summer of 1866 one of Tait's friends wrote a letter which said that he "found such a mob of people (men, women and boys) on Raquette, that I do (did) not go to Constable Point. . . . One day (last Sunday) there were eighteen persons on Constable Point, and a minister among them performed church."

Reverend Murray chose a site on Osprey Island to erect his "Terrace Lodge." For a while the island became known as "Murray's Island." During the summers of 1867, 1868 and 1869, Murray and his friends camped there regularly using Alvah Dunning and Alonzo Wood as guides.

In 1868, Murray was invited to become Pastor of the Park Street Congregational Church of Boston, a very fashionable but conservative parish. He accepted the position. Meanwhile, he had written about his Adirondack experiences for a Connecticut newspaper and in April 1869 his sketches appeared in book form. The book, *Adventures in the Wilderness or Camp Life in the Adirondacks*, was an immediate success. Murray appointed himself an authority on almost anything connected with the outdoors. Where previous books told of adventures in the Adirondacks, Murray made an appealing presentation to those weary of city life and business pressures, their wives, avid sportsmen and even the ill, enticing them to the woods, where they too could find excitement, good sport, good health, and seclusion if that was their preference. It was probably the first Adirondack guidebook with instructions helpful for the north woods traveler. Unfortunately his enthusiasm clouded his judgment and his writings proved to be more fiction than truth.

By June 1869, the book had created a stampede to the woods. After all, that which was printed had to be true—for wasn't it written by a distinguished clergyman? All too soon the crowds flocking to the Adirondacks found, to their dismay, all was not as written. Those who read of the simplicity of his words, "You choose the locality which best suits your eye and build a lodge under unscarred trees, and upon a carpet of moss, untrampled by man or beast. There you live in silence, unbroken by any sound save such as you yourself make, away from all the business and cares of civilized life," did not expect to find primitive dwellings in place of the hotels they envisioned.

Others, ill and disheartened, rushed to the mountains after reading Murray's words: "Another reason why I visit the Adirondacks, and urge others to do so, is because I deem the excursion eminently adapted to restore impaired health. Indeed, it is marvelous what benefit physically is often derived from a trip to these woods. To such as are afflicted with that dire parent of ills, dyspepsia, or have lurking in their system consumptive tendencies, I most earnestly recommend a month's experience among the pines." Those with "consumptive tendencies" soon found they were not welcome and were forced to seek shelter elsewhere. Sportsmen too were disappointed when they found they could not "land two huge trout on one cast, catch deer by following them in a boat and jumping out and hanging on to the stub of a tail until the animal gave in, and shoot a high waterfall in a guide boat and live to write about it." The "distinguished clergyman" was soon labeled "liar" and his book a "hoax."

The Boston newspapers criticized Murray for his book and played up the fact that Murray was involved in projects "most improper for a Boston minister" including breeding race horses as well as betting on them. Much to the relief of his church, Murray resigned his post. He started a church of his own, but in 1880 left his religious calling to travel the continents. By this time he had divorced his wife who went abroad to study surgery. It was said she was the first American woman to receive her diploma in Vienna.

Upon returning to Boston, Murray decided he was no longer happy there. He later moved to Montreal, Canada, where he ran a restaurant. The establishment attracted many ex-parishioners from Boston who came to see the former clergyman "dressed in a white robe, serving food." Once again, disenchanted with his life, he returned to lecturing until he died on March 3, 1904, a month before his sixth-fifth birthday.

To this day, Murray is credited with having done more for the Adirondacks than any other person in history. Yet, as Wallace wrote in this 1894 *Descriptive Guide to the Adirondacks*, ". . . there is not a place in the Adirondacks which commemorates the name of him who opened the eyes of the world for this Grand Sanitarium and Pleasure Ground!"

ALVAH DUNNING AND OSPREY ISLAND

The next inhabitant to make his home on Raquette Lake was Alvah Dunning. Dunning, considered by many the "hermit guide" of Raquette Lake, truly deserved his reputation of having a primitive dislike and distrust of his neighbors. His whole nature was of a simple man who greatly resented the intrusions of progress.

Alvah's father was Shadrack Dunning, born about 1787 in South Parish, Weedbury, Connecticut. He moved with his family to Wells, New York and around 1809 Shadrack married Mary Nichols of Lake Pleasant where they took up residence. Following her death in about 1815, Shadrack married Dorcas Greene of Lake Pleasant who became the mother of Alvah Green Dunning, born June 14, 1816. Shadrack died in 1872 at Lake Pleasant.

Alvah Dunning joined his father trapping and hunting at the age of six. He is said to have killed his first moose at age eleven and by the age of twelve guided his first white man into the Raquette Lake area. It was small wonder, with the guidance of his father and Nick Stoner (a veteran trapper), he grew to be a man with the same skill and love of the woods as his mentors.

From his youth and until he was very old he was tall, slender and straight of form. He was known not only to possess the stealth, strength and endurance of an Indian, but his features have been likened to that of one. A most apt description is made by Donaldson in Volume II of his *History of the Adirondacks*:

> Most prominent was his vulturesquely beaked nose, arching beneath rather small but clear, keen eyes, to whose deadly vigilance the red men paid tribute by calling him "Snake-Eye." The forehead was broad and sloping, and all that was needed was a crown of feathers to give the last Indian touch to the head. The mouth was small, and the lips were thin and tightly pressed together when closed, but could part in a

> pleasant smile when humor moved them. The chin was covered by a scraggly beard that trellised up over his ears. Both hair and beard turned a pure white in his later life, and his skin became as creased and crackled as the bark of an old cedar.

Dunning's nature appeared to many as passive. However, he had a primal tendency to wage war with newcomers and had, from some accounts, a barbarous sense of cruelty. Two instances of his fierce temper have been told and retold.

The early years of his life were spent in Lake Pleasant and Lake Piseco. It was during this period he married and the first incident of his anger is related. It is said he found his wife to be unfaithful and his treatment of her was so severe the law stepped in. To avoid punishment for his deed he fled deep into the forest and finally to Blue Mountain Lake.

While there he met Ned Buntline, the author, and it was during this association that the second episode of his violent disposition occurred.

One summer a misunderstanding arose between the two men. Dunning decided the solution was to perforate a boat belonging to the novelist until it sank. In retaliation, Buntline shot the old man's dog while it was standing between Dunning's legs. Alvah counter attacked with a barrage of profanity and a threat to set fire to Buntline's "Eagle's Nest." It is said the author chased Dunning all over Blue Mountain Lake with intent to kill. The old trapper escaped to Eighth Lake. In 1865 he arrived at Raquette Lake, settling on Indian Point.

In an essay about Alvah Dunning in 1897, Fred Mather had this to say: "He built a camp where he lived alone, trapping, drawing his fur on a hand sled fifty-five miles to Boonville and bringing back provisions. It took a week to make the trip. One winter his skins of otter, fisher, marten, mink and bear brought him $743."

During his stay on Indian Point, Dunning acted as guide for Reverend Murray and author, Fred Mather. After many trips with these men, they eventually became friends.

Dunning had no respect for game laws. He felt one should be able to fish and hunt for food as needed. However, he did not approve of hunting and fishing "just for sport." He had little regard for most of the men he guided since he felt they were "the durndest lot of cur'osities you ever seen an' many of 'em's fools."

In the autumn of 1869, Alvah Dunning took possession of Murray's then vacated camps on Osprey Island, saying Murray gave him the property. He enclosed the open camp and lived in it until it burned in 1875 destroying what few possessions he owned.

Rowena (Roblee) Bird, Reuben Mick and Frank Carlin, old time Raquette Lakers, recalled some stories about Alvah Dunning.

Mick related this story of Alvah's mistrust of people: "Alvah was encouraged by one of his friends to put his money in a bank in Utica. On one of his few trips out of the mountains he decided to take their advice. He was most suspicious of this "gimmick of civilization." After depositing his money, he sat watching the cashier. As he watched, he saw some customers withdrawing money. He returned to the window and demanded his money back, saying: "If you're gonna give it to ev'body, I won't leave it here." This episode reinforced his feelings against the "civilized world."

Rowena Bird recalled her mother telling how she wasn't allowed to go past Carlin's livery when she was little because "Alvah sat in the village waiting with a gun on his knee for trespassers."

A favorite story of Carlin's happened one winter. "The lake was frozen over and Mary Bryere of Brightside, while sweeping the porch at Stotts, saw a bear chasing her cat. Donning her snowshoes, Mary walked to Antlers, where some men were working, to obtain their assistance in retrieving her cat. They took after the bear, chasing it all day unsuccessfully. The next day, her husband, Joe, trailed the bear all day. He managed to get in a shot and broke one of the bear's legs as he crossed from Needle Island to Indian Point. The next day, Alvah was going to Stotts and saw the bear crossing from Kenwells on Tioga Point. He shot him and and broke another leg. The bear, wounded and in pain, couldn't run away. Dunning had no more shells so he approached the bear with gun in hand. Frightened, the bear stood up on his hind legs ready to attack. Alvah started swinging with the stock of his rifle, succeeding in killing the bear by battering in his head. 'I had to do it,' said Dunning, 'I couldn't let him suffer.' It is said the bear was used to hold umbrellas at Little Moose Club House."

Alvah Dunning was destined to be constantly uprooted. In

1879, Durant's cousin, Charles W. Durant, Jr., wished to own and occupy Osprey Island. He approached Dunning about purchasing the land and was greeted by the barrel of Alvah's shotgun.

When Charles Durant was unsuccessful in his approach, his cousin W. W. Durant, submitted an application to the Land Office in Albany on behalf of Charles on the grounds that "Osprey Island had become cut and burned over by temporary camping parties who had no interest in its preservation." Charles Durant was designated as "custodian." In the 1886 report by the Forest Commission (successor to the Land Office) the word custodian was never defined nor were the rights gained by the custodian upon his appointment.

It is said Mrs. Durant intervened and after some persuasion, in 1880, Dunning vacated his shanty and island for the sum of $100. He received another $100 when he signed over the deed to Charles.

When Dunning left Osprey he moved back to Eighth Lake. In 1896, the influx of inhabitants drove him back to Raquette Lake. This time he built a hut near the Inlet to Brown's Tract, living quietly in the solitude he enjoyed. Three years later, he was approached and informed his property was needed for a railroad station.

Discouraged by his constantly being disturbed by outsiders and by progress, he released his claim for $600. Shortly after, he decided to leave the area and head west. Within a year the old woodsman, then eighty-three years of age, longed to return to his beloved Adirondacks. He returned tired and weary from his quest to find seclusion and, finding a remote spot on Golden Beach, he set up camp near South Inlet.

In March 1902, he traveled to New York to attend the Sportsmen's Show. On his trip home, he stopped to spend the night at the Dudley House in Utica, planning to continue to his sister's home in Syracuse the next day. The crowning irony of this "rugged individualist" who rebelled against "newfangled" inventions, was his death. Upon retiring that night, the old woodsman blew out the light . . . a gas jet which leaked all night. The next morning he was found asphyxiated.

For weeks after, papers all over the country carried the story of "The Last of the Great Adirondack Guides."

CAMP FAIRVIEW

When Charles Durant acquired Osprey Island, his intention was to build a camp for his family. The building, built on the western tip of Osprey was started in 1879. By 1881, the lodge was completed and work started on other buildings and servants' quarters.

It is believed that Ed Bennett built Camp Fairview for Charles Durant and Camp Echo for Phineas C. Lounsbury, both having similar architectural features including a lodge with twin towers flanking a gabled center. It is also a distinct possibility he built Camp Cedar on Forked Lake.

The deed to the property was not recorded until May 6, 1891. About this time J. Harvey Ladew, a leather merchant from New York City and one of the incorporators of the Raquette Lake Railroad, became interested in purchasing the property. He acquired the complex consisting of the lodge and an adjoining cottage containing a dining room , kitchen and servants' quarters. Other buildings included a hen house, stable, barn, ice house and cooler. A boathouse with servants' quarters above was near the dock. Durant's boat *Stella*, which Ladew renamed *Osprey*, was included in the sale. The grounds comprised a country garden and tennis court as well as a bridge that joined Osprey with Little Osprey Island, used as a play area for the children.

It is said the interior wall decor was similar to many of the larger camps of that time, with Oriental prints and fans. The furniture was rustic, built of native wood, perhaps by some of the best carpenters of the time including Joe Bryere and Seth Pierce. The furniture and floor coverings of fur and hides scattered throughout the rooms were decorative as well as useful.

Sometime during the late 1920's the lodge and several buildings were destroyed by fire.

Ladew had two sons, Joseph and Oliver. "I remember," said Carlin, "until they reached their teen years, they never rode in anything but a chauffeur-driven Rolls Royce and were always accompanied by a tutor or guardian."

Carlin also recalled that Ladew insisted the "Osprey" be fired twenty-four hours a day when he was in residence, "in case of emergency."

It was told, in the mid-1920's, that Ladew signed a contract to buy leather from Argentina, which would have made him a fortune. After the contract had been signed, the U.S. Government flooded the market with surplus leather from the U.S. Cavalry of World War I and Ladew lost in excess of twenty million dollars. The venture rendered him penniless.

The property was then acquired by Bernon K. Tourtelot, an attorney from Utica, New York. He sold the *Osprey* to the Adirondack Museum in 1957, where it is now on permanent display.

After the death of Bernon Tourtelot, his wife married Ernest Berry. Mr. Berry has since passed away and the property remains in the family name.

CHAPTER III

ACCOMMODATIONS AND PROPRIETORS THROUGH THE YEARS

THE PAYNE FAMILY

With the increasing number of sportsmen visiting the area, more comfortable housing accommodations became necessary on Raquette Lake. One who foresaw this need and felt he could make a living out of both guiding and providing lodging was Samuel Payne.

Samuel Payne was born in Oxfordshire, England in 1828. His wife, Mary Callon, and their two sons, Charles and William M., were also natives of Oxfordshire.

In 1845, the family migrated to Canada where two other children, Jane and Samuel Jr., were born. Early in the 1850's the family moved the the States, settling in a log house at Indian Lake, New York, on the site later to be known as the Cedar River golf course. The family increased in size by five: John, George, Lucy, Joanna and Henry.

In 1855, Payne chose a parcel of land (240 acres) at the foot of West Mountain in Sucker Brook Bay on Raquette Lake. His intent was to build a hunting lodge. Farrand Benedict owned the property at the time, but having no further interest in it, deeded it to Payne.

A closed-in camp and ice house were built on the land first, and several years later a sawmill was added. Until 1879, Payne operated a commercial camp for hunters and fishermen, acting also as their guide. Tiring of that life, he moved to the Dakotas. The property remained unoccupied until his son, William, and

and his family took possession in 1883.

William M. Payne was eleven years of age when his family moved to Indian Lake. He chose farming and guiding as his profession, although he was also an excellent carpenter.

While living at Indian Lake, he married his first wife, Sarah Brooks, who died in 1879 after bearing him nine children: Walter E., George S., Mary L., Phebe M., Lovina, Benjamin H., Ashel (Asa), Huldah and William H.

On December 6, 1879 he took his second wife, Martha M. Washburn Porter, (born in Schroon Lake, 1837) a widow with six children: Sidney, Orillie, Florence, Frederick, Olive and Lewis (Lou) Porter (fathered by her deceased husband, Jesse Porter, whom she had married in 1852). On September 2, 1880, a son, William Harry Payne, was born to the couple.

"Old Billy Payne," as William Payne later became known, only visited the camp on Sucker Brook Bay occasionally, until he decided to settle on Raquette Lake after his father deeded the parcel to him.

He was a small man, only five feet tall, yet was not hindered by his size. A born woodsman, he was considered a genius with ax and saw, and proved to be one of the finest builders in the area.

"Old Billy" is credited with building the first year-round house at Sucker Brook Bay, the original Payne homestead building, later called "Lone Pine Camp." (At this writing it is used as a vacation home by his great-grandson, Jim Payne, and his family.)

The home was strategically placed on a high bank commanding a magnificent view of the large bay and its islands. The logs for the building were floated in by flat boat and cut at the Payne sawmill. The roofs were built at a very steep pitch (to avoid damage from the heavy snow) with shingles Billy had made. The shingles were hewn from white pine blocks split into thin slabs. After clamping them on a sawhorse, Billy shaved them to a taper. The results were thick, heavy shingles, built to last a lifetime and much in demand by other builders in the area.

The complex Billy built was done with one thought: to be self-sufficient. When he inherited the camp he also got the ice house and sawmill, which he put to good use. Next to the woodshed was a skidway for logs. It was here, year after year, that he sawed and split cords of wood from the beech and pine he logged for himself and to sell to others.

Along the edge of the woods near the ice house was a back-house, a carpenter shop and barn of log construction. The barn contained stalls for the milking cow, its heifer when there was one, and "Tommy," his ox. There was also the frame forge where his tools could be built or repaired.

Nearby was a clearing where Billy hand-mowed oats and hay for the livestock. The area was fenced to keep out the deer and other animals. A root cellar was built to store the vegetables and a smoke box was dug into the side of a hill. A large sugar bush and sap house occupied another section of the land. The yield of syrup was both for family consumption and for sale.

On October 3, 1910 Billy's wife, Martha, died and he took his third wife, Hannah M. Dugar, who had been employed by the neighboring Andersons.

Everyone had to work for his keep as money was scarce. Billy, in addition to taking in boarders and guiding, kept the neighbors' ice houses and woodsheds full. Hannah added to the cash flow by selling the balsam pillows, syrup and maple cakes she made, as well as the cold drinks always available for those climbing West Mountain. At the time access to the mountain was across the Payne property.

Billy always had a dog or two around; they too were trained to work, rounding up the barn animals, or dragging wagons or toboggans across the lake for supplies.

"Tommy," the ox, was known to one and all. He weighed at least a ton and was the predecessor to the modern-day tractor. Whenever it was necessary to haul heavy loads, Tommy was put to work. Despite the fact the ox was an asset, his stubborn temperment was a constant source of irritation to Billy.

By the late 1800's, several sections of the Payne property had been acquired by summer residents. For a period, Richard Morle leased a camp built by Payne on a one-acre parcel referred to as "Furlough Camp." On September 12, 1913 it was deeded to Lucy Platt, and as of this writing remains in the possession of the Platt family.

Charles Anderson and his wife, Annie, acquired a parcel of about ten acres. The Anderson and Platt families were related by the marriage of Dorothea Anderson and Lester Platt, Sr. Currently a small part of the Anderson Camp has been retained by Anne Thompson. The remainder, having changed owners several times, is in the name of Randolph. These parcels of about five acres bordered either side of the property owned by Lewis (Lou) Porter, stepson of Old Billy Payne.

By 1894, most of Old Billy Payne's children and stepchildren had left Raquette Lake; only a few remained.

William H. Payne, son of Old Billy and Martha Washburn, married Florence Turner and stayed at Raquette Lake for a while running the Payne's boarding house. Later they moved to Inlet. Young William Payne offered property owned by him and adjacent to the Inlet Golf Course, to the town for use as a cemetery. The town rejected the proposal. There is however, one grave on the parcel—that of William Harry Payne.

In the census of 1905, Billy's son, Benjamin (born of his first wife, Sarah Brooks) and Benjamin's wife, Lillian Blanchard, were listed as living in Raquette Lake. They moved to Indian Lake shortly after.

Billy's son Asa (also born of his first wife) married Delphine Thibado, September 25, 1898. He built a home for his family on the Payne tract of land now occupied by the Bennetts. A year later his stepbrother, Lou Porter, built a home at Sucker Brook Bay. They were neighbors until 1904 when Porter left Raquette Lake.

While at Raquette Lake, eight children were born to Asa and Delphine: George, Richard, Nellie, Louis, Lawrence, Joseph, Lavinia and Esther. Richard and Joseph were the only ones who attended Raquette Lake School. The Paynes moved to Inlet where their ninth child, a daughter, Dorothy, was born. Their Raquette Lake property was acquired by Ruktessler and at present is owned by Henry Bennett. Delphine Payne died July 20, 1949, Asa Payne died October 16, 1953.

Lou Porter, born in 1874 in Indian Lake, was the son of Martha Washburn Porter Payne and her first husband, Jesse Porter, stepson of Old Billy. Lou was in great demand as a guide portaging hunters and sportsmen throughout the Moose River Plains area south of Inlet. Being adventurous, he eventually moved to the West. He returned in 1899 and married Esther Thibado (Canadian born) of Indian Lake. Reuben Mick, Raquette Lake Justice of the Peace, officiated at the ceremony.

The couple settled at Sucker Brook Bay, living in a platform tent while Porter put his craftsman's skills to work, and by 1900, he completed the family home which is still in existence (now a summer residence of the Phinney family).

Two daughters, Orilla and Louise, were born to Lou and Esther Porter. They lived with their parents in Raquette Lake until 1904 when the property was sold to Mary (Minnie) Gordon DeForest who purchased it as a surprise for her husband, Ezra.

The DeForest family visited the area together at a later date and Minnie DeForest decided to purchase the adjoining Porter homestead when it became available. The family named the camp, "Camp Sunny Cliff," a name it still maintains, and added an addition to the back of the house.

Upon the death of Minnie Gordon DeForest in about 1939, her daughter, Dorothea, inherited the property. Dorothea and her husband, Charles Cole of Philadelphia, contracted Larry Payne to add two cottages and two lean-tos. Rachel Cole Phinney inherited the property upon her mother's demise in 1985. She and her husband, Rod, lived in the little cottage when they vacationed at the camp until 1977. "I love it," stated Rachel. "I wouldn't think of tearing it down."

Louise Porter Payne of Inlet, a charming lady in her 80's, refers to herself as "the old lady of the hills." Perhaps old in years, but not in spirit. She spoke about her home on Raquette Lake and her parents, Esther and Lou Porter.

"The site on which Porter built his home was originally intended for the Village of Raquette Lake," she said. "The Raquette Lake railroad was planned to go to Sucker Brook but it was decided that there were too many hills around there, and the location of the station was changed to where the village is now. Freight and supplies would be brought to the head of the lake on the railroad, then loaded on boats or sleighs to be transported to the lake."

Her mother, Esther Porter, was said to have named the neighboring islands, "The Hen and Chicks Islands." Most of the islands on Raquette Lake have been named for the inhabitants on the island, often for no apparent reason. The naming of the "Hen and Chicks" had a very simple reason behind it. To keep raccoons from eating the chicken eggs, the Porter hens were deposited on the larger island called "Hen Island." It followed naturally, the small islands near Hen Island be named "The Chicks."

Louise remembered her father, Lou, fondly. "He had a laugh that came up from his toes. One of the things I remember most about my father was his courage."

She smiled as she continued. "Once when my mother and we girls started out to town, the team of horses bolted and ran away with the wagon. My father hopped on his bicycle, caught up with the wagon and stopped the team shortly before it reached the edge of a cliff. Just like in the Wild West."

Although very young when her family went west in 1904, she recalled traveling in a covered wagon. When they returned from California they moved to Sixth Lake near Inlet where a son, Orvis, was born to the couple.

Their home burned and Lou Porter built another house known as the Golf Course House, which still is in use today as the clubhouse at Deer Run Golf Course in Inlet. Porter died in 1944. His wife Esther succumbed in 1976.

On February 21, 1925, Louise Porter married Richard Payne, son of Asa Payne, her father's stepbrother. Their children, Richard, Jr., Theodore, Sidney and James all live in Inlet with their families. Their only daughter, Rosemary, who is married to George Hardin, lives in Syracuse. They all maintain vacation camps on the Payne property at Sucker Brook Bay in Raquette Lake. Louise does not visit Raquette Lake any more but keeps herself busy knitting and enjoying her position as grandmother to more than thirty Payne descendants and great-grandmother of seventeen.

On July 27, 1930 "Old Billy" made out his will, witnessed by James L. Harding and Lester B. Platt. The property was willed to his son, William H. Payne of Inlet, New York, subject to life use by his widow, Hannah. Later she married Philip Andros who had been living and working with them for several years.

Hannah remained on the property deeding it to Asa's youngest son sometime before 1945. After the death of Hannah on May 6, 1949, Joseph and his family used the camp.

Joseph built a small camp on the lakeshore of the parcel and sold the original homestead to Richard and Louise (Porter) Payne. They sold the camp to their son, Jim, in the early 1970's.

Joseph Payne also built a larger year-round camp on the lakefront which was deeded, with acreage, to his daughters, Mrs. Levi and Mrs. Townsend. Later Levi also acquired the smaller lakeshore camp. In the early 1940's, Joseph Payne deeded parcels to Sid and Dolores Payne, and George and Rosemary Hardin who maintain them as vacation retreats.

THE BLANCHARD FAMILY

Shortly after Samuel Payne settled at Sucker Brook Bay another woodsman, Charles William Blanchard, moved to Raquette Lake intending to operate a sportsmen's camp.

Blanchard was born in 1842 in Barnard, Vermont, son of Charles and Mary A. (Maxhan) Blanchard. During the Civil War he served with Company 1, 25th Massachusetts Infantry. In 1873 he and his wife, Harriet (Baty), joined Samuel Payne in occupying the peninsula, building on what is known as Green Point. There he built "Blanchard's Wigwams," conducting a commercial recreational business for hunters and fishermen. On a very early map designating residences on Raquette Lake from 1830-1876, it shows Blanchard also having occupied what is known as "Beecher's Island" in the 1860's. Several years after building the Wigwams, Blanchard built himself another house on the westerly part of the peninsula, some three-quarters mile distant from the camp, on property later occupied by Lou Porter. While continuing to operate the Wigwams, Blanchard also acted as caretaker, keeping watch over Samuel Payne's buildings.

Between 1885 and 1890, Blanchard's father joined him on the Point. About 1892, ignoring his son's protests, his father chose to stay alone on the Point during the winter. Because of his concern, Charles Blanchard returned to Raquette Lake in early spring, only to find his father had frozen to death.

Charles and Harriet Blanchard had six children. Herbert, born April 1876, was killed in a boating accident on Raquette Lake near Silver Beach in 1886. A daughter named Minnie was born in 1881 and married James Sutliff, settling on Poplar Point in Raquette Lake.

Another daughter, Florence, born in 1891, married Francis Haischer who was said to have been the first teacher at the Raquette Lake School. He also served as agent for the Raquette Lake Transportation Co. from 1911 to 1929. They resided on property originally owned by Frank Carlin, now partially owned by Richard Lauterbach, with the remaining portion in possession of Eva Humphrey.

Charles and Harriet Blanchard's first-born son, Arthur (born 1874), married Lucy Hunt of Indian Lake. The ceremony took place at North River in 1921. Arthur and Lucy took over opera-

Courtesy Rachel Phinney

Old Billy Payne hand mowing oats for his livestock near his "Lone Pine Camp" in Sucker Brook Bay. Circa early 1900's.

Courtesy Rachel Phinney

When the tower on West Mountain was built, Old Billy and "Tommy" the ox carried the materials up the mountain. Circa early 1900's.

Courtesy Rachel Phinney

"Furlough Camp." Circa 1913

Courtesy Rachel Phinney

Charles and Annie Anderson's boat house. Circa early 1900's.

Courtesy Louise Porter Payne

Lou and Esther Porter pose (she in her wedding dress) in front of their home. Circa 1900.

Courtesy Rachel Phinney

Mary (Minnie) Gordon DeForest
Circa early 1900's.

Courtesy Rachel Phinney

One of the lean-tos on the DeForest property, shown here ready for guests. Circa 1940.

Courtesy Rachel Phinney

Hannah (Dugar) Payne, and Philip Andros, whom she married in the early 1930's. Circa 1930's.

Courtesy Earl Blanchard

Earl Blanchard transporting his house boat to the north end of the lake. Circa late 1880's.

Courtesy Doris and Glenn Martin

John H. Blanchard purchased the home shown here in 1908. The house was originally built in 1878 by guide Henry Taylor. Circa early 1900's.

Author's Collection

Ed Bennett's hotel "Under the Hemlocks" was built on the north shore of Long Point in the early 1880's. Circa late 1880's.

Courtesy Bertha Conley

In 1903 Patrick Moynehan built the Raquette Lake House. Circa 1910.

Author's Collection

Hotel guests mingle on the verandah at "Under the Hemlocks." Circa 1890's.

Courtesy Bruce Cole

The main structure of the Antlers built on Constable Point. Circa early 1900's.

Courtesy Bruce Cole

The Casino at the Antlers. Circa early 1900's.

Courtesy Jerry Halsband

Campers were housed in these tents behind Antlers Hotel after the property was purchased by the Cedar Island Corporation in 1920. Circa 1920.

tion of the Wigwams while Charles Blanchard continued to live in the house near Payne. Harriet Blanchard died in 1921 and six years later, Charles Blanchard died at the age of 85. Both are interred at Blue Mountain Lake.

Arthur and Lucy Blanchard had one son, Earl, born in 1907. There is no record of Arthur other than that already mentioned. However, according to the records of the Hamilton County Historian, Earl and his mother lived at Raquette Lake until 1925, during which time she ran a boarding house.

In 1932 Earl, having married Merry Hall, built a houseboat on which they lived while he pursued his career as a guide. The structure was moved from place to place on the lake until they purchased Pine Island in 1942.

Some of the old maps listed the island as Harding Island. Raquette Lakers at the time referred to it as Judd Island. Judd Landon acquired the land sometime before or during the 1920's and, although he did not frequent the area often, he maintained possession until it was sold to Blanchard.

Judd owned a light cedar guide boat which was occasionally "borrowed" by local youngsters wishing to fish in Sargent Pond. Its light weight made carrying it into the area easy. One of the culprits gave this explanation:

"We were always careful not to let anything happen to it. When someone on the pond would comment 'What a beautiful boat. Where did you get it?' we would make believe we didn't hear. It sure was great to have a boat like that even for a little while and we all treated it like it was our own."

For many years during Earl Blanchard's ownership, Pine Island was referred to as Blanchard's Island. Formed during the Ice Age, it is estimated to be at least 10,000 years old, and is composed mainly of rock and dead vegetation. In one of the camps on the island hangs a framed one-page history of the island. It reads as follows:

> At about the turn of the century, the cottage which is now Pine Cottage was built. The shore of the mainland which the cottage faces was not developed as it is now. The only road north through the area ended at the village, so the cottage was very private.
>
> Pine Cottage had no heat except from the fireplace and no running water, phone or electricity. The section that is now the kitchen and bathroom was part of

> the porch. Toilet facilities were located in an outhouse, and the kitchen, separate from the cottage, was located in the approximate position of the present tool house.
>
> Spruce Cottage was originally the houseboat which was moved ashore the winter of 1943. The bedroom was converted into a bathroom and two bedrooms were added.
>
> What is referred to as Maple Cottage was the original Blanchard homestead built on Green Point. The understructure of the cottage is made of handhewn logs. The bathroom was originally an open porch. In the winter of 1948 it was slid across the lake and brought ashore. It is because both cottages had to be moved on to land at low elevations that the south side of the island was developed first.
>
> A gasoline generator was installed on the island to maintain a 32-volt electrical system. To bring town water to the island, a pipe was laid in the winter across the ice on the lake. In the spring the pipe sank to the bottom.

Other cottages and buildings were added and improvements made through the years. The cottages served as summer rentals.

When Earl's mother, Lucy Blanchard, died in 1950, he inherited the property on Green Point. He became involved in litigation with the state, as did many other landowners. The dispute continued for years. Eventually all cases resulted in court rulings in favor of the property owners. The parcel on Green Point was eventually split and sold.

Earl and Merry Blanchard continued to summer on Pine Island, wintering in Syracuse. Later they moved to Florida for the winters, still maintaining the camp during the summer. In 1974 the island was sold to Douglas Madden. The Blanchards became permanent residents of Tampa, Florida.

Another son of Charles and Harriet Blanchard who lived in Raquette Lake was John H., born in 1878. He and his wife, Nancy (Hughes), lived in Blue Mountain until they purchased a parcel of land on Raquette Lake in 1908. The house was originally built in 1893 by a guide, Henry Taylor, who lived there until John McLaughlin, Hamilton County Sheriff, took possession from Taylor for an overdue bill and in turn sold it to James McGovern who sold it to Blanchard. At the time, Blanchard's first-born, Paul, was three years of age.

Paul is now in his 80's and lives at Indian Lake. He believes his father was interested in that particular piece of land because he had a shack there in earlier years which he used occasionally when hunting. Paul recalled his father, a carpenter and boat builder by trade, telling that when he arrived on Raquette Lake there were two other boat builders on the lake. "Old Man Graves" who lived in the bay on the south side of Big Island and "Charley Cole" who lived in Lonesome Bay.

When John H. acquired the land from McGovern, he added a guideboat shop, storage and woodshed as well as a boathouse. As he was a highly skilled and sought after boat builder, the construction of boats during the winter months became a family project. John's wife, Nancy, and daughter, Ruth, caned the seats while Paul assisted with other phases of the development process. John also built launches and power boats as well as repairing engines. During the summer they ran a tourist home.

Paul attended Cornell University in the 1920's where he obtained a degree in civil engineering and met his future wife, Edith Nash, whom he married in 1923. After living in Auburn, New York for eleven years they moved to Indian Lake. When Paul's father died in 1948, he and his family helped his mother continue operating the tourist home during the summer months. When Nancy died in 1959, Paul inherited the property and family members lived at the house seasonally.

In 1976, (James) Jim Blanchard, the youngest son of Paul and Edith, moved to Raquette Lake from Rochester and acquired the property from his father. The following year he married Mary DeShaw from Tupper Lake. Jim, also a carpenter, and Mary operate a jewelry and craft business at Tupper Lake.

Mary Blanchard is the sister of Theresa (DeShaw) Cleaveland and Roy DeShaw who both reside in Raquette Lake with their families. Their parents, Edith (Gale) and Bernard DeShaw came from Tupper Lake in 1960. Edith worked at the Old Station, and Bernard was employed by the Raquette Lake Supply Company. Several years later they returned to Tupper Lake.

Roy DeShaw, employed by the state on road maintenance, lives with his wife, Pam Meari, children Bob, Leslie, Andrea, Jeff and Michelle and grandson, Joshua. Theresa DeShaw Cleaveland lives with her husband, "Dayt," and their children, Dayton and Tara. Theresa is employed by the Raquette Lake Supply Co. and her husband is a state employee.

Ernie (Ernest) Clarence Blanchard, the last son born to Charles and Harriet Blanchard was born January 7, 1877. He married Maude Myrtle Gray who bore him four children, one of whom died at two years of age. Maude succumbed in 1925 at the age of thirty-seven. Ernie found it necessary to send his children, Nancy, Mary and Ernest to live with their Uncle John and Aunt Nancy at Raquette Lake.

On May 9, 1927, Ernie took a second wife, Lavina Gates, born in 1900 at Blue Mountain Lake, daughter of David Gates and Huldah Payne. (Huldah was the daughter of Old Billy Payne and his first wife, Sarah Brooks.)

Six children were born of this marriage. There is a record of only one returning to Raquette Lake. Ella Pauline, widow of Gordon Walter Gauvin, married Dayton Cleaveland of Raquette Lake. Cleaveland was employed as custodian-bus driver at the Raquette Lake School until he retired in November 1975 when the couple left Raquette Lake.

Ernest Blanchard, son of Ernie and his first wife, Harriet, returned to Raquette Lake as an adult. In 1949 he married Carol Fish of Indian Lake. The couple served as caretakers of Tioga Point until it was razed in 1967.

In the December 21, 1958 edition of the *Albany Times-Union*, an article entitled "Last of the Old Guides" was written about Ernie Blanchard. The following excerpts are taken from it:

> At the age of ten Ernie shot his first deer, with an old single-shot Ballard rifle. The incident occurred in the desolate country along the Moose River while Ernie and an older brother were hunting game for the winter food supply. They had tracked an old buck to a clearing and sneaked noiselessly up on him. Without saying a word, the brother handed Ernie the rifle and extended his arm under the barrel. Resting the 38.55 caliber across his brother's arm, Ernie dropped the deer with a bullet clean through the head.
>
> At twelve years old, Ernie was a full-fledged fishing guide, earning a top-scale two dollars a day taking sportsmen back into the woods to find hidden trout streams.
>
> If the outdoor life was a hard one, it was an extremely rewarding one, both in self-satisfaction and money. In 1919 when the boys were returning from

> France and the nation was heading into its deep post-war slump, Ernie was making close to $4,000 a year from his fur trapping and guiding. . . . The pay for a guide had risen from a skimpy $2 to $10 a day, and those who could afford the services of a guide tipped big.
>
> "I couldn't say," said Ernie, "if it was a hard or soft one, because it was the only life I ever knew, and I just couldn't draw any comparison. I know one thing for sure, though, and that's that I couldn't live indoors. Some things are just meant to be out of doors, and I'm one of them. I have to be out in the fresh air, and the wind and rain and snow, if it has to be. . . . I found something a lot of men are looking for."

Following the article, Ernie Blanchard worked for two years as fire watcher on Blue Mountain and worked at the Adirondack Museum for one season. He died October 12, 1961 at age 84.

THE BENNETT FAMILY

The Bennett brothers played an important role in the early development of Raquette's tourist trade. Their father, Thomas Bennett, was born in Ireland in 1824. He became a U.S. citizen in 1849 while employed as a gardener in Hyde Park, New York. He later moved to Peekskill and then Long Island, where he and his wife, Ellen, raised four sons: Edward (b. 1854), Thomas (b. 1856), Richard (b. 1857) and Charles (b. 1858).

Charles Bennett was the first of the brothers to arrive at Raquette Lake, setting up as a guide on Long Point in 1873. A year later, his brother, Ed, joined him. They put up tents and erected a small cabin where they took in tourists. Among their clients was Dr. Thomas Clark Durant, who started making occasional explorations of Raquette Lake in the late 1860's while building the Adirondack Railroad from Saratoga to North Creek. Occasionally, he was joined by his brother, C.W. Durant.

In the Fall of 1879 and Spring of 1880, Ed Bennett erected the first frame house on Raquette, on the north shore of Long Point. He set it up as a hotel with a capacity for twenty guests. His brother, Charlie, took over their original camp on Long Point and continued to guide visitors.

In June 1880, Ed Bennett married Mary Shaughnessy of Warrensburg, New York, who later gained quite a reputation for her culinary pursuits.

The hotel burned two years later and was replaced with a larger structure, "Under the Hemlocks," which could accommodate forty or fifty guests. It consisted of a main building with spreading verandas cooled by shade trees. Two rustic cabins were on the premises, one of which had been constructed for concert vocalist, Madame Gerster.

The first wedding at Raquette Lake took place at The Hemlocks. On July 8, 1884, Joseph O.A. Bryere and Mary Agnes Gooley (of Brightside) were joined in matrimony by Father Gabriel from Troy, New York. "Their marriage certificate was written on the hotel stationery," states Frank Carlin in his diary. "The bride's corsage was a water lily and their honeymoon trip was a ride on Raquette Lake."

Harold Hochschild, in his *Township 34*, states Ed Bennett sold his hotel to Eugene C. Finck and his brother, Frederick, in 1889 for the sum of $15,000. According to the Bennett family history as supplied by the County Historian, "Under the Hemlocks" with ten acres of land, was sold at a mortgage foreclosure at Indian Lake on February 7, 1889 to Edwin A. McAlpin of Sing Sing, for $6,250. It was sold again the same year to Eugene and Frederick Finck and was renamed the "Raquette Lake Hotel."

In the early 1890's Jack Daly took over management of the hotel. After the sale, the Bennetts moved to Warrensburg and eventually to Glens Falls where Edward Bennett died July 1932.

In 1899 Daly's Raquette Lake Hotel burned. A news item in a Saratoga paper included in Frank Carlin's notes gave the following account: "'Under the Hemlocks,' the second largest hotel in Raquette Lake, was destroyed by fire involving a loss of $15,000, said John J. Daly, proprietor. The fire was caused by chimney sparks igniting the roof. The temperature was 24 degrees below zero with high winds prevailing and ice on the lake was 21 inches thick making it impossible to obtain water from the lake to extinguish the fire."

Before Daly had an opportunity to rebuild, the land was bought by Collis P. Huntington. Daly moved to Eckford Lakes.

Charlie Bennett left a permanent mark on Raquette Lake. In 1885 he bought Constable Point across the lake from Long Point. Two years later he opened his own hotel, the "Antlers."

Wallace, in his *Guide to the Adirondacks*, described the Antlers as "set in a beautiful location on Constable Point, consisting of a picturesque grouping of wall-tents, open camps and neat little cottages, affording the retirement and comforts of home-life, all clustering around the main structure, a building well fitted with modern conveniences. . . . From here a wagon-road has been opened to Raquette Lake Station on the Adirondack & St. Lawrence Railroad, some twelve or fifteen miles west, where stages from this place will connect with the principal trains. A line of rowboats and carry-wagons, also ran to the head of Fourth Lake, connecting with the steamer *Fulton*, and forming daily connections at Old Forge with the A.&S.L.R.R. Fare was about $3.00."

The Antlers had accommodations for approximately 200 guests and was the largest in the area. It also maintained a huge vegetable garden (located where the present parking lot stands), affording fresh vegetables daily. A pasture occupied the area used as a golf course later on.

Donaldson, in his *History of the Adirondacks*, had this to say about Charlie:

> From the first, his camp-like hotel was so good and so well patronized that he could soon afford to travel, and the more he traveled the better his hotel became. His globe-trotting was done in the winter, of course. He wandered all over America and visited the leading countries of Europe. Wherever he went he stopped at the best hotels, chiefly to discover why they were the best. He mixed not only with the guests but with the management. He liked to watch the wheels go round, and was always nosing about for some new trick of the trade. If a new dish were set before him, especially abroad, he made connection with the chef and learned how to concoct it, for he was an excellent cook himself. After every winter trip, he returned to apply something appropriate of the knowledge he had gleaned to the betterment of the Antlers, and it gradually acquired touches of comfort and surprises in food which were to be had nowhere else in the woods. . . . This was what gave the place a distinctive charm. This was Charlie the caterer.
>
> There was also Charlie, the host. He liked to meet and mix with his guests, but he did so with discrimi-

> nation. . . . He was quick to sense the difference between men of inherited culture and ancestral wealth and those who had been suddenly tossed to prosperity by a bull market. To the latter he gave of his hotel but not of himself. To the former he gave of both.

Charles Bennett never married. A housekeeper, Miss Amelia Keller, and later a sister, Margaret Bennett, assisted him. Despite all his good qualities enumerated by Donaldson, Charlie was revealed by his associates and acquaintances as a practical joker, a vindictive man, either loved or hated.

One particular instance of his revengeful nature was repeated many times as well as being previously recorded in *Township 34*.

In or about 1886, John Holland planned to rebuild his Blue Mountain Lake Hotel utilizing an old mill that stood at the foot of Raquette Lake. He asked Charlie Bennett if he would go into partnership on the mill. The idea was to move it up the Marion River to Bassett's Carry, where it could be used advantageously for both Raquette Lake and Blue Mountain Lake. Charlie agreed to bargain with Durant who owned the mill and who subsequently gave permission to move it. Bennett and Holland had a disagreement and the matter was referred to Durant who sided with Holland, giving him the mill and excluding Charlie from the deal.

Holland started to move the mill on a raft which became caught in the early ice, so he had to wait until the ice became thicker, then resume the project. He had the boiler placed on a sleigh and started up the river; the load broke through the thin ice and sank to the bottom. Charlie was elated at the mishap and found some fire-balloons and rockets left over from the Fourth of July, setting them off to celebrate the misfortune of his former partner.

Charlie Bennett was known for his habit of imbibing! Natives laughed as they recalled the saying, "Antlers is full - and so is Charlie!" Reuben Mick's favorite story of Charlie was when the doctor told him if he didn't quit drinking it would kill him. Charlie had no intention of quitting and his retort was, "I don't drink half as much as Joe Bryere."

Charlie Bennett ran the Antlers with a flair until 1915 when he died. Margaret Bennett then ran the hotel until 1920.

In 1875, Thomas Bennett came to Raquette Lake as a guide, presumably for Dr. Arpad G. Gerster, husband of the renowned vocalist, Madame Gerster, who occupied a camp near "Under the Hemlocks."

In 1886, Bennett planted a huge strawberry patch on Big Island, with plans to ship the berries to the hotels in Saratoga Springs via Blue Mountain Lake and North Creek. Unfortunately, the long journey by steamboat, stagecoach and railroad proved too much for the fragile fruit. A financial disaster, the strawberry raising was abandoned. About 1890 Jerome Wood leased the property from Bennett, who continued as his guide until his death in 1894 at the age of 38.

Richard Bennett and his wife, Elizabeth, came to Raquette Lake in 1878. They brought their two children, James (b. 1872) and Margaret (b. 1874). After moving to Raquette Lake, two other children were born, Nellie M. (b. 1887) and Edward (b. 1890).

The following information was obtained from a brochure supplied by Horace Bartow, a resident of Sunset Camp since 1956.

Richard Bennett opened his Sunset Camp on Woods Point in 1880. The camp "takes its name from the panorama of kaleidoscopic color that greets one as the sun sets behind the mountains across the lake."

Bennett never felt his hotel was finished. Every year additions and improvements were made, until the camp became quite modern and the property quite expensive. The camp included a two-story main house in the center with cottages, lodges and tents scattered through the trees and along the lakeshore accommodating eighty-five guests. The dining room was on the first floor of the main house commanding a fine view of the lake. Guest rooms and baths occupied the second floor. Swimming, boating and fishing, as well as hiking from camp or boat trips, were offered. The camp also boasted a badminton court, quoits and shuffleboard. A special attraction was the service of the camp's seven-passenger Cadillac available for trips to other lakes and points of interest including Lake Placid, Saranac Lake and Lake George.

After the Raquette Lake Railroad entered the picture in 1900, information on train service was included in an advertising brochure:

> TRAIN SERVICE: Sleeping cars leaving Grand Central Terminal at night, arrive alongside the boat pier at Raquette Lake Village the following morning,

> guests arriving at camp for breakfast. There is also a morning train from New York arriving in time for the evening meal. The rail fare one way is $11.77. Our launches meet all trains and convey guests and baggage to camp.

A train schedule was included noting any changes in time. It continued,

> Guests motoring up will find splendid macadam or concrete roads all the way from New York to Raquette Lake Village via Albany, Saratoga, Glens Falls, Lake George, Chestertown, Weavertown, Indian Lake and Blue Mountain Lake. Individual garage accommodation available in the Village at $1.00 per day or $5.00 per week.
>
> Automobiles cannot be taken to camp. This is an advantage, for it does away with the noise and bustle and odor of arriving and departing cars. On your arrival at Raquette Lake village you call the camp (26-F12) and in fifteen minutes the camp launch picks up you and your luggage.

Bennett ran his Sunset Camp for 30 years. He died November 29, 1925, The December 11, 1924 edition of the *Warrensburg News* ran the following obituary:

"The passing of Richard Bennett, who died on Nov. 29, in Utica, removes from Raquette Lake the last of the Bennett brothers who did more to open up and develop that section of the Adirondack region than anyone else except Thomas C. Durant."

A short commentary followed on the accomplishments of the Bennett brothers. "Richard Bennett was a type of the old-fashioned hotel keeper who is fast passing away."

"He was personally always looking out for the interests and pleasures of his guests and not leaving their welfare to the subordinates of his employees. He was of an agreeable and pleasant disposition and always ready and willing to lend a helping hand to anyone in trouble."

After mentioning his survivors, the article continued, "The following beautiful lines which were written in 1858 by Col. E.Z.G. Judson, better known as "Ned Buntline" when he lived at Eagle Lake, near Blue Mountain Lake, at that time and which were so appropriate then seem to be just as appropriate now, for 40 years Richard Bennett made Sunset Camp his "Wildwood" home.

"Where the silvery gleam of the rushing stream
  Is too brightly seen on the rocks dark green,
Where the White pink grows by the wild rose red,
  As the Bluebird sings 'til the welkin rings
Where the antlered deer leaps and the panther creeps
  And the Eagle screams over cliff and stream,
Where the lilies bow their heads of snow
  And the Hemlocks tall throw a shade over all
Where the rolling surf leaves the emerald turf
  And the sportive fawn crops the soft green lawn,
Where the trout jumps high at the hovering fly,
  And the crows' shrill cry bides the tempest nigh,
There is my home, My Wildwood home."

Richard Bennett's wife, Elizabeth, died in September 1928 and Sunset Camp passed on to their daughter, Nellie. She and her husband, Maurice A. Jones, ran the camp until the early 1950's when it ceased operation. In 1955 the property was sold to James Bird. A year later the camp was broken up and sold to individual camp owners.

THE ANTLERS

In the March 20, 1920 edition of the *Warrensburg News*, it was reported: "The Antlers, a summer hotel at Raquette Lake, has been sold to New York parties. The hotel grew up from a small camp and was developed by the late Charles Bennett, who made a fortune from it. . . ."

"The hotel, conducted by Miss Margaret Bennett, and sold by her recently, was purchased by a company known as the Cedar Island Corporation. The price is said to have been $80,000. The new owners intend to use the property as a summer school and also to provide accommodations for relatives of the students who may desire to spend the summer at the lake. The school at present has 150 enrolled students."

Mrs. Ray K. Phillips, a member of the Cedar Island Corporation, established the Cedar Island Camp on Fourth Lake in 1916. When Antlers was purchased she moved the camp to the property and the campers were housed in tents behind the hotel or "main house" as it was known.

In 1922, H.L. Dabler was commissioned to hire a crew and

construct the Girls Camp as it is today. The corporation also acquired property on Woods Point, accessible only by water, on which a boys camp was to be built. Dabler remained as superintendent of maintenance for both camps. Max Berg, a partner of Mrs. Phillips, took charge of the Boys Camp maintaining a residence there while Mrs. Phillips directed the Girls Camp.

In 1951 Berg and Phillips retired and sold the hotel and property to S.&I. Hotels, Inc. from New Jersey who operated the Antlers as an American plan hotel from the date of purchase through the summer season of 1955. They also operated the golf course which had been built by Berg and Phillips about 1925. S.&I. Hotels, Inc. sold the Antlers of Raquette Lake, Inc. in March of 1956. The operation of the hotel and golf course continued through the summer of 1956 and 1957. It was then broken into units and resold.

In April 1958, Donald and Mary Elizabeth Langham purchased a sizable portion of the Antlers property. Don made his first visit to Raquette in 1935, hunting with his father and Gerry Lanphear, a Raquette Lake native and guide.

"I fell in love with the woods and often returned," says Langham, "staying at Ma and Pa Taylor's or with Ott and Hazel Lanphear."

Before acquiring the property at Antlers, the Langhams maintained a family cottage on Rondaxe Lake where Don was a licensed guide.

The parcel at Antlers consisted of the former Canteen, boat livery, four terrace cottages and Cedar cottage with 300 feet of shoreline. Twelve rooms in the cottages served as motel rooms. The Canteen operated as a restaurant and bar. The business, known as "The Antlers Motel," derived most of its business from the nearby Boys and Girls Camps.

In 1959, Langham purchased an additional lot from Antlers of Raquette Lake, Inc. on which they built a home as their permanent residence. The Antlers Motel property was sold to the Faculty-Student Association of State University Teachers College at Cortland, Inc. in 1965. Langham retained sixty feet of shoreline at the north end of the property where he built a sportsman's lodge. The following year the lodge was sold along with thirty-five feet of shoreline to George and Marguerite Fuge. The Fuges used it as a winter residence until 1985 when Fuge retired as Director of Cortland State Outdoor Center. It is now their permanent home. At the time Cortland purchased the motel property from Langham they also purchased the large main building (one of the original Bennett structures) from Antlers of Raquette Lake, Inc.

With the exception of the Girls Camp and Cortland property, Antlers is now owned by private camp owners.

RAQUETTE LAKE BOYS AND GIRLS CAMPS

In 1951 when Berg and Phillips sold the hotel property, they also sold the Girls Camp to Lee Krimsky. The Boys Camp on Woods Point was sold to Gordon Liebowitz and Phil Drucker and in 1967 the Boys Camp was again sold, this time to David Gold.

On July 17, 1973, after 17 years experience and ownership of other camps, Jerry Halsband of New York purchased both camps and once again they were run as a unit.

The Girls Camp is in the original form except for the dining room which burned in 1943 and had to be rebuilt. The camp is comprised of fourteen bunkhouses, dining, hall, recreation hall, gymnasium, trading post, first aid station and assorted utility buildings. There are tennis courts and a large outdoor arena with huge fireplaces. In the 1950's the original dining room was moved to its present site where it is used as a gymnasium.

Accommodations at the Boys Camp are similar to those at the Girls Camp. Both have excellent water sport facilities in addition to many other activities.

Three buildings used as dormitories were damaged extensively when a tornado-like disturbance passed through Raquette Lake on the evening of August 30, 1984. Fortunately the boys, numbering between 40 and 50, were in the dining room at the time.

"It had to have been a mini-tornado," said Dean Pohl, in charge of maintenance at the camp. "We had a wooden dugout on a masonry foundation and it moved 20 feet."

The camps maintain a large, wooden, gas-propelled launch, called *The Antlers*, built to handle well in shallow water. Built in 1924 at Alexandria Bay, it was purchased by Berg and Phillips in 1926 to be used as a means of transport between the camps. Getting the launch to Raquette Lake was quite a feat since it was necessary to use special tractors to transport it down the old

Uncas Road coming from Eagle Bay into Raquette. At that time that was the only road into the Antlers.

From the time of its acquisition until 1934, Norton Bird and Arthur Baker alternated as pilots of the craft. In 1934 Charles Bird took over serving as pilot until 1952. In 1977 it was necessary to ship *The Antlers* off to be refurbished. This time it was transported back to Raquette by Sid Payne and his crew from Inlet. When the craft was delivered to the village, it was lifted from its trailer by the claws of a logging truck and carefully dropped into the water. George Brownsell, then maintenance man for the camps, drove the launch back to camp. Hubie Gauthier served as pilot intermittently between 1952 and 1985. Another boat, *Raquetteer*, purchased from the Lake George Fire Island Ferry Company, is also in service.

In 1982, the camps purchased a used ferry boat to replace *The Antlers* while it was again being refurbished. It has a capacity for 50 passengers, much larger than either of the other craft. It was named *Killoquah V*. Four other Raquette Lake boats have also been named *Killoquah*, the Indian name for lake.

Jerry Halsband, owner of the camps, stated that in the 67 years of the camps' existence there have been only three superintendents of maintenance: H.L. Dabler, Joe Gauthier, and at present, Dean Pohl, a local contractor and builder.

Joe Gauthier and his wife, Maggie Tassier, were first employed at the camps in about 1943 or 1944. Their children, John, Joanne and Steve were born in Tupper Lake. While Joe worked in maintenance, Maggie cooked for the help at Antlers. Later she worked at Hunter's Rest. Joe retired from the camp in 1979, wintering in Florida. Gauthier's son, John, was one of the last two students to graduate from the Raquette Lake School in 1949. John, who had married Joan Cole, daughter of the late Howard and Mae Cole, maintains the Cole summer home at Raquette Lake. After Joe's retirement, he and Maggie summered in Raquette Lake until 1983 when they settled permanently in Florida. Maggie Gauthier died February 3, 1987.

Dean Pohl and his wife, Donna, are employed at the camp summers. They have four children: Bill, Rachel, Jim and Rebecca.

Halsband has made a practice of employing native Raquette Lakers whenever possible. Jane Tracy, another Raquette Laker has been in the camps' employ for "more years than I care to remember."

The Raquette Lake Boys and Girls camps have become a tradition in Raquette. The tourist seasons begin and end with camp openings and closings. They not only afford recreational and learning experiences for the young, but camp owners have worked diligently to maintain the camps in their original forms. The camps remain visual reminders of Raquette Lake's historical past.

CHAUNCEY HATHORNE

Accommodations on Raquette Lake were sparse when Chauncey Hathorne arrived in 1877. Sam Payne at Sucker Brook Bay, Charles Blanchard on Indian Point, and the Bennett brothers on Long Point maintained the only camps on the lake catering to sportsmen.

In 1855 Hathorne visited Blue Mountain Lake for the first time. During the winters of 1856 and 1857 he spent time on Eagle Lake. He then returned to Saratoga where he operated the Avery Lake House for a short period. Suffering from tuberculosis, he returned to Blue Mountain Lake, settling on the eastern shore where he built several crude cabins to board sportsmen he guided.

He moved to Raquette Lake in 1877, settling on Golden Beach, and built rough accommodations known as "Chauncey Hathorne's Summer Camp" with a guest fee of $1.00 per day.

A year later, Hathorne built Hathorne's Forest Cottages, described as built in the Swiss style and nicely furnished, which he maintained until his death in 1891.

Chauncey Hathorne was described in Frank Carlin's diary as "being tall and slim, well educated but rather odd. In later life he became a heavy drinker and a recluse. His only contact was his housekeeper, Elmira Rose."

On November 9, 1891, Hathorne went out in his guideboat alone. When he did not return, a search was begun. The next day he was found with one leg hooked in the boat, floating in shallow water between Echo Camp and Big Island. It was believed he may have suffered a heart attack, dying before he fell out of the craft. He is buried at Blue Mountain Lake.

Durant, who had acquired Hathorne's property, sold it to the state in 1897. From 1903 until 1909, it was occupied by Freeland Jones of Blue Mountain Lake. Joseph Murray of Troy took possession of the Golden Beach property in 1910 which he used as a summer residence for several years. New York State repossessed the land which the Conservation Department now maintains as a public campsite.

WILBUR'S RAQUETTE LAKE HOUSE

The only hotel in the Raquette Lake area in the 1850's, known as Wilbur's Raquette Lake House, was primitive. Through the years after its construction in 1856, it changed hands several times, first to Cyrus Kellogg, then to Thomas R. Cary and later to his son, Reuben Cary of Long Lake.

In *Adirondack Country*, White relates, "One old hotel register of the Raquette Lake House, . . . tells something about the visitors who came in its first fifteen years. By 1871 the hotel had entertained twenty-five hundred guests. One party appeared in 1864 about whom someone noted in the register, "all drunk." . . . In July one guest wrote, "Going home to Chicago where there is whiskey," and another added, "Been temperance man for eight days from necessity." In August of the same summer, one gentleman commented, "Been sleepless all the time. My home is Heaven, my rest is not here."

For sixteen years the Raquette Lake House served visitors and sportsmen, ceasing operation in the fall of 1873. After laying idle for a while, George Leavitt, a lumberman from Warren County acquired it in 1878. He moved part of the old log structure to the Forked Lake end of the carry, enlarged it and operated it as "The Forked Lake House." Eventually it changed hands again and became a popular hotel known as "Fletchers."

KENWELL'S RAQUETTE LAKE HOUSE

During the mid to late 1880's sportsmen found meager accommodations at Payne's at Sucker Brook Bay, the Bennetts on Long Point, Hathorne's on Golden Beach and Blanchard's on Green

Point. However, Isaac Kenwell's hotel, the "Raquette Lake House" (the second so named) on what was then Kenwell's Point, was the only real hotel on the lake.

The two-story hotel flourished for thirteen years before it burned in 1887. It was never replaced. Kenwell sold the property to the Honorable Dennis McCarthy of Syracuse who erected a private camp on the site. Kenwell then moved to Indian Lake.

In addition to the McCarthy cottages on what is now known as Tioga Point, there was also "Camp Deerhurst," owned by Frank Platt, son of U.S. Senator Tom Platt of New York City. In the 1890's McCarthy sold his property to William A.T. Strange of Paterson, New Jersey. Sometime after 1915, Strange sold out to Platt.

Frank Carlin's notes reveal that Strange owned a black-hulled clipper-front boat called the *Lorna Doone* which was included in the sale of the property.

MOYNEHAN'S RAQUETTE LAKE HOUSE

In 1903 Patrick Moynehan built the Raquette Lake House which remained in operation for almost twenty-four years. The three-story, wooden structured hotel sat in the center of the village, with a tennis court beside it on an attractively landscaped parcel. George R. Swarthout became its second proprietor.

George Reardon, who operated the hotel on lease for many years, was listed as proprietor in the 1915 census. During that time employees included John Morse Jr. house detective, George T. Burns chief clerk and Elber Burnham chef.

An advertising booklet printed by Reardon in 1915, embellished with pictures of the establishment and surrounding attractions gave the following description of the hotel and services:

> Raquette Lake House is a modern summer hotel, with spacious airy rooms, well lighted, and the rooms and large piazzas give beautiful views in all directions. The hotel is up-to-date in equipment, facilities and furnishings, with electric lights, rooms with bath, and a long distance telephone. The offices and public rooms are comfortable and convenient, and the parlor and assembly hall are provided with victrola and

> pianos. The hotel, although in the heart of the Adirondack wilderness, is easy of access, for the railroad station and steamboat docks are near at hand, also the post office and telegraph office, and modern store.... The cuisine of the Raquette Lake House is unexcelled and the table plentifully supplied with fresh vegetables, eggs, milk and dairy products. An excellent orchestra furnishes music.... Open all year ... rates $15.00 and up per week, transient rates $2.50 and up per day.

Rates were later raised to $16 and $3 when a new dining room, guest rooms with open fireplaces and private baths were added.

The Raquette Lake House was destroyed during the fire of 1927.

TIOGA POINT

The exact date that Kenwell's Point was renamed Tioga Point is unknown. The earliest information obtained was from a 1903 edition of a U.S. Geological Survey Map which shows the point as Tioga Point.

The most comprehensive information available on further activities at Tioga Point is after 1919 when the property was sold to Dr. Samuel Evans of New York by a Livingston Platt.

Robert Morley Evans of Shelton, Connecticut, (grandson of Dr. Samuel Evans) tells that Platt had the camp greatly expanded. "Platt prepared the camp for full use," said Evans. "The story goes that the first full summer there Mrs. Platt died and he left and never returned."

Dr. Evans and his wife, Ellen Hoe, had three children, Ellen, Robert T. and Samuel. When Dr. Sam's wife died at an early age, he took upon himself the task of raising them alone. During the summer months the children spent their time at Tioga. As they grew older and married, they spent the summers at the camp with their children. Before Dr. Evans' death in 1932, he sold the property to his daughter, Ellen, and her husband, Robert Lewis.

In August 1982, Mrs. Ellen Lewis Parisot of Wilton, Connecticut, granddaughter of Dr. Sam Evans, visited Raquette Lake for the first time in forty years. She boated to Tioga Point (accessible

Courtesy Jerry Halsband

The Raquette Lake Girls Camp, built in 1922 is in its original form. The boat house pictured remains in service. Circa 1922.

Courtesy Horace Bartow

Richard Bennett's "Sunset Camp" opened in 1880.

Author's Collection

"Forest Cottages" established in 1878 by Chauncey Hathorne. Circa 1890's.

Courtesy Robert M. Evans

Dr. Sam Evans. Circa early 1930's.

Courtesy Robert M. Evans from Walter Burg

Evans' boat "The Weneederagin" was bought about 1930 from the Albany Boat Works. Circa 1930's.

Courtesy Robert M. Evans

The "New House" at Evans' Camp. Circa 1930's.

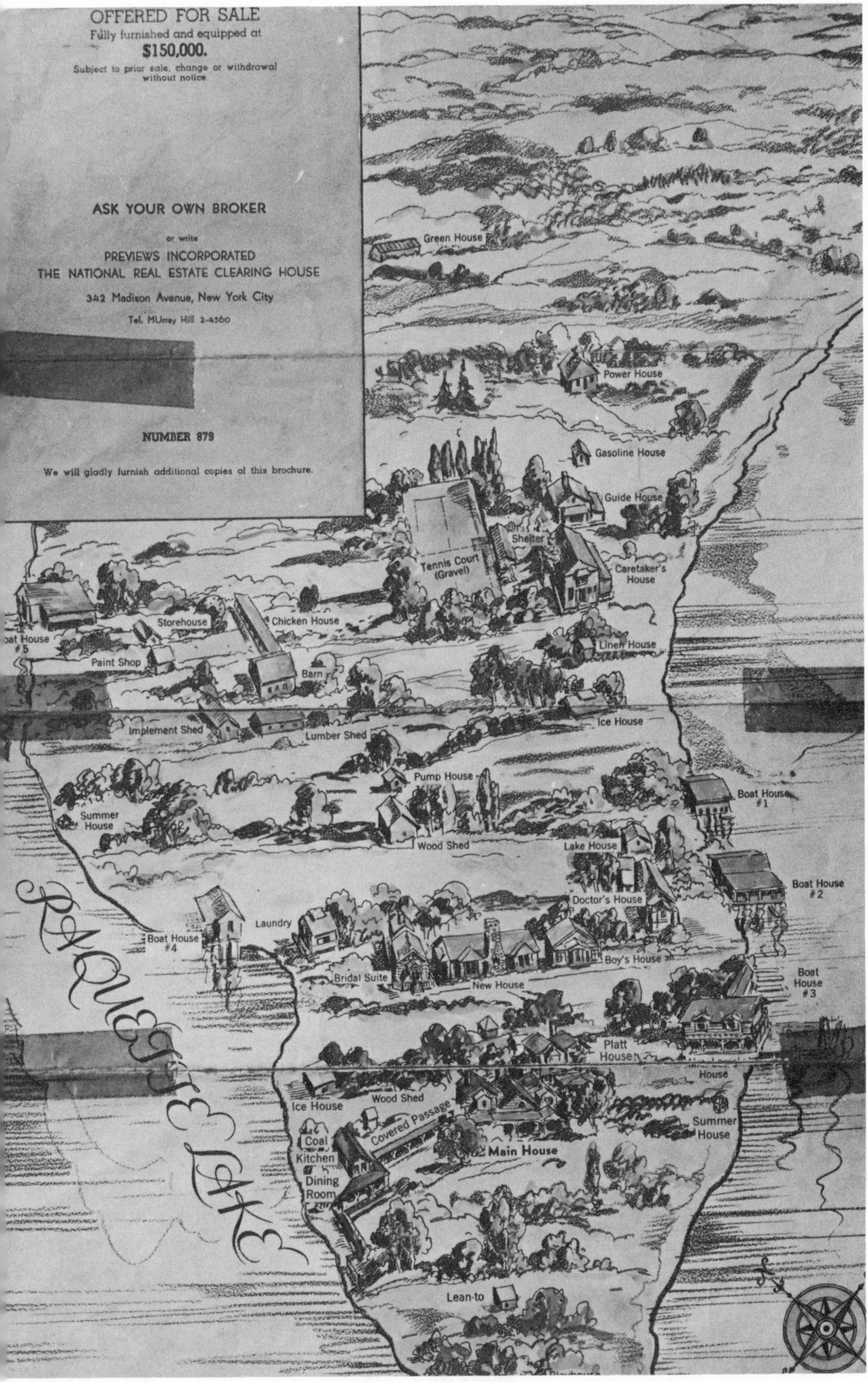

Courtesy Robert M. Evans from Burg Collection

Map of Evans' Camp illustrating buildings on premises when it was put on the market for sale. Circa 1930's.

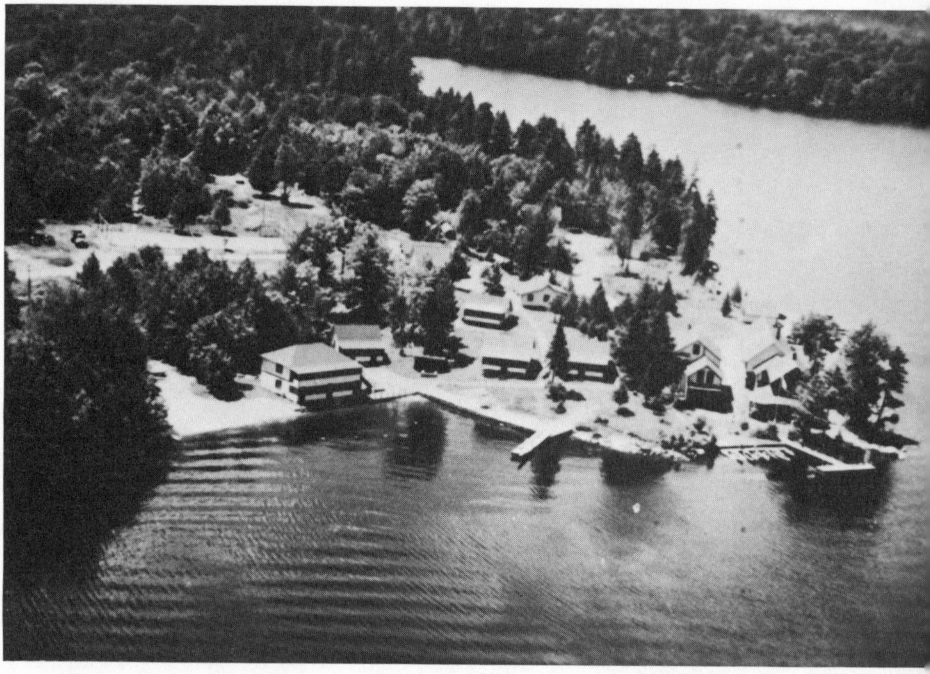

Courtesy Edna Colligan

Aerial view of Hunter's Rest. Circa 1930's.

Courtesy C.H. Carlin

Frank Carlin in "Twildo." Circa 1900.

Courtesy C. H. Carlin

Frank Carlin set up the first marina on Raquette Lake in the 1890's renting canoes and selling fishing gear. Circa 1900.

Courtesy C. H. Carlin

Frank Carlin and son Charles Henry hauling wood for sale. Circa 1915.

Courtesy C. H. Carlin

Carlin's Livery. Circa early 1940's.

Courtesy C. H. Carlin

C. H. Carlin as a boy with friends in large guideboat. L-R: Alfred Egenhofer, C. H. Carlin, Everett Jones, Arthur Mick, Richard Collins Jr., Earl Blanchard, Andrew Sims and Roscoe Carlin. Circa 1920.

Courtesy C. H. Carlin

Mary Ann Carlin, whose hobby was photography, had many of her photos made into postcards which she sold at her gift shop adjoining the boat livery. Circa 1920.

Author's Collection

Henry Carlin visited his old homestead, the Raquette Lake Marina. Circa 1982.

only by water) and "had the happy experience of unexpectedly meeting her cousin, Robert Morley Evans." Evans had been coming to Raquette for a summer holiday for many years, camping at Tioga.

"I was very surprised," stated Mrs. Parisot, "to find my cousin camping in lean-to #6 where the old sailboat house used to be on the back side. I hadn't seen my cousin for a number of years. It was a joyous reunion."

"A semi-professional photographer," she continued, "Robert had taken many pictures of the buildings now burned down. We used his photos to examine the foundations and matched each house to each foundation and path."

"I remember," recalled Ellen, "when there always seemed to be so many people visiting the camp. Tennis, speed-boats, canoes and climbing Blue Mountain or fishing Sargent Pond seemed to take up our time. When everyone was not eating in the main dining room served by a large staff, they were up on the bluff roasting marshmallows and singing the camp song."

The camp song she referred to is the Camp Fire Song, written by her Uncle Sam Evans who was a musician. Walter Edmonds, a frequent guest at Tioga and author of *Drums Along the Mohawk*, wrote the words.

Robert Lewis, Ellen's father, told her of some of the escapades he remembered. "He recalled his visits to Collier's camp and bowling in their large alley," she related. "He laughed as he told of going to church on Church Island where Dr. Sam was in charge of the music and the choir. The family and their house-guests all sang out of tune and then would sneak out of the church window one by one until no choir was left singing and Dr. Sam was left playing the organ—alone and furious."

Dr. Sam's brother, Reverend Anthony Evans, also of New York City, arrived at Raquette Lake in 1889 and set up a camp. He performed Sunday services at the Church of the Good Shepherd on St. Hubert's Isle. According to Robert Evans, he was still conducting occasional services during the 1920's when the Evans family was in residence.

Ellen recalled that her father talked about one of the Evans' boats, the *Weneederagin* (We-need-er-agin), which he used for aquaplaning (with Ellen on his shoulders). This boat replaced their boat, the *Weneeder*, which her father felt was not satisfactory.

Robert Evans was most helpful describing the architectural details of the Evans estate.

> "There were five boathouses, three on one side of the property and two on the other. The dock house was called the Lewis house or boathouse number two. The number one boathouse was to the left. Additions had been added to the original Platt construction which had a little covered stoop and became what was referred to as the "Bridal Suite." The buildings were distinguishable by the outside siding, all of log construction."
>
> The large estate included a playhouse, summerhouse, lean-to, two additional summer cottages, the doctor's house, lake house, pump house, woodshed, barn, linen house and laundry. There was also a paint shop, storehouse, chicken house, and caretakers house named "The Harvey House" (resident caretaker Harvey lived there with his family). A guide house, gasoline house, power house, tennis court and green house were also on the premises.
>
> "I never saw the buildings in back too much," said Evans. "They were servant's quarters and we were not allowed to play there and disturb them."

Ellen Parisot possesses a family guest book dated from 1924 to 1939 which shows one of the last names recorded in 1936 was L.V. Groves, who later became the head of the Atomic Bomb project in Los Alamos under Oppenheimer during World War II.

On June 1, 1940, Tioga Point was sold to Mr. and Mrs. Walter Burg of New York City. They operated the camp as a resort hotel, "Tioga Point Hotel," but it never did well and on September 15, 1950 the Burg's sold it back to the Evans family.

The camp, offered by Evans for $150,000, was purchased on July 31, 1951 by the New York State Conservation Department from Ellen Evans Lewis and Robert J. Lewis. Records show a purchase price of $12,000 for up to twenty-two buildings and forty acres.

The camp lay dormant until it was opened as a Conservation Camp in 1952. It operated as the Raquette Lake Boys' Conservation Education Camp through 1966 during which a total of 5,241 boys attended the camp. It was administered, along with three other similar camps, by the Division of Conservation Education, New York State Conservation Department.

From 1952 through 1955 the camp program was supervised by Nicholas Drahos. LeRoy G. Irving, Conservation Educator, took over supervision from 1956 through 1966. At one point, Irving's son, Roy, worked at the Camp. Fred Thomas of Raquette Lake, the first caretaker, was replaced by Ernest Blanchard of Blue Mountain Lake in about 1958.

"As the buildings and physical plant were rapidly deteriorating and with no hope of adequate funding for maintenance or capital improvements forthcoming," related Irving, "the decision to discontinue the camp after the 1966 camping season was made."

During February 1967, all usable equipment was transported by truck over the ice and taken to the Lake Colby Camp outside Saranac Lake. Irving and his son assisted in the operation. With the exception of the caretaker's residence and the stone power house, the entire complex was burned to the ground under the supervision of New York State Forest Rangers.

Blanchard stayed on as caretaker until the spring of 1967 and supervised the moving of the 26-foot Steelcraft Cruiser which had serviced the camp. The cruiser was transferred to the Conservation Department Fish Research Facility on Lake Ontario.

On April 4, 1967 the property was transferred to the Division of Lands and Forests, New York State Conservation Department for Forest Preserve purposes.

Tioga Point has been operated as a public campsite since. All that remains of the original complex is the stone power house and a few original stone fireplaces that were built into the cottages.

THE CARLINS

Two brothers who came to Raquette Lake in the 1880's contributing to the growth of the area were George and Frank Carlin. George H. Carlin was born in 1870 in Bangor, New York, the son of William and Margaret Smith Carlin. Two years later, his brother, Frank D., was born. Migrating to Raquette Lake at an early age, both have left their mark on its history.

George was first to arrive in Raquette in 1885. Frank followed in 1888. For the first eight to ten years they worked at various jobs acquainting themselves with the area, while they decided how they would "make their fortunes." George chose the hotel business.

In 1893 George Carlin opened an establishment at the camp of guide John Jones, a short distance from Bryere's Brightside, which he named "The Bear Trap." In addition to being a meeting place for gentlemen, it served as a store supplying staples to the residents on that side of the lake.

The following year he found a parcel more to his liking on a point close to Antlers. At the time, Dr. Sherwood maintained a one-room camp on the property. Carlin purchased a quit claim deed from Sherwood for one hundred dollars. (Later the property claim was contested by the state and after a lengthy legal battle, it was decided in Carlin's favor.) It was on this site George Carlin built his famous Hunter's Rest.

Frank Carlin described his brother as "a strange businessman, but successful. In about 1896 or 1897," Frank recalled, "George purchased about $2,000 in goods, which for some reason he hid and went into bankruptcy. I had to run Hunter's Rest that season while he served thirty days. Guess he learned his lesson, or it served his purpose, he never did anything so stupid again."

George Carlin is also remembered as being quite frugal despite his wealth. "He never went to a doctor or dentist that I recall," said Frank, "and from April 20 to November 20, Mattie Jones, his housekeeper, cut his hair."

Rowena Bird recalls George Carlin as "a saving man with a good sense of humor. If someone tried to borrow money, he would step outside his store and look up and say, 'Do you see a bank sign up there?' He always had funny sayings to make us laugh," continued Rowena. Although he remained a bachelor, "he was good with little kids. He'd give them a chocolate bar and set them on the back of Tippy, his big Collie, to give them a ride."

George Carlin ran Hunter's Rest successfully until he retired in 1948. Jim and Marion Bird purchased it in the fall of that year, running the camp as an American plan hotel until 1962 when they sold it to Mr. and Mrs. Joe Picinich. The camp was converted to a co-ed camp, "Camp Eagle Feather," and operated until 1979 when Dean Pohl purchased the property. He immediately sub-divided and sold parcels to Jay Cummings and Jim Bird. Bird sold his parcel to Dr. John Sammon, Jr., who at this writing owns nearly all of the land area where the original hotel buildings were located. Most of these old buildings were moved or torn down with the exception of the dining room building and tap room building. These were converted into second homes for the Sammon family.

The former two-story boathouse building was moved and completely rebuilt by Eunice and Jay Cummings, It is now their year-round residence.

In May 1942, after a brief illness, George H. Carlin died at age 72 at the Good Samaritan Hospital in West Palm Beach, Florida. His interment took place in Mt. Olivet Cemetery, Utica.

Carlin's estate was estimated at approximately $300,000. His nephew (Charles) Henry Carlin said of his uncle, "I visited him on several occasions, but had no hint of his financial worth."

When the Carlins arrived at Raquette Lake, although the only transportation was by boat, there was no marina. Frank Carlin saw a future in operating a boat livery. He set up the first marina on Raquette Lake in the 1890's on property in the village, now known as the Raquette Lake Marina. At first he only rented canoes and sold fishing gear but later added row boats, and when they became available, motors.

Carlin had gained title to much of the surrounding land behind the marina and on the hill above where the railroad siding was later built in 1900. He also maintained title to property on the shore where Route 28 now passes. "There was a wooden tower that was the boundary towards Lamphears Poplar Point," explained Frank's son, Henry Carlin, "and the end was just short of what was Gardener's house, including what is now Bird's Marina."

"Dad had a marina annex where Bird's is at one time. Later he gave a piece of the property to Henry Taylor who was guiding for Morgan, in exchange for Taylor's services renting boats for the marina on the site."

In 1900 the large marina building containing a shop on ground level and apartments occupying the second and third level was built. It is still in service.

On March 2, 1904 Frank Carlin married Mary Ann Pelletier. The ceremony was held at St. William's on the point with Father Fitzgerald officiating.

Mary Anne Pelletier, one of five children, was born April 17, 1875, daughter of Jane Bannon and Joseph Pelletier, a Civil War veteran. Henry Carlin remembers his mother telling of their fear of Indians when the family lived in Beloit, Kansas. He could not comprehend the situation. He chuckled as he related how his "hillbilly grandmother, Jane, smoked a corncob pipe."

"Would you believe," he said, "my grandmother and grandfather were both addicted to playing poker, and kept a sack of silver dollars on hand ready for a game at anytime and with anyone?"

Henry Carlin spoke of his childhood. "When I was young at the livery-marina," reminisced Carlin, "we had, on the village side, a barber shop with a pool table and a slot machine. That was where the post office was, with Mrs. Farrington as Postmistress."

"We had the apartment over the shop which was rented to teachers or families most of the time." With a chuckle, he added, "The saying was, to be a native Raquette Laker one had to have worked at Antlers or one of the other camps, or had to have lived over the marine shop."

Continuing with his description of the marina, Carlin elaborated. "The third floor was used as a residence for some of the family including me. Behind there was a concrete cellar and canoe and rowboat storage. Next came the ice house. We also had a small shop where mother sold items of interest to visitors. In addition to mother's hobby, photography, she was an excellent craftswoman."

Rowena Bird, who still lives on the hill above the marina near the adjoining Raquette Lake Chapel, remembers "The shop always smelled so good from Mrs. Carlin's sweetgrass baskets and balsam pillows. She was a very energetic, strong woman who took pictures, bailed boats, ran motor boats on occasion and was very active in the Catholic Church."

On May 26, 1925, Mary Carlin was stricken with a cerebral hemorrhage. Her son, Roscoe, who was attending school at Glens Falls, was summoned. At that time the road had not been built to Raquette Lake and he was brought by auto to Forked Lake where he had to obtain a motor boat to reach Raquette. Within a day of her seizure, Mary Carlin died.

Frank and Mary Carlin has a son, Daniel, born June 5, 1915 who died three days later. Two other sons, (Charles) Henry and Roscoe, were born of that union.

Henry Carlin, born 1906, became a Colonel in the U.S. Air Force. His service career began when he enlisted in the Army

Infantry in 1935. He was later transferred to the Signal Corps and then the Air Corps. Carlin was in Pearl Harbor on December 7, 1941 and participated in the invasion of Europe and was engaged in the opening of the Korean War.

When he retired in 1956 he was recipient of sixteen decorations including fourteen battle stars. Henry died January 14, 1986 in Auberry, California.

Roscoe Carlin was born about 1907 or 1908. He remained in Raquette Lake assisting his father in the Marina business until Frank Carlin retired in the late 1930's. Roscoe later inherited part of his father's holdings.

Roscoe died in Old Forge around 1965 at the age of 58. He was survived by his wife, Lillian Peak, a son, Roscoe, in California, a son, Stephen G., serving in the Coast Guard at Camp May, New Jersey and a daughter, Mary, of California.

His livery was sold to Virgil Masters on August 24, 1960. The name was changed from Carlin's Boat Livery to Raquette Lake Marina. Edgar Lamphear managed the operation until 1966 when Al Timm of New Jersey took possession. By then only the original marina building remained and a covered boathouse which Masters had built.

RAQUETTE LAKE MARINA

The Timm family began vacationing at Raquette Lake in the 1940's, becoming property owners in the early 1950's. Upon purchasing the marina, Timm urged Edgar Lamphear to remain in his employ for a time. Gregory and Richard Timm, who were attending college during the first few years of operation, joined their father working summers.

In 1968 Raquette Lake Marina acquired the McCoy Cottage adjoining the marina property where manager Greg Timm resided with his children, Tina, Bob and Heather, his wife, Dawn and her son, Dieter Erdmann.

Increased parking facilities and dock space have been added. Four huge storage sheds have been built on level ground carved out of the rock ledges on which much of the marina property sits.

A subsidiary business, Raquette Lake Ceramics, was also maintained during the first seventeen years. The first classes were held in the lean-to adjoining the marina building. After an indoor stairway and other carpentry work was completed by local carpenter Art Jenkins, the ceramic business utilized the entire third floor of the building.

In addition to six classes a week, prospective studio owners came to the "first ceramic studio in the North Country," traveling within a radius of 300 miles to purchase supplies and learn how to set up and operate studios of their own. Teachers traveled from parts of the U.S. and Canada to participate in specialized classes in porcelain creation. For thirteen years the Town of Long Lake Recreation Department sponsored ceramic classes for all students from third grade through twelfth. In 1979 the shop was closed to the public and classes discontinued. Only the mail order ceramic book and supply business continued.

In 1986 it became necessary to place new siding over the original on the marina building for easier maintenance. At the same time an addition was built, increasing the service area. A second office was also built to be used as the branch office for the Rivet-Eldridge Better Homes and Gardens Realty. The real estate office, managed by Dawn Timm, serves the Raquette Lake, Blue Mountain Lake and Long Lake areas.

CHAPTER IV

RAQUETTE LAKE GUIDES

Even before Reverend Murray enticed city sportsmen to come to the Adirondacks to "find good sporting," hunters and fishermen had started coming to the northernmost part of the country, especially to Raquette and Long Lakes. Unaccustomed to living with nature in strange surroundings, they needed the services of an experienced woodsman. Almost anyone living in the area, eager to earn money, would take time from their normal occupations to guide.

As the need for guides increased, many moved to Raquette Lake from Indian and Blue Mountain Lakes. The duties of a good guide included, in addition to guiding, obtaining supplies, carrying the heavy loads, cooking and making arrangements for transportation and sleeping accommodations. They were also expected to entertain clients with outlandish stories around the evening campfire.

In 1894, Wallace's annual *Guide to the Adirondacks*, stated guide fees ranged from $2.50 to $3.00 a day, and he advised against "the practice of penetrating these wilds unaccompanied by a guide. . . . These useful and trusty men, generally noblemen at heart if not in pretension, are really indispensible to those who visit the Adirondacks."

In addition to Raquette Lake guides mentioned elsewhere in this volume, there were others. Many have been completely forgotten, some remain but names on a page of a history book. Numbered among the latter are Wesley Bates, Phillip Bell, George Bentley, John Grogan, William Cullen, James Harrington, John Higgins, Orrin LaPelle, Francis (Doc) and Alexander (Cal) LaPrairie, John Richards, Warren Steeves and his brother, Hy, and Arthur Sheldon for whom Sheldon Bay was presumably named. One of the earliest guides arriving in the North Country in the mid 1870's was Joseph O.A. Bryere.

JOE BRYERE

Joseph O.A. Bryere was born in April 1859 of French parents in the village of St. Anne de la Parade in Quebec. During the gold rush, his father, Pierre, left for California to find a great fortune and never returned.

As the years passed, Joseph grew tall (six-foot-two), lanky and strong as a "bull elephant." Like his father, he became a trapper and a woodsman. It was said he was known in St. Anne as "number one" at wrestling, doing his share of kicking, gouging and biting. The story is told how Joe met a bull moose on the trail, face to face, grabbed its wide horns, wrestled it and cut its throat, then dragged the 1,200 pounds of meat into the village.

Joe left home to find his fortune. In the mid-1870's, he arrived in the North Country, where he first worked as a lumberjack, then as a guide. When Charles Durant built "Camp Fairview," Bryere became its caretaker.

One summer day, while visiting Blue Mountain, Joe was introduced to Mary Gooley (b. 1861, Albany), who was working as a salesgirl in the local store. The two were immediately attracted to each other. To be close to Bryere, Mary remained in the North Country that winter, moving in with the family of George W. Turnicliff, proprietor of the Prospect House where she obtained employment. The following summer, on July 8, 1884, the couple were married at Ed Bennett's inn, "Under the Hemlocks." Their first home was the boathouse at "Camp Fairview" where Bryere was caretaker.

Bryere, realizing the increased number of city visitors who required accommodations, decided he and his bride would own and operate a boarding house. He looked all over Raquette Lake in search of the perfect spot where they could settle. Finally he decided upon a site on Indian Point under what is known as "The Crags" (steep, rugged rocks) extending into the lake for a distance of one and a half miles. Without deed or title, he and Mary "squatted" and began building "Brightside."

The couple pitched a tent and Joe moved some leftover logs from the building at Fairview to the site. Using these, they built an open three-sided log cabin with a huge fireplace in front. They began clearing their land of trees, moving them down to the water where they were towed by guideboat to the sawmill at the foot of the lake. The logs were cut into lumber and delivered back by steamboat. They then built a bark cabin to protect them from the winter blizzards and below zero temperatures.

Mary was considered one of the most beautiful young women in the North Country, and one of its great cooks. In addition to these virtues, she could swing an axe or pull a cross-cut saw with any man. She was a dead shot with a rifle or shotgun, doing her share of hunting bear, partridge and deer for meat during the winter. Supplies were brought to camp by guideboats. When the lake froze, the Bryeres cut ice and buried it in sawdust for the summer. In spring, they tapped the maples for sugar, and as soon as weather permitted, worked on their dream—a hunting and fishing lodge for city "sports." They built a barn, bought a cow and horse and finally built their first real house. The structure contained a living room, dining room, kitchen and six guest rooms (there were no baths). The first guests registered at Brightside in May 1891.

In the 1900 census of Raquette Lake, Joe and Mary Bryere were listed as innkeepers and their four children, Franklin, Florence, Clara and Kathleen as students. The children attended school first on Long Point, then later at the school in the village when it was moved to its present site. When the lake was frozen over, they crossed by snowshoe. When the water was free of ice they were transported by boat. Arthur Martin, their first teacher, was a boarder at Brightside. He transported the students by guideboat, picking up others along the way.

Others listed as permanent residents at Brightside included: Libbie Gooley, Mary's sister who was housekeeper, Dennis Dillon, school teacher, John Carlisle, a painter, James Sutliff, a servant and Seth Pierce, a carpenter.

In 1900, Joe and Mary built a second and larger building joined to the first by a covered walkway. It contained eleven guest rooms and a beautiful living room. This time they were assisted with the construction by their boarder, Seth Pierce.

When the first house burned in 1905, the three once again cut the timber from below "The Crags," boomed it to the sawmill, and in one year, rebuilt the house, this time with nine bedrooms. Both buildings are still in service. The architecture, especially of the second building, is a combination of "gingerbread" trimming and Quebec roofs, designed to shed the snow readily.

The Bryeres and their guests shared a mutual admiration for each other. Some, in the earlier days, had to travel thirty miles by buckboard after an overnight journey by train. When they arrived, they were greeted warmly and assured of privacy, good service and excellent food. Joe, always in control, did or supervised everything, including, much to her annoyance, his wife's cooking.

In addition to being a conscientious hotel keeper, Bryere was in demand as a guide, carpenter and caretaker. In one of his books, Seneca Ray Stoddard singled out Bryere as "an artist of rustic work." For four years, Camp Stott's on Bluff Point was under Bryere's care during the winter months.

SETH PIERCE

Seth Pierce was born in December 1828 in New York State. By 1850 he was living in Newcomb where he married Eleanor Heath. The couple apparently moved to Wisconsin where their son, Edward Clifton was born in 1855. Another son, Seth M. Pierce, Jr. was born in New York in 1859.

The 1880 census shows Pierce's son, Edward, as a guide at Kenwell's Hotel. Three years later Ed moved to Long Lake. Seth, Jr., also a guide, married Annice Skinner in 1866 and fathered four children. The family left Raquette in the early 1900's. Seth, Sr., described by Frank Carlin as "a slim man with large hands and one of the best rustic carpenters and guides in the area," remained in Raquette Lake to pursue his occupation. For a while he lived in a small house he built at Conwells.

Seth, a veteran of the Civil War, was a great delight to the Bryere children. He lived at Brightside for a number of years, and even after he moved to a closed-in lean-to on Ladew's property on Osprey, he continued spending Christmas with the Bryere family. Young Clara remembered him fondly, "On Christmas morning, each of us children would stand on a step on the enclosed stairway of the inn, "Uncle Seth," dressed in his Civil War uniform, at the top. It was a regular rite with us." Pierce died at Brightside.

Rowena Bird recalls working for Joe Bryere in his later years. "When I worked for him, he was an old man. He had frozen both feet and gangrene had set in. Mr. Bryere was still very distinguished looking, but he couldn't walk or get around by himself. An old Russian who worked for him would wheel him around the grounds in a wheelbarrow. That was his big event of each day—to get out and see his big beautiful garden."

Joe Bryere died in 1941 at the age of 81. His wife, Mary, died in the 1950's.

After her father died, "Miss Brightside," as young Clara was called, gave up her nursing career and returned to Raquette Lake to assume active management of Brightside. During World War I, Clara had been a surgical nurse with the Roosevelt Hospital Unit at Base Hospital No. 15 - General Pershing's headquarters. After the war, she continued her career with a prominent New York doctor.

Mary remembered how, "at the turn of the century, the Game Commission brought in moose from the north and elk from the west in the belief they would propogate and increase the interest of hunting sports. The Raquette Lake country was barren of food for both species, and those that did not die became "domesticated." She recalled meeting "a big bull with huge blades who only wanted a little affection and the lady moose who moved into the village and mooched handouts."

When Clara Bryere first took over Brightside she found things difficult. Her father had apparently managed almost everything and she found her mother of little help when it involved business. Clara soon learned she had to solve problems using her own judgement. One of the first things she acquired was a pump. Until then, she had to keep a water hole open all winter. She took other problems one at a time and solved them.

When asked, "Don't you ever get bored? . . . Are you ever frightened? Is it worthwhile?" she replied, "There is no time for boredom . . . We are never frightened because there is nothing to be afraid of, and here, with the manifold offerings of the Adirondacks, it is very easy to forget the outside world you knew so well, but somehow, no longer seem to care about."

In 1955, Clara sold her property, reserving life use of her residence, to "Brightside on Raquette Lake Inc." It was operated as a hotel until about 1963 or 1964, with "fewer guests than family."

In 1975, five pieces of furniture Bryere had built for the hotel, Brightside, in 1888 were donated to the Adirondack Museum by his daughter, Clara Bryere.

The property at Brightside has been divided and sold to individual owners.

PAUL TIBBITTS

Paul Tibbitts was a guide who came to Raquette Lake around 1878 settling on Long Point near the Marion River. Although he did not remain in the area as long as some, he is important since the property he settled upon became known as Camp Marion. At one time he also owned Silver Beach. In the late 1880's Tibbetts was forced to vacate the premises because of ill health. He sold the land to John McLaughlin, then a merchant on the point. His death is recorded in 1891.

CAMP MARION

Joseph Grenon arrived at Raquette Lake the winter of 1889 working for W. W. Durant at Mohegan Lake. In 1892 he purchased Camp Marion from McLaughlin and built a one-story log cabin for himself. From 1892 until 1897 he added an ice house, root cellar and a second building.

When he married Margaret Guylander of Raquette Lake in 1897, he enlarged the camp. A year later he built a new two-story building adjoining the cottage to satisfy his family's needs. The couple had three children: Margaret, Lula and Robert Lawrence (Larry).

Joe Grenon became game protector in 1905. In the census of 1915 he is listed as running a boarding house and in 1925 as a hotel proprietor. There is no record of the date Camp Marion became a hotel.

An old advertising brochure of the camp noted that Grenon

boasted accommodations "equipped with a bath, hot and cold water and modern conveniences making life both comfortable and enjoyable. Its table is excellent and wholesome, supplied with fresh vegetables, eggs, milk and poultry"—and all this for as little as $18.00 and up per week. He also advertised an excellent tennis court, open camps for the guests who enjoyed life in the open and tents with platforms arranged as a sleeping room in the main building for those who liked tent life.

Grenon was an ambitious man. By 1916 his complex included a 16 x 13-foot addition (built in 1914 and still standing) with a second floor, a laundry, power house, barn, root cellar, three open camps, seven cottages, an ice house, boat house and wharf for the private launch which ran from the train station in the village. He sold the property to Wallace Yeaple in the late 1930's.

SILVER BEACH

In addition to Camp Marion, Paul Tibbetts also owned the property referred to as Silver Beach which he deeded to Grenon. On December 10, 1923, Joseph P. Grenon and his wife sold the property to Arthur J. Cunningham. Cunningham had possession of the property until about 1963 or 1964 when he sold to Joseph P. and Mary Edna Uzdavinis and Richard and Judith L. Cohen, reserving a small pie-shaped piece of the parcel for Matthew H. Gooding.

About 1972 or 1973 the larger parcel was divided into four equal parts in the names of Joseph P. Uzdavinis, Mary Edna Uzdavinis, Richard Cohen and Judith L. Cohen, and in April or May of 1986, the four parcels were sold to New York State with Gooding still maintaining his.

BILL BALLARD

Bill Ballard was born in Nova Scotia, son of William and Bridget Ford Ballard in December 1951. He arrived in Raquette Lake in the early 1880's where he met and married Mary Stretch in 1894.

The couple had six children, only two of whom lived. A son, William, born in 1899, followed in his father's footsteps, becoming a guide. He left Raquette Lake sometime before 1925. Their daughter, Sarah, was born in 1901 and married Arthur Baker, a carpenter at the Antlers, in 1922. They had two children.

Bill Ballard guided until he died of pneumonia in 1916. His wife, Bridget, succumbed in 1925. Both are interred at Blue Mountain Lake.

HENRY TAYLOR

Henry Taylor, born in Franklin Falls, Saranac in 1858, came to Raquette Lake with his first wife, Julia, in 1880. She died two years later at the age of nineteen. He then married Addie "Mae" Treadwell from Keyesville.

Taylor built a house (now occupied by the Blanchard family) in South Bay, where they started a small tourist home. In 1893 he lost the property in a sheriff's sale. He then moved to property owned by Frank Carlin. Carlin had a boathouse near the Taylor camp which he used as an annex to the Carlin Boat Livery in the village. He made arrangements for Taylor to rent boats in exchange for the land.

The Taylors built a small house, thought to be the first in the area with a cellar and wallpapered rooms. They set up five or six platform tents and took in seasonal guests. Each dwelling had its own woodburning stove which afforded comfortable temperatures during the cold winter.

Edna Colligan, who worked for the Taylors during the summers of 1927 and 1928, said Mae Taylor was extremely "fussy" about her boarders accommodations: "The tents were kept immaculate and the beds were covered with bedspreads and had embroidered pillow cases. They also had a dresser, bedside table and hooks to hang clothes.

Taylor claimed to have seen the railroad at North Creek in 1878 and gas used for the first time at the Tupper Lake Hotel. He guided for J.P. Morgan at Uncas for twenty-four years and numbered among his other clients A.G. Vanderbilt and J.D. Rockefeller, Jr. He enjoyed boasting that he refused to guide Lt.

Gov. Woodruff when he offered $50 a month to do so—because he "just didn't like him!"

Taylor died about 1938. His widow moved to Saranac and in about 1940 sold the property to Alex and Charlotte Lauterbach. They set up a small tackle and bait shop which they operated until they sold the property in 1968 to the present owner, Bob Skiba.

FRED MAXAM

Fred "Mossie" Maxam was born in 1856 of Henry and Lydia Patten Maxam in Baker Mills, New York. In 1885 he married a much younger woman, Ada May McNeill, a native of Illinois. The couple lived on a farm in the town of Johnsburg for many years. During this time two of their children died in infancy; two sons, Edward and George, and a daughter, Ethel, survived.

Mossie, a mason by trade, moved to Raquette Lake settling on South Bay next to the property occupied by Henry Taylor. Maxam earned his living as a trapper and a guide with his main source of income as house guide, first for Morgan at Camp Uncas, then at Kill Kare for ex-Governor Woodruff.

Ada Mae Maxam left Mossie in 1895 right after their daughter Ethel was born; she moved to Glens Falls, taking Edward and Ethel. George went to live with a school teacher aunt, Jennie Davidson, in Millcreek. When George was fourteen years of age, the aunt died and he returned to live with his father in Raquette Lake. Edward had already returned to Raquette.

In 1909 Ada contacted Mossie requesting financial aid for Ethel. He agreed on the condition Ethel live with him. Ethel was sent to the "Advance School" in Utica until 1911. During this period she spent her vacations at Kill Kare where he father was employed. Maxam then made arrangements for Ethel to board with a friend while she attended Indian Lake School.

"I recall seeing my father only twice until I was fourteen years of age," said Ethel. "He had a problem but was always a good father to me."

Ethel Maxam married Roscoe Tripp in 1914. The couple resided at Indian Lake where Roscoe died in 1943. Ethel is still a resident of Indian Lake.

Edward Jr. married Mae Maron, a native of Ireland. They moved to Portsmouth, New Hampshire where they had a son, Arthur. Edward died of influenza during the 1918 epidemic one week before Mossie received notice of the death of his other son, George, who was stationed at Camp Mead, Maryland. George Maxam, who is buried in Arlington National Cemetery, is listed as the only World War I casualty from Raquette Lake.

Mossie Maxam remarried, and in 1920 at age 66, fathered two girls, Molly and Kate. It is said that his favorite description of the twins was "Kate and Duplicate." In 1922, a son, Richard, was born.

Maxam died July 14, 1930 at Raquette Lake and was interred at Johnsburg. His family remained in Raquette until the children graduated from the twelfth grade at the Raquette Lake School. Ethel Tripp believes Molly now lives in Tampa and Kate in Miami.

Dayton Cleaveland and his wife Ella leased the property, using the cottages as rental units during the summer, until 1975 when they left Raquette Lake. The Maxam family still maintains ownership.

JOHN JONES

John Jones remains one of the few guides who has descendants still residing in the North Country. His granddaughter, Rowena Roblee Bird, remains in Raquette Lake.

Jones, born in Vermont in 1866, was the son of Melanchton and Jane Nobel Jones. The family moved from Vermont to Indian Lake around 1880. By the late 1880's, John Jones and his wife, Martha "Mattie" Gylander (b. 1869), were in Raquette Lake operating "Deerhurst Camps" which was situated between Bryere's Brightside and the Martin Homestead.

Three children were born to John and Mattie Jones, Elsie, Elmer and Anna Mae. No record has been found of Elsie. Elmer became a lineman on the Raquette Lake Railroad. In 1912, Anna Mae married Beecher Roblee (b. 1881) of North Creek, who was employed as a carpenter in Raquette Lake.

In 1916, Roblee became caretaker and guide for J.H. Ladew on Osprey Island. "Summer and winter," recalled Henry Carlin, "we, at the livery could set our morning clock by his passage. No matter the weather, he was never late." Roblee worked at Osprey until his death in 1934.

Anna Mae and Beecher Roblee had two children. Rowena, born in 1913, moved to the village to be closer to the school. She stayed with her paternal grandmother who lived on the hill behind what was then the railroad barn that housed private railroad cars (now the Raquette Lake Chapel). The couple's son, James, born in 1915, served in the 53rd Infantry 4th Division during World War II. He survived the war, but was drowned in Raquette Lake in 1950.

When John Jones died, Mattie continued the operation of Deerhurst Camp. Later she went to work at Hunter's Rest as George Carlin's housekeeper. The camp was rented to Dr. Foley who used it as a Catholic boys summer camp for about ten years. It was then acquired by a niece of Dr. Foley who was married to Gardner Callanen, an attorney from Utica.

Mattie's granddaughter Rowena says, "Mattie was still painting and varnishing the dining room floor at Hunter's Rest when she was 72. She was a remarkable woman and well-liked." Mattie died in 1943 at age 74, a year after the death of Hunter's Rest owner George Carlin.

Rowena, who resides in the Roblee family home, left Raquette Lake after graduating from the Raquette Lake School. She attended Plattsburgh Normal School for Teachers, returning to Raquette in 1933. In 1939 she married a classmate, Charlie Bird, who was working at Antlers. They continued to live with their children, Kathleen and Jim, in the old homestead. As the children grew older they left Raquette. Charlie died in 1978 leaving Rowena to live alone in the old homestead with only her memories —memories of the "good old days' which she shared.

> "I first remember the railroad men and caretakers of the camps lived on the hillside. There were lots of blueberries and raspberries along the tracks and roads. The whole shoreline was built up beautifully with heavy planks. There was boat signs for all camps' boats and a sidewalk from the station to the hotel and store.
>
> For about ten years after the end of the first World War, there were good times. Every summer an Italian organ grinder would come on the train with his

monkey. The monkey wore a little jacket and red cap and danced with his tin cup, going to the people to collect a penny or two. We had such a good time as we danced with him.

We had movies twice a week at the Casino—Hoot Gibson, Clara Bow! Sometimes power went off in the middle of the silent movie. People would leave, walk around for 15 minutes and then come back to see *Who Kisses Her?*, another movie.

We had a great 'pick up band' for our weekly dances; all of them played by ear except Bert Gardner. He played the piano and was the only one to ever take lessons. The other members 'picked up the tune' and included Hiny Gutlith, Charlie Egenhofer and the barber, William Hill, whose shop was at Carlin's livery then. The hotel hired an orchestra from out of town every weekend.

The dances were always fun, but the square dances were the best . . . and the Irish Jigs. Someone would always come in and do a jig.

George Jinks was one for that. He would put his hands behind his back, look up at the ceiling, and dance all around the room. He was really good, too.

We played tennis, and swam and watched the people coming and going; some with little Chinese dogs under their arms. Everyone met the 5:15 and saw the 8 p.m. sleeper out. It sure was a good life."

REUBEN MICK

In the 1960's, one of the oldest guides still residing at Raquette Lake was Reuben Mick. Mick was born in 1878 in the Town of Denmark in Lewis County, coming to Raquette Lake in 1896 to live with his sister, Rose Shied.

He guided and trapped on his own until 1905 when he signed on as guide at the Hasbrouck Camp on the north shore of Raquette Lake. Fifty years later he was still on the job. Outliving all of the Hasbrouck family, he saw the camp become part of New York State's Forest Preserve.

In 1905, Mick was appointed one of two Republican Election Inspectors. In 1908 he was elected Justice of the Peace, a position

Author's Collection

After the Bryeres built their "Brightside" on Raquette in 1890, they built this second, larger building in 1900 in which they resided. Circa 1970's.

Courtesy Doris and Glenn Martin

When the Bryeres built their second home, they were assisted with construction by Seth Pierce shown here with Joe Bryere. Circa 1900.

Courtesy Charlie Egenhofer

William "Bill" Egenhofer followed in his father's footsteps as a guide in the Raquette Lake area. Circa 1914.

Courtesy Buster Bird

Moses Leonard (Raquette Lake Forest Ranger), Gerald Kenwell and Reuben Mick out for a ride in one of Morgan's original guide boats. Circa late 1930's.

Courtesy Craig Gilborn

Mary Agnes Gooley and Joseph O.A. Bryere on their wedding day, July 8, 1884 at the Hemlocks.

Courtesy Edgar Lamphear

Guide Orrin Lanphear, on left, with two unidentified hunters. Circa 1930's.

he held for sixty years, the only unopposed Justice in the Town of Long Lake.

Mick often recalled time spent with the Morgans, Durants, Colliers and Vanderbilts who built fantastic camps in the early days. He boasted he had lived through two World Wars and remembered the gleaming spectacles and flashing teeth of Teddy Roosevelt when he was at the Lewis County Fair making his campaign speech. He always considered himself one of the pioneers, for when he arrived at Raquette Lake in 1896, the only inhabitant was Alvah Dunning. There was nothing much south of there until the settlement of Old Forge.

Mick liked to talk about the largest deer he remembered taking which weighed 220 pounds, and seeing elk on the ice. Sometimes he'd boast about taking a 30-pound trout using a 1½-pound sucker for bait.

Reuben and Julia Mick had six children: Mildred, Arthur, June, Charles, Reuben and Vincent.

Vincent, the youngest, was born in May 1915 and served in World War II. An excerpt from an unidentified newspaper reads:

> "Lieutenant Mick graduated from Raquette Lake High School in 1934 and the following year he attended St. Lawrence University at Canton. In 1936 he entered the Michigan State College of Mines at Houghton and three years later was graduated from there as a mining engineer.
>
> In the fall of the same year he accepted a position as mining engineer with the Neilson Gold Mining Co. and was sent to the Philippine Islands at Parcale Camarines Norte on Luzon to do research work for the company. He remained on the Islands and when the Japanese invaded the Philippines following the attack on Pearl Harbor, Mick joined the U.S. Army Engineer Corps and was commissioned a Second Lieutenant.
>
> A Christmas card received December of 1941 was the last word the Mick's received from their son."

In a 1948 *Adirondack Arrow*, the following appeared:

> Lt. Mick was taken prisoner during the fall of Bataan and after surviving the death march he was taken to the prison camp in Fukuoka on the island of Kyushu, Japan where he died from cruelty and ill-treatment at the hands of the Japanese in 1945.

In 1948 his body was shipped to the west coast, then to Thendara under special Army escort. An honor guard from Leonard-Mick-Roberts Legion Post of Inlet and Raquette Lake met the train to accompany the body to Raquette Lake where prayer services were held at the home of his parents. Reverend Father Julian officiated at a Requiem High Mass at St. William's Catholic Church before interment in the family plot in Lowville.

In 1958, at age 80, Reuben Mick was heard telling visitors at Uncas he was still in the guiding business, "for men who can't go too far or walk too fast."

It is said, after Mick retired, he drove to Florida to spend winters, the last trip at age 90. In their later years, Reuben and Julia Mick moved to Port Chester, New York living with their daughter, Mrs. June Johansen. Each summer, however, they managed to spend some time at their home on Mick Road in Raquette Lake.

On January 15, 1976, the couple, then 97 years of age, celebrated their 75th wedding anniversary. Mick recalled meeting his bride at a square dance. "She had a braid long enough to sit on," he said with a smile. When asked what secret he had for his long marriage, he replied with a twinkle in his eye, "Never getting the last word."

Reuben Mick died August 1, 1977 at age 99. Julia Mick died October 28, 1978 two months before her 100th birthday.

ORRIN LANPHEAR

Descendants of "Ott" Lanphear still remain a part of the Raquette Lake community.

Orrin "Ott" Lanphear was born in 1889 in Lake George, the son of George W. and Emma Plue Lanphear. At age twelve he started work as a chore boy at the lumber camp in Loon Brook. Ott migrated from Indian Lake in the early 1900's working as a guide earning $1900 a year, which was considered good money at the time.

In 1911 he married a teacher, Hazel E. McCane, and settled in Pug Bay, also referred to as Twin Bay, on Raquette Lake. He gained employment with Carnegie who owned North Point.

The couple had five children: Edna and Edgar, twins born

April 27, 1913, Stanley, born 1916, Gerald "Jerry," born 1918 and Frank, born in 1920. That same year Lanphear left Carnegie, moving to Poplar Point so the twins would be closer to the school which had been moved to the village. The Poplar Point property was bought from James and Minnie Sutliff who took in occasional boarder; the Lanphears continued the practice.

The Lanphears had two more children, Jean and Shirley. Ott continued working as a carpenter and guide during the deer season. He was employed by Dr. Evans on Tioga Point for many years.

In the late 1930's the Lanphears added a cottage to their camp, the beginning of "Lanphear's Cabins." During the war, building was continued resulting in a total of eight cabins.

Ott Lanphear died January 30, 1964. Hazel, who celebrated her 93rd birthday April 10, 1986, resides in her home on Poplar Point.

The Lanphear twins, Edna and Edgar, talked about Pug Bay and their father. "There were only two families that lived in Pug Bay when we were there," said Edna, "the Lanphears and the Waldrons, and both had twins. That's how the bay got its name Twin Bay. People used to come up there and get water from the spring." Edna laughed as she continued, "Must be they thought there was something in the water that made twins!"

Edgar said, "My sister Jean wouldn't drink from the spring."

Edgar also remembered being told about the winter his father was courting his mother who lived in Cedar River at the time. "He walked from North Point, rode the Carry to Eagle's Nest on a sleigh with the mail carrier, then walked the rest of the way in 45° below zero temperature." When the trip was discussed, Ott's only comment was, "The horse ran so fast, I couldn't wait to get off. I was so cold."

The Lanphear children were all educated at the Raquette Lake School, which at that time consisted of grades one through twelve. Stanley died in 1940 and the remaining children are still residing at Raquette Lake.

Edna Lanphear met Ray Colligan in 1930 while he was working for the Conservation Department at Raquette Lake. Colligan (b. 1904) originally came from Port Henry. Shortly after their meeting, Edna left Raquette to study nursing and in 1935, after she graduated from St. Luke's Hospital in Utica, the couple married. They moved to Port Henry where Ray was employed by the

Delaware and Hudson Railroad. Six children were born to the couple: Pat, Gerry, Jim, Bob, Peggy and Lanny.

In 1955 the Colligan's returned to Raquette Lake where Ray was employed as caretaker at the Cortland Outdoor Education Center at Pine Knot on Long Point. They resided at Pine Knot until he retired in 1971 and they moved to Poplar Point.

Ray Colligan died on August 4, 1981. He was 77 years old. Edna remains at Poplar Point, visited frequently by her son, Jim, who flies in by seaplane.

Edgar Lamphear, Edna's twin brother, worked as caretaker at Baekeland Camp until he entered the U.S. Army March 1942. During World War II he served as a Corporal in the Army Amphibian Engineer Corps in the South Pacific. He suffered severe shrapnel wounds requiring several operations. His injuries led to his receiving the Purple Heart.

While on leave during his recuperation at Rhode's Hospital in Utica, he returned to Raquette Lake where he met Anne Gibbs who was residing in Old Forge. Anne had the mail run from Old Forge to Raquette Lake. During the summer there were two trips a day. After four years of delivering mail, she went to work at Hunter's Rest.

In March of 1946, Edgar married Anne. Upon Edgar's discharge from the service he worked again as caretaker at Baekeland Camp. For a while he worked for the state and then at the Raquette Lake Marina in the village for eight years. He is now retired, living in Raquette Lake. Edgar is listed in official records as Lamphear instead of Lanphear. "The service decided to change my name," laughs Edgar, "and it's too much trouble to straighten it out."

Gerald "Jerry" Lanphear is next in the line of boys. Following in his father's footsteps, he has always been a guide and caretaker. In 1936 or 1937 he was employed as Caddy Master at the Antlers Golf Course and is credited with being the only local person to hold that distinction, as well as being the youngest.

He married a native Raquette Laker, Mary Bird, in 1940. The couple exchanged vows at Echo Camp which was owned by Maxwell Griffith at the time. Mary's brother, Hod, who was caretaker, was best man and Jerry's sister, Jean, was maid of honor. During the war, Jerry served a four-year tour of duty as Sergeant in the U. S. Army.

From 1954 until 1963, Jerry and Mary owned and operated the

Marion River Cabins. From 1963 through 1969 they operated North Point Cottages. The couple then moved to their home on a parcel at Poplar Point. One child was born to the couple, a daughter, Marcia, who married James Roblee. They have one grandchild, James (Jamie). All reside in Raquette Lake.

Frank Lamphear is the last of the boys in the family. Due to an error on his birth certificate which has never been corrected, his name is also recorded as Lamphear instead of Lanphear. After completing his education, he worked with Joe Bird until 1940. When his brother Stanley died, he replaced him working at Baekeland Camp. He entered the Marines in October 1942 serving in Hawaii and then in the occupation force in Japan and he was discharged as a Corporal in April of 1946.

Upon his return he met Doris Murray from Chadwicks, New York who was working for his mother at the Lanphear Cabins. They were married in March 1949. The couple had seven children, none of whom are living at Raquette at this time. They include Joel, Jane, Paula, Murray, Donald, Craig and Brian.

After the war, Frank returned to work with Joe Bird, then back to Baekeland Camp. In the summer of 1950 he guided and that October he was appointed Game Protector. After thirty-two years of service, Frank retired January 1983; his friends at Raquette Lake honored him with a surprise retirement party.

The couple continue living in Raquette Lake in their home on the hill above Mick Road.

Jean Lanphear Beckingham graduated from Raquette Lake High School in 1939. The following year she took a post graduate course in business at the school. Upon completion, with the help of her teacher, Lydia Elliott, she applied for and received a six-month scholarship at the Adirondack Business School in Malone. She then worked with Burkhard Insurance in Inlet for a year and a half.

In 1944, Jean married Richard "Bud" Beckingham of Old Forge, in Fort Worth, Texas. Bud served as a B24 bomber pilot in the U.S. Air Force during World War II flying thirty-eight missions over Europe. Jean returned to Raquette Lake while Bud completed his tour of duty. She was granted a temporary certificate to teach business shorthand and typing in Raquette Lake High School until Beckingham's return.

Upon his return to Raquette Lake in 1945, the couple rented Dr. Warrick's house (now owned by Bartow) in the village. For a while Beckingham worked for Joe Bird. In 1946 he signed on as Highway Light Maintenance foreman for the state. Meanwhile, Jean stayed at home to raise a family. The Beckinghams have three children: Richard, Thomas and Sandy, none of whom live at Raquette. Another daughter, Sherri, died of pneumonia in 1962 at the age of thirteen.

In 1950 Bud and Jean moved to Pulling's house (now DeMarsh) and later that year purchased their home, the old Freeland Jones homestead between Maxim and Blanchard.

Bud's job with the state required the family to move to Indian Lake in 1960. Jean was employed by the county, then the state, working with Judge Curry and Judge Martin. Although she was stationed in Indian Lake, she was assigned to the Hamilton County Court, Surrogate Court and Family Court which necessitated frequent traveling to the county seat at Lake Pleasant.

In 1973 the Beckinghams moved back to Raquette Lake, commuting to their jobs in Indian Lake. Bud retired as Highway Heavy Maintenance foreman in 1978. Jean retired the same year. The couple has continued to maintain their home in Raquette Lake.

Shirley Lanphear Forsell, the youngest of the Lanphear children, started working part time in the Raquette Lake Post Office in 1943, her senior year in high school. After graduation she worked for a while at Utica Insurance, returning later to Raquette Lake as a part time worker for the Post Office, a position she still holds.

In about 1949 or 1950 she met Kurt Forsell who was working for the Boys and Girls Camps at Antlers. The couple married in Old Forge in 1951. From that time until 1965, the couple resided on Mick Road in the home now owned by Jim and Marcia Roblee.

Forsell held various jobs at local camps and in the 1960's started his own construction business. The couple then moved to Poplar Point taking over the Lanphear Camps. In 1970 Kurt gained employment with the state working at Tioga Point Camp Site, a position he now maintains.

The couple have three sons, all residing in Raquette Lake. Gary works at Tioga Point for the state. Jeff works for contractor, Dean Pohl, and Mark works on the town road crew. Mark and his wife, Liz Richer, reside at Poplar Point with their daughter, Kathryn Elizabeth.

CHAPTER V

RAQUETTE LAKE AND THE FOREST PRESERVE

In 1894, not quite ten years after the formation of the Forest Preserve, an amendment had been passed affirming the industry of the Adirondack country would be recreational. The following year, the Forest Commission combined with the Fisheries Commission to deal with the problems of the forest preserve and the fish and game. That same year (1895) funds were allotted to stock Raquette Lake with trout.

Raquette Lake was stocked with bass in 1871. Seth Green, a pioneer in fish culture engaged in "teaching the county how to conduct the delicate operation successfully," and with his assistant, Johnathan Mason, made a trip to Little Moose and Raquette Lakes to plant fish he had raised himself.

Mason recorded the event in the January 18, 1871 entry in the Forge House register with the following notation: "Put 31 Black Bass in Rackitt Lake and 2000 White Fish in Little Moose Lake. Anyone should take any of these fish will please put them back."

Since the early 1900's Raquette Lake has had three conservation officers (game wardens), four forest rangers and, since campsites were established in the 1920's, numerous Raquette Lakers have been employed in various other capacities.

GAME WARDENS

The first recorded Raquette Lake Game Warden was Joseph Grenon of Camp Marion who was listed as such in 1905.

The next warden noted was Ray Burke who assumed the position in the 1920's. Burke, a resident of Utica when he served during World War I, migrated to Raquette Lake working as a steam engineer for the Raquette Lake Transportation Company. He met his wife, Barbara Zweifel, while she worked in the Long Lake Hotel. Two children were born of this union, Fredolin and Margaret. The family eventually purchased Rush Point from the estate of H. Robert Beguilin. During the years 1930 and 1931, Barbara Burke ran the Marion River Hotel and then ran Rush Point cottages until her death in 1951.

Ray Burke served as Game Warden until 1945 when he received the political appointment at the Hamilton County Veteran Service Agency, a position he held until 1961. Burke died the following year at Raquette Lake.

Margaret Burke, who had married Bruce Risley, acquired Rush Point Cottages which the couple ran during the summer months until her death. The cottages remain in possession of the Risley family.

When Fredolin (Fred) Burke returned from the service in 1945, he and his father purchased the property then known as Huntington Wood Lot, now Burke's Marina.

Fred, a carpenter by trade, did the building himself. In 1947 and 1948 he built two cottages and in 1949 a counter hot dog stand. He married Gloria Cordani from Long Island in 1950. They met when she rented one of Burke's cottages. Fred built his first gas station that same year, and the following year, his home. In 1953 four more cottages were added to his other two rental units. In 1954 an additional five cabins were built totaling eleven. In addition to the Marina and rental units, Burke also owns a restaurant in "Burke Town" which he leases.

Fred and Gloria Burke were the parents of two children, Linda and Louis. Linda eventually left Raquette Lake. Louis is employed by the Raquette Lake School system and is married to Holly Gauvin. The couple have two adopted children, Jeeun (June) and Soo Bin (Ben). Holly is the librarian at the Raquette Lake Library.

Following Gloria's death, Fred married his second wife, Helen (Lennie) Carfel, a teacher from Buffalo. Three children were born of that union: Monica, Nora and Michael.

Ray Burke was replaced as Game Protector by Frank Lamphear in 1950. Although Lamphear could be placed anywhere in the County or State, at any time, he was assigned the territory from Inlet to Blue Mountain (east and west), and from West Canada Lake to the north end of Brandreth Park (north and south). In the 1960's his title was again changed to Environmental Conservation Officer and in the early 1980's to Environmental Conservation Police Officer.

"The biggest change," commented Lamphear, "in addition to the name, was to include in our job overseeing landfills, navigation, vehicle traffic, snowmobiles and other things—too broad a field!"

"The first twelve or fifteen years I served," continued Lamphear, "I only had to enforce the hunting and fishing laws. The past fifteen years I've had to join the forest ranger in "search and rescue" operations in addition to everything else."

Since Lamphear's retirement in 1983 he has been replaced by officers not residing in Raquette Lake.

FOREST RANGERS

The first recorded Forest Ranger in Raquette Lake was Daniel Lynn. He was the son of Daniel and Ann Ward Lynn and was born at Minerva, New York on November 13, 1867. He arrived in Raquette Lake in 1889 and resided at Pine Knot for several years. In 1909 he was appointed Forest Ranger and he served in that capacity until 1935 with the exception of 1914 when he was temporarily replaced by Joseph Lahey and in 1915 by Frank Carlin.

Lynn married Margaret Oley in 1924, maintaining his residence at Raquette Lake until 1958. For several years before his death on December 17, 1958, he and his wife wintered in Brooksville, Florida. In addition to his widow, Lynn left a daughter, Mrs. Carol Thornton of Pennsylvania.

In 1936, Moses Leonard was transferred as Forest Ranger from Big Moose to Raquette Lake. A widower, he and his family moved into the home previously occupied by Dr. Beals, next to the McCoy cottage which is adjacent to the Raquette Lake Marina. His children all attended Raquette Lake School.

His five daughters eventually married. Inez married Gordon Rudd of Inlet, Betty married Ted Harwood of Eagle Bay, Frances married Barney Lepper of Big Moose, Ada married William Pearce of Whitesboro and Emma Lou married Howard Waldron of Raquette Lake.

In addition to his daughters, Leonard had one son, Philo. Philo worked at Kamp Kill Kare, then enlisted in the Army Air Corps during World War II. He served as Staff Sergeant and was recognized as an expert machine gunner and navigator. On December 17, 1942, Philo Leonard was killed when a light bomber, on which he was a gunner, was shot down over North Africa. The craft burned leaving no survivors. Buried in the National Cemetery in Kentucky with other crew members, Philo Leonard is listed as the first youth "killed in action" from the Central Adirondacks. On March 8, 1943, Moses Leonard was informed by the War Department that the Purple Heart had been awarded posthumously to his son.

Replacing Moses Leonard was Morgan Roderick who had been transferred from Syracuse to Raquette Lake. He served at Raquette Lake from 1958 until 1964 when he was transferred to Canton, New York. In 1969, although no longer stationed in Raquette Lake, Roderick and his wife, Judy, purchased a second home at North Point. They have two children, Lynn and Eric.

Gary McChesney replaced Roderick in September 1964. He had served as a Forest Ranger for two and a half years at West Canada Lake before being transferred to Raquette Lake.

In 1960 he married Donna McDonald. Three children were born to the couple before moving to Raquette Lake. Theron was born in Carthage in 1961, Theresa, born in Gloversville in 1963 and Thera, born in Piseco in 1964.

Gary and his second wife, Pat, a campsite supervisor at Golden Beach, reside in the Ranger's home on Route 28 opposite the school.

RAQUETTE LAKE FISH AND GAME CLUB

In a recreation area where hunting and fishing are the main sports, the natural course of events would be to organize a local Fish and Game Club. The date when the Raquette Lake Fish and Game Club was begun has not been determined.

When the constitution was amended in 1970 raising dues from

$1 to $3, it was noted the date of the previous constitution was 1948. This date may not be correct, but rather the date of a revision of the constitution. The first fishing derby sponsored by the Raquette Lake Fish and Game club was held in 1946.

It is also difficult to establish when the first Fish and Game Newsletter was printed. The first one available to the author was the 1958 issue when Art Howe was president. Several interesting items from that publication are herewith noted:

"In 1957 wild rice was planted on Big Island in an amount that should produce a heavy growth. Results of previous planting of duck food is questionable . . . however, a noted increase of ducks on the lake."

"For your safety and convenience, the rocks on the most traveled routes have been marked." Included with the letter was a map drawn by member Ken Bieber showing water depths.

A most important notation of fish stripping was made: "It is difficult to oppose the New York State Department of Conservation's practice of taking eggs from lake trout in Raquette Lake as the entire Adirondack area is supplied with fish hatched from the spawn taken. The other side of the story is that Raquette Lake is now getting their proportionate share of the eggs hatched.

In addition to Art Howe, other club presidents noted in newsletters include William Meisburger, Jerry Lanphear, George Fuge, Don Langham, Greg Timm and Gary McChesney.

In 1975 the APA "scenic" river classification of the Marion River almost brought about the elimination of motor boats and snowmobiles in the area. Through the efforts of the club, the river remained open to motor boat traffic although the class remained "scenic" rather than "recreational."

In 1976, the group sponsored, for the first time, a local child to attend Camp Colby. They have done so each year since then.

A Junior Class membership for those fifteen years and under was established in 1977, and the first canoe raffle was held to help subsidize the feeding of the deer. The cost of feeding the deer for the winter of 1985-1986 was $1629.28.

In 1979 a shooting range was established and reloading sessions held for young hunters.

Each year members of the club assist in stocking the lake. In the spring of 1986, the lake was stocked with 14,000 lake trout, three to six inches long.

The Raquette Lake Fish and Game Club, with an approximate

membership of 318, remains a vital link with other conservation organizations whose main concern is the preservation and maintenance of wild life in the area.

CHAPTER VI

WILLIAM WEST DURANT

The man responsible for a great part of the early growth of Raquette Lake was William West Durant. Durant pursued his father's, Dr. Thomas C. Durant, and his own dreams for developing the Adirondacks.

Dr. Durant's dream of developing a railroad across the continent became an obsession. He started by building several lines through the Midwest and became an active promoter of the Union Pacific. He built the Adirondack Railroad from Saratoga to North Creek, opening up the Raquette Lake and Blue Mountain Lake area. It was during this period in the early 1860's that he made occasional explorations of Raquette Lake.

Dr. Durant initiated a telegraph system and set up a stagecoach line from North Creek to Blue Mountain Lake, and he also owned a fleet of rowboats for crossing the Eckford Lakes into Raquette Lake.

In April of 1863, under a special legislative act, he reorganized the Adirondack Railroad as the Adirondack Company. (In 1890 the railroad was sold to the Delaware and Hudson Railroad.)

Frank Carlin's diary, referring to a conversation he had with W.W. Durant in about 1929, stated: "W.W. visited Raquette Lake for the first time in the summer of 1875. He returned that winter, taking ten days to reach the lake from North Creek traveling by way of Long Lake in sixty inches of snow. He reached Long Point with only food, tent and a stove."

The record continued: "W.W. spent the entire winter there with his friend, Will Stone. Alvah Dunning and Charlie Bennett joined them, living with them in their tent. It was during this time Charlie and W.W. became good friends and Durant learned about Raquette Lake."

In the summer of 1876 William West returned to the lake with his father, Dr. Tom, sister Heloise Hannah Durant and several friends. They were guests at Charlie Bennett's camp. The following year, Dr. Durant decided to build his family's summer camp on Long Point which was the beginning to the famous Camp Pine Knot.

William succeeded his father as president of the Adirondack Railroad. He not only continued his father's projects, but went on to inaugurate many firsts in the history of the central Adirondacks. His accomplishments in the field of transportation are explained more fully in the chapter on transportation.

In 1880, W.W. Durant was instrumental in building the first church at Raquette Lake - the Episcopal Church of the Good Shepherd on St. Hubert's Isle.

W.W. Durant and Janet Stott were married October 15, 1884 settling in Saratoga Springs during the winter months, convenient to both his Adirondack interests and those in New York City.

While on a trip to Mt. Marcy with photographer Ed Bierstadt, William was notified that his father was ill; Dr. T.C. Durant died in North Creek in 1885.

The 1880's brought about an influx of people to the area. Camp Pine Knot became the nucleus of the town. In 1889, W.W. Durant organized and became president of the Adirondack, Lake George and Saratoga Telegraph Company. That same year he petitioned for a post office at "Durant" on Long Point, becoming its first Postmaster. An employee of Durant, John McLaughlin, opened a store in 1891 on land on Long Point given to him by Durant. Shortly after, the first school was initiated behind the establishment.

Upon completion of Camp Pine Knot, W.W. Durant began acquiring large tracts of land, becoming the owner of nearly a million acres of real estate in the Adirondack region.

Many of Durant's employees were Catholic. Perhaps that is why he felt a strong need to build a Catholic Church, St. William's, on the point in 1890. Durant also donated separate cemeteries for the Protestants and Catholics at Blue Mountain Lake.

Among his acquisitions Durant owned Mohegan Lake, located in part of Township 6 and including all of Township 5. He also owned Sumner Lake in Township 6 and Shedd Lake. On these parcels he built Camp Uncas (1890), Kamp Kill Kare (1893) and Camp Sagamore (1896). Although the camps are not on Raquette Lake, they have played an integral part in the economy of the hamlet. They have been a source of employment for many.

Durant is remembered by historians for all his accomplishments and for his gradual defeat. His life was deeply affected by the sudden death of his close friend, Collis P. Huntington. The tragedy, following his divorce, was compounded by the lawsuit brought against him by his sister, Heloise (Ella) Durant Rose over the settlement of their father's estate. When the courts awarded Mrs. Rose a heavy judgment, Durant was forced to gradually dispose of his Adirondack holdings.

By his own admission Durant was not a practical man, which contributed to his financial problems. He was no longer the driving force behind the growth of the region. In 1904 he left the area moving to Utica. Several years later he married a Canadian, Annie Cotton, twenty-three years his junior.

For the next thirty years Durant tried numerous occupations, returning only occasionally to his beloved Adirondacks. In an article printed in the March 17, 1926 edition of the *New York Times*, it was reported he was "employed in the real estate brokerage business conducted by his wife."

On June 1, 1934 William West Durant died following surgery at Mount Sinai hospital in New York City. He was 83. On August 12, 1936, his widow Annie, took part in a ceremony dedicating a stone and bronze marker in memory of Durant which was installed on the site opposite Lake Durant two miles east of the village of Blue Mountain Lake.

Notations in Frank Carlin's diary reveal W. W. Durant to be a considerate, sensitive individual, remembered by many:

> "Outside of being addicted to his high silk hat, W. W. was a regular guy. One time when things were starting to look bad, W. W. came to sit awhile. He (W. W.) told me his employee Callahan offered him all his money if it would help him any, but I guess that wasn't enough. Looking kinda sad, he said the one thing he had to be thankful for was most of his money went to the working man."

This statement proved true from some of the other entries in the log.

> "The spring of 1893 most of the men had no way of earning money. W. W. hired 50 men to cut the ice from the Carry to Pine Knot so his wife could come in the steamboat. The job took 9 or 10 days. It finished on a Sunday and Durant gave a party for the men and his family - telling them to take home whatever was left over. This was the first good food many of them had seen for quite a while."

Another entry read:

> "W. W. hired a crew to burn dead timber just because the men were unemployed at the time.
>
> Every holiday Durant would give a gift of liquor to his employees who drank and a turkey to all the families. If he heard of anyone in the village who didn't have one (a turkey) he would see to it that they did.
>
> Durant was a proud man and understood pride in others. He never gave anything outright—always made it look like you earned it."

CAMP PINE KNOT

Camp Pine Knot (referred to as Camp Huntington) is located on Pine Knot Point, a projection of the main Long Point which lies between East Bay (into which the Marion River empties) and South Bay. The point runs east and west and is roughly two miles long and about a mile wide. It is accessible by boat, by driving across the ice in winter or by hiking or snowshoeing some two and one half miles from the Golden Beach Campsite.

In 1876, Dr. Thomas Durant elected to build a summer home on Long Point, on a site which had been acquired from Charlie Bennett in exchange for Dr. Durant's assistance in obtaining land titles. There he built two or three simple cabins near the cabins previously built by Charlie and Ed Bennett. Another cabin owner on Long Point at the time was Colonal McAlpin. The land sold by the state to these men had been owned for a quarter of a century, with nearly all the rest of the Raquette Lake area, by Farrand N. Benedict. It had been allowed to revert to the state by tax default.

Later that year, W. W. Durant became aware of a more favorable location half a mile away on a promontory extending from the southwest shore of Long Point into South Bay. Here, he constructed what has become historically known as the first of "The Great Camps" . . . Camp Pine Knot.

At first, the main building was a one-story structure. Several log cabins, a building for the kitchen, an open dining area and several platforms for tents were also constructed.

By 1882, a two-story building (now known as the "Chalet") was completed. Evidence of log construction on the first level of the building and frame construction on the upper level indicates the possibility of an addition being made to the original building. The structure which contained a large living room and four bedrooms became the center of the unique complex of buildings to follow. Instead of the traditional house with many rooms, each room was a separate building. Pine Knot included many buildings for various activities—dining, cooking, sleeping, working and playing. Most were connected by covered walkways.

In an interview with George Fuge, once Director of Cortland College Outdoor Educational Center (of which Huntington is now a part), Fuge stated, "Durant wanted to give a feeling of being outdoors, even while you're inside. The buildings' interiors have what is believed to be the first knotty pine paneling. Durant used unpeeled logs for the exterior of some buildings and "paneling" of cedar bark on others."

Fuge went on to describe the camp: "Durant built stone fireplaces, some with five foot mantels cut from one stone. Adirondack style tables, beds and chairs abound. They were made from tree limbs and twigs, the bark still attached. Curved furniture, of gingerbread trim on the buildings were made from limbs that grew bent . . . they weren't steamed into shape."

Among the relics remaining in use is a large desk built for Durant covered with white birch bark. The drawers were outlined in maple twigs and branches. One interesting note brought out by Fuge was the unique manner in which Durant incorporated the letter W somewhere, either in the interior or exterior of the buildings and on some of the furniture.

Durant designed the buildings combining Swiss architecture with the rustic style of the Adirondacks. Utilizing native Adirondack materials and craftsmen, he built a complex of buildings that blended into the wilderness surroundings. Their durability sustained the years and they remain today.

Of Pine Knot, Donaldson in *A History of the Adirondacks* wrote:

> "It became the show place of the woods. Men took a circuitous route in order to gain a glimpse of it, and to have been a guest within its timbered walls and among its woodland fancies was to wear the hall-mark of the envied. . . . While they were building, one of the family ran across a wonderful pine knot on the shore of the lake. It was shaped like the hilt of a sword, and measured some three feet across. This curious relic of the forest was made an ornament of the camp and suggested its name. . . . Pine Knot became the prototype of the modern Camp Beautiful. Before it was built there was nothing like it; since then, despite infinite variations, there has been nothing essentially different from it."

One of the most unique detached buildings was a bark cabin, built on a raft of pine logs, and moored near the boathouse. It was originally built by Durant as a refuge from the black flies. Durant seemed to share White's opinion of the pest:

> "The chief nuisance of the Adirondacks is not reptile or beast but the notorious black fly, shaped like a house-fly and one tenth its size. He is the flying form of a nymph which is hatched in running water and is a favorite food for trout. Black flies appear about the middle of May and stay around for six weeks. They are at their worst on hot windless afternoons. Some people are immune to their bite; others get welts that swell to the size of a baseball. The punkies, mosquitoes and "no-see-ums" that follow are a nuisance that stay around all summer, but the black fly, enemy of any warm-blooded animal is supreme in its persistence and viciousness."

The detached cabin was later supplanted by an elaborate houseboat containing four rooms, a kitchen and bath and the luxury of running water. It could be towed by a launch any place on the lake. The sixty by twenty-six-foot boat was named the *Barque of Camp Pine Knot*.

During Durant's period of prosperity, 1889-1892, further building was pursued. A bedroom, dressing room, bathroom and stove room were added to the cottages reserved for his mother, Mrs. T.C. Durant. To this was also added an annex containing rooms for the children and the governess. The covered walkway from the nursery to the summer house is presumed to have been constructed at this time also. In addition, the Durant cottage which contained three rooms, a bath and two fireplaces was built for Durant and his wife.

Collis P. Huntington, a wealthy industrialist and friend of William, first stayed at Pine Knot with his wife in 1890. In 1895 he purchased the entire camp and 200 acres from Durant.

Between the years 1895 and 1900, John E. Tillson, then caretaker, reported three other buildings were built. The buildings now serve as staff house, dorm and recreation buildings.

In 1900, while staying at Pine Knot, Collis P. Huntington died of a heart attack.

In 1920, John and Grace Moore, originally from Ticonderoga, came to Raquette Lake assuming the position of caretakers of Pine Knot.

During their stay, their three children, George, Phyllis and Robert were born and raised. The children attended the Raquette Lake School, traveling by boat when the water was free and across the ice during the winter. Moore was said to have told Frank Carlin, "During our 35 years at Pine Knot, we saw a member of the Huntington family but once. The camp remained unused during their ownership and I had to keep up with repairs and other things myself." The Moores retired to their summer home near the school on Route 28.

In 1955, Edna and Ray Colligan replaced Moore. They held their positions as caretakers until they retired in 1971.

Dr. Harlan (Gold) Metcalf and Dr. Walter Thurber, faculty members of the State University of New York College at Cortland discovered the unused Camp Pine Knot during a canoe trip on Raquette Lake. Dr. Metcalf established contact with Archer M. Huntington and in December 1947, Dr. Metcalf and Professor William Clemens of the Science Department, journeyed on snowshoes to the camp to further inspect the property.

The Huntington family was interested in Metcalf and Clemens' proposal to convert the camp into an educational facility and agreed to donate the property to the college. On April 16, 1948, the New York State Board of Regents voted to approve "acceptance by the Commissioner of Education of the lands owned by the Huntington family for use by Cortland College as a memorial to Collis P. Huntington."

CORTLAND STATE COLLEGE OUTDOOR EDUCATION CENTER

On June 29, 1948 the first educational program sponsored by the college was conducted at Pine Knot.

George Fuge, class of 1949, was among the first group of students to participate in the summer program of 1948. In 1962, Fuge took over directorship of the camp, a position he held until 1985. George, his wife Marguerite (Muggsy), and their three daughters, Heidi, Debbie and Jill, moved from Suffern, New York to take up year-round residency at Pine Knot.

In 1963 the Outdoor Center was expanded through the purchase of a 240-acre tract, including Camp Marion on Long Point, from Mrs. Wallace Yeaple. On January 15, 1965 the facility was expanded once more through the purchase of five acres of land of the Antlers from then owner Donald Langham.

Jay Cummings was introduced as assistant director in 1970 and shortly after he and his wife, Eunice (Kris), arrived at Raquette Lake to take up residence at Antlers where a daughter, Holly, was born.

A new dorm was constructed in 1970 on the north side of Camp Huntington with a capacity of 28 persons. With the new addition, the camp could house 100 persons at a single time.

In 1971, a group of Cortland College students and faculty conducted a fund-raising campaign to preserve *The Barque of Pine Knot*. They moved the former houseboat of the Durant family off the water's edge to higher ground. Future plans are to renovate the boat as a museum for Camp Huntington.

A combination dining hall and laboratory/classroom building was constructed in 1979 replacing the aging and inadequate facilities for the growing program which serves close to 2,000 students each year.

In 1983 the center celebrated its 35th anniversary. The center, used year-round for faculty and student programs only, was open to the public for the first time for a total of four days, during which guided tours were given.

At approximately 3:30 a.m. on Tuesday, October 18, 1983, the residents of Raquette Lake were awakened to the sound of fire sirens. The night sky over one section of the lake was lit up by what appeared to be brilliant pink clouds rising above the trees on Big Island. Camp Huntington was on fire!

It was learned from director George Fuge that he and his wife were alone at the camp at the time. They were awakened when they heard a blast which they thought was an earthquake; minutes later they heard another one.

As Fuge started outside in investigate, he heard a third blast. As he rounded the corner of the Chalet he could see the ice house was totaled, a shed next to it was in flames and the flames were creeping toward the kitchen. It appeared the fire had started in the ice house either in the heater or compressor and spread to the propane tanks nearby which had exploded.

The flames were shooting about 50 feet high, hitting the power lines. Fuge immediately ran toward the kitchen-dining hall and tried to use the fire hook-up. However, the burned power lines rendered it useless, as was the phone. The couple ran to a boat and headed for help at Antlers.

Neighbors had also seen the light in the sky and reported the fire. By the time the Fuges and the Assistant Director, Jay Cummings returned to the camp, the fire fighters had reached the point and were using the portable fire equipment which they had transported by boat from the village. The cottage known as Mrs. Durant's was covered with flames and the fire was underway in the adjoining library.

In addition to the Raquette Lake firemen, those from Blue Mountain Lake and Inlet responded to the call for assistance and were transported by boat to the point. The firemen worked for hours before the last embers were dissipated. Fortunately they were able to control the blaze and minimize the damage to adjoining buildings. The last of the fire equipment was removed by 9 a.m. and cleanup began immediately. The blaze caused damage estimated at over $500,000 and destroyed four of the original buildings.

Following the fire, the College Alumni Association and the College Development Foundation of Cortland Inc., joined forces in raising money for the "Raquette Lake Rebuilding Fund."

Several years prior to the fire, as a result of a project involving the National Historic Trust, Adirondack Museum and Princeton

University, drawings had been made and pictures taken of the inside and outside structure of the buildings at the camp. An architectural history student at Princeton was sponsored by the Adirondack Musuem to render the architectural drawings. Plans were started to restore the damaged buildings as exact duplicates of the original Durant buildings. By the fall of 1986 the rebuilding contract was completed, and the library complex and Mrs. Durant's cabin were finished.

George Fuge retired as Director of Cortland's Outdoor Education Center on August 23, 1985 after serving twenty-three years. Dr. Charles Warren, acting president of the college announced the appointment of Joe Pierson to fill the vacancy. Pierson, who joined the Cortland faculty in 1966, moved with his wife, Nancy, and their children, Lance and Michelle, to Pine Knot where they have taken up residence. The Fuge's have moved to their permanent home on the Antlers property.

KAMP KILL KARE

Upon the completion of Pine Knot, W.W. Durant began acquiring large tracts of land outside Township 40. The parcels included all of Township 34 which contained the Eckford Chain of Lakes, a part of Township 5 and Township 6 which included Sumner Lake (now Lake Kora).

Prior to 1888, Durant built a cabin on Sumner Lake to be used as a "hide-away hunting camp" accommodating two to four people. "Camp Omonsom," as it was named, was used mostly by Durant and his friend, Dr. Arpad Gerster, who maintained a camp on Big Island in Raquette Lake.

In 1896, Durant sold 1,030 acres of land around Sumner Lake to Timothy and Cora Woodruff for $12,360. At the same time, with the sale of 23,872 acres in Township 6 completed, the New York State Forest Preserve Board surrounded Kamp Kill Kare completely by Forest Preserve.

Woodruff, who was elected Republican Lt. Governor for the first of three terms in 1896, took possession of the camp August 27, 1897, immediately renaming the lake, Lake Kora. This was the fourth change of name for the lake. Originally known as Fonda Lake, then Sumner Lake, the name was changed by

Durant to Lake Tuscarora.

Camp Uncas, Sagamore and Kill Kare form a triangular shape of land with Sagamore located on the northerly end.

By 1898, Kamp Kill Kare was greatly extended and improved. At first the kitchen was made into a dining area and part of the wooodshed converted into a kitchen. Later the cabin Omonsom was absorbed into the main building which consisted of five attached or semi-attached buildings connected on ground level by a large verandah covered by three roofs supported by wooden columns.

In 1901 Woodruff had a cottage, known as the "Kabin" built on an island on the lake. Constructed as a place of recreation, among other conveniences, it contained a piano, victrola, library with mounted specimens, ping pong tables and a well-stocked bar.

Cora Woodruff died in 1904. The following year Woodruff remarried and from then on spent less time at the camp. Sometime before Woodruff's death in October 1913, the property was deeded to Alfred G. Vanderbilt. On December 11, 1914 Vanderbilt conveyed title to Mr. and Mrs. Francis P. Garvin, friends and frequent guests of Robert J. Collier of Bluff Point.

The Garvans had owned their camp only a short time before it was destroyed by fire in 1915. They managed to salvage some of the furnishings and several of the original buildings were saved including the Kabin on the island, the casino and Mrs. Garvan's personal cottage which contained a bedroom, bath, office and lady's maid quarters on the upper level.

With the services of Captain Hiscoe who had assisted the Woodruff's with their renovations, the main building was rebuilt and refurnished along the lines of the original.

Extensive expansion was undertaken under the supervision of John Russell Pope, one of the foremost architects of the day. Most impressive were the added buildings often referred to as a "Cyclopean mode of construction" built with huge native stones giving the appearance of being held together without mortar. Included in the eight stone buildings was a stable said to have cost Garvan one million dollars. The irony of the situation, according to some people, was that it never stabled a horse. The new construction also included a cow barn and dairy. It has been said that during World War I, Mrs. Garvan supplied milk to all Raquette Lake families with children.

Mrs. Garvan was the daughter of Anthony Brady, a multi-millionaire who made a fortune in public utilities. The Bradys, non-Catholic Irish, later converted to Catholicism. A reproduction of a Norman Chapel was included on the grounds with the other stone structures. The stones used in the exterior construction were allegedly picked one by one so the moss would show when the structure was finished. The interior panels, doors and beams were made of teakwood.

The chapel, completed in 1921, was built by Schuyler Kathan of Blue Mountain assisted by George Starbuck, Frank Flynn and Seth Allen. Kathan had come to Blue Mountain in 1879, studied masonry with Henry Wheelock, and worked for W. W. Durant before building the chapel.

Through the pastor of the St. William's parish, Mrs. Garvan made arrangements to have Mass said for the employees of Kill Kare, Uncas and Sagamore since nearly all of them were Catholic. The chapel had never been dedicated and the Bishop of Ogdensburg sanctioned Mass through "knowledge of practice." Later, however, according to Father Paul Knapp "Mrs. Garvan received a special indult from the Pope to have the Blessed Sacrament exposed in the chapel while she was in residence."

"Mrs. Garvan was a very religious woman," said Father Paul. "She was extremely generous to the church and those who needed help and spent many hours during the day on her knees in prayer."

It is not known if any baptisms or marriages ever took place in the chapel. However, on August 31, 1975, Angela Lewis, daughter of the caretakers, Mr. and Mrs. Calvin Lewis, received her First Holy Communion in the chapel, administered by Father Marcian Kandrac.

Between 1949 and 1964, Leo and Katherine Small, caretakers who specialized in horticulture, kept the altar supplied with prize roses when Mrs. Garvan was in residence.

Helen and Edwin Wires replaced the Smalls as superintendents in September 1964. They described the camp which at the time encompassed thirty buildings or structures.

"In addition to the usual service buildings which included a blacksmith shop and carpenter's shop (still in service during the 1970's), several greenhouses, a boathouse which included a guest house above, used by Mr. Garvan, a recreation hall which housed a bowling alley, a baseball field, a handball court and two tennis courts occupied the grounds. The main lodge included fifteen rooms for the servants quarters, five bedrooms, a living room and a large dining room which included two large alcoves. Steam heat was used to warm the buildings. There was also a men's camp, "Kamp Keen Kut," for the use of the ground crew, and year-round homes for the superintendent, caretaker and electrician."

Mrs. Garvan is remembered fondly by Raquette Lakers for her generosity, thoughtfulness and her passion for baseball.

Jerry Lanphear recalled a typical week in July and August during the late 1930's:

> "A group of us were hired, each with a different job - gardener, life guard, and so on. We'd go to work at seven a.m. and work until noon. After lunch we'd go to the ball field and practice baseball until five o'clock. This would go on six days a week; there was but one exception. On Wednesday and Thursday, my brother Stanley and I would catch brook trout at the lake for Friday night supper for the family and friends. What was left over was fed to the workers.
>
> On Sundays, Mrs. Garvan would hire teams from other towns, Newcomb, Long Lake, Boonville and so forth, to play against us. I don't remember us ever losing. After the game there'd be a big pitcher of orange juice for us and then a big dinner.
>
> There were eighteen of us altogether, including three Garvan boys, Pat, Tony and Pete. Me, my brother Stanley and Philo Leonard were from Raquette Lake. The rest of the team was from Savage Arms in Utica and worked at Kill Kare during the summer. The only qualifications to get a job was that you had to play ball!
>
> Sagamore had its own team which included Alfred and George Vanderbilt, their help and some locals including Denny and John Dillon. Later in the 1940's, my brother Frank replaced Stanley and we played against the "Dillons-Birds" local team. Every other week we'd play against the hired teams. In about 1946 Frank played for the Pony League in Wellsville, a semi-professional team, but when he hurt his arm he couldn't play. I think it was about 1947 or 1948 when Chiang Kai-shek and Marshall came to see us play."

Mrs. Garvan, although enjoying the pleasures afforded her by wealth, appreciated the simple things in life. She loved the natural scenery of the woods, not allowing human presence to destroy what nature intended. During her ownership, with the exception of clearing brush and fallen timber, the surrounding forest acreage remained untouched.

After sixty-four years of ownership of Kill Kare, Mrs. Garvan died in 1978. With the exception of the small portion of land for the camp itself, the property inherited by family members remained much as it was in the 1890's.

The estate was later purchased by Kora Woods Incorporated.

Riley Parsons and his family resided in the electrician's cottage for over thirty years. Parsons, known as a "genius with radios and electricity" was sought after by such companies as General Electric, but chose to stay in the North Country where he was born and raised. In 1947 he was offered a full time position maintaining the electric and telephone lines at Kamp Kill Kare.

Riley, his wife Phyllis and their son, Frederick, moved from Old Forge to Kill Kare. The camp, which is six miles from the Raquette Lake Village, is accessible only by a dirt road. At times in the spring, it was necessary for their son Frederick to make a portion of the trip to the village on foot to attend school. He had a record of never being late or absent during his school years. After completing his eight elementary grades in six years, he attended Indian Lake Central School. This necessitated traveling by bus from the village making a total of approximately 60 miles daily to attend school.

In 1957 Frederick graduated from Indian Lake Central High School as valedictorian. Parson's classmate, James Colligan, who graduated as salutatorian, found traveling to school just as difficult. Living on Long Point, he had to cross the lake to meet the school bus. In spring and fall when the ice was unsafe it was necessary for him to walk a half a mile around the shore to the village.

One of Riley Parson's larger accomplishments while at Kill Kare was rebuilding the telephone line at the camp in its entirety after it was destroyed during the hurricane in 1950. Riley Parson retired from Kill Kare in 1972 returning to Old Forge where he died in April 1984.

During the winter months, Kamp Kill Kare maintained a staff of about ten or twelve. Thirty or forty were employed during the summer months including, at times, a chef hired from Delmonico's or some other New York City restaurant to prepare fresh caught trout or other specialties for prominent guests.

Many Raquette Lake residents were employed at Kill Kare throughout the years. Two of them, Margaret McLaughlin and her husband Fitzhugh (Fitz) Vogan became permanent residents, raising a family, with members still residing in Raquette.

Fitzhugh Vogan was born 1885 in Cadyville, New York. His father was warden at the state prison and Fitz is said to have even witnessed an execution when he was a kid.

Vogan arrived at Raquette Lake about 1914 or 1915 gaining employment rebuilding Kill Kare. In 1920 he met Margaret McLaughlin, born in 1901 in Olmstedville, New York. She was hired as a school teacher at Kill Kare. After what was considered a comparatively long courtship at that time, the couple were married in North Creek in June 1927. They then moved to Penagrove, New Jersey.

About 1931 the Vogans moved back to Raquette Lake with their daughter, Patricia (Pat). Vogan was employed by the State Highway Department as foreman for the area from Eagle Bay to just outside of Tupper Lake. He retired in 1957 and died in July 1961.

The Vogans had four other children: William, Margaret (Peg), Katherine and James. Pat and Peg remained in Raquette raising families.

Pat Vogan Gauthier returned to Raquette Lake from Utica when her mother died in 1948. She married Hubert (Hubie) Gauthier in 1955. The couple managed Lil & Gerry's Bar and Restaurant from September to June 1950 to 1955. During the summer months, owners Lil and Jerry Kavanaugh returned from Ohio to resume business operations.

A daughter, Laurie, was born to the couple in 1957. Before and after Laurie's birth, Pat worked part time at Camp Sagamore.

Hubie was caretaker at the Boys Camp from 1945 until 1956. For a time he worked in Utica, returning to Raquette in 1960 when he became employed by the Town of Long Lake Highway Department. He retired in 1976.

The Gauthiers operated the Old Station Restaurant summers from 1966 until 1969. Pat has been employed at the Cortland Outdoor Recreation Center since 1970. Hubie worked on and off as pilot of the Boys Camp boat until shortly before his death in 1985.

The couple's daughter Laurie, married Tom Murdock, who is employed by Waldron's Construction Company. The Murdocks reside in Raquette Lake with their sons, Kurt and Steven.

Pat Vogan Norris has the distinction of being one of the last two students graduating from the twelfth grade at the Raquette Lake School in 1949. In 1951 she married Harold (Buz) Norris, who was employed by the state. The couple moved to Vernon, New York for several years, returning to Raquette Lake in the early 1960's.

Peg has been employed by the Tap Room, Lil & Gerry's Restaurant, Raquette Lake Supply and has held a part time position at the Raquette Lake Post Office for over twenty years.

The Norris children include Mike, Jim, Tom, Kevin, Dick (deceased) and Cindy. Although Mike and his wife, Jill (Ponder) reside in Inlet, Mike participates in many Raquette Lake activities. Cindy is attending college. Jim and his wife, Linda, reside in Raquette Lake with their children, Jessie and Danny. Tom, who served a three and a half year hitch in the U.S. Marines is employed at Raquette Lake Marina where he has worked since his early teens. Kevin works for the Raquette Lake Supply Co. and his wife, the former Susan Schafstall, is employed at Sagamore Institute.

CAMP UNCAS

Durant started to build his "Camp Uncas" in 1890 on Lake Mohegan. The name and setting were taken from Cooper's tale *The Last of the Mohicans*. He built two cottages close to the lake and named them Chingachgook and Hawkeye after Uncas' father and Natty Bumpo.

Besides its beauty, Mohegan Lake, on an isolated preserve of over 1,500 acres, is considered to be one of the finest brook and lake trout lakes in the Adirondacks. Public fishing has never been allowed.

Several buildings, placed in a stand of towering white pines, were built of perfectly matched pine logs. Other buildings have facings of spruce and white pine logs with the bark left on.

The masonry work, all of native stone, is unexcelled in the Adirondacks. The hardware was hand made in the blacksmith shop on the premises, which was still in service in the early 1960's. Huge walk-in fireplaces, also of native stone, were raised off the floor.

The furniture was handmade of native wood . . . most of it done by Raquette Laker, Charles Hunt. Durant went to great lengths to find the right pieces for balustrades for the stairs and the many unique chairs.

According to an article in the August 21, 1966 *New York Times*, Durant's (later Morgan's) dressing room was a small alcove off the bedroom with a built-in chest of drawers. Local logs were meticulously joined forming the entrance arch. The living room "entertainment corner" contained an elaborately encased piano with cupboards for storing sheet music, cards and games, and a small library. On the inside of the dining room door were mounted two versions of the turtle, the symbol of Uncas. One was a hat rack with deer feet and the other was an iron door latch.

The bathroom was the ultimate in luxury with wood paneled walls, a pedestal sink, silver fittings and embroidered linens. Bright red blankets with the Uncas emblem were woven in England. Furnishings, pottery and bric-a-brac were accumulated from all parts of the world by Durant (and later Morgan).

The dining hall, a one-story building was changed in later years by Anne Morgan to a one and one half-story building with a bedroom and bath on the top. When J.P. Morgan owned Uncas, it was said that after dinner he enjoyed reclining on a large bench in front of the dining hall, "drinking in the beauties of the lake and the forest."

A pasture and garden were on the east side of the lake. Farm buildings, the carriage house and sheds, although not far from the main house, were not in view. The camp also included a greenhouse, lean-to and boat shed. Behind the kitchen, with a view of the lagoon, stood the superintendent's cottage.

John Callahan, who had gone to work for Durant in 1889 at Pine Knot, assumed the position of superintendent of Uncas the following year. His wife, Mary Buckley, was considered the finest cook in the area, which was an added bonus for Durant, who was said to be an excellent cook himself.

Durant summered at Uncas during its construction, visiting Pine Knot occasionally. Completion of the camp is dated 1892 and was said to have cost $120,000.

Courtesy Adirondack Museum

Original one-story structure of Camp Pine Knot. Dr. Tom Durant (white hair) seated. William W. Durant conversing with woman through window. Photograph by Seneca Ray Stoddard, circa 1877.

Author's Collection

Chalet of Pine Knot completed in 1882. Circa 1970's.

Courtesy Adirondack Museum

William West Durant descending the stairs of the Durant Cottage built for Durant and his wife at Pine Knot. Circa 1889.

Courtesy Cortland Outdoor Education Center

Building used as original Pine Knot living room, now used as the recreation hall of the Cortland Outdoor Education Center. Note Durant's trademark, the letter "W" on the portico.

Courtesy Cortland Outdoor Education Center.

Interior of the original Pine Knot living room. The bark and limb ceilings and the beveled wall boards have withstood the time and elements since it was built in the late 1890's. Circa 1967.

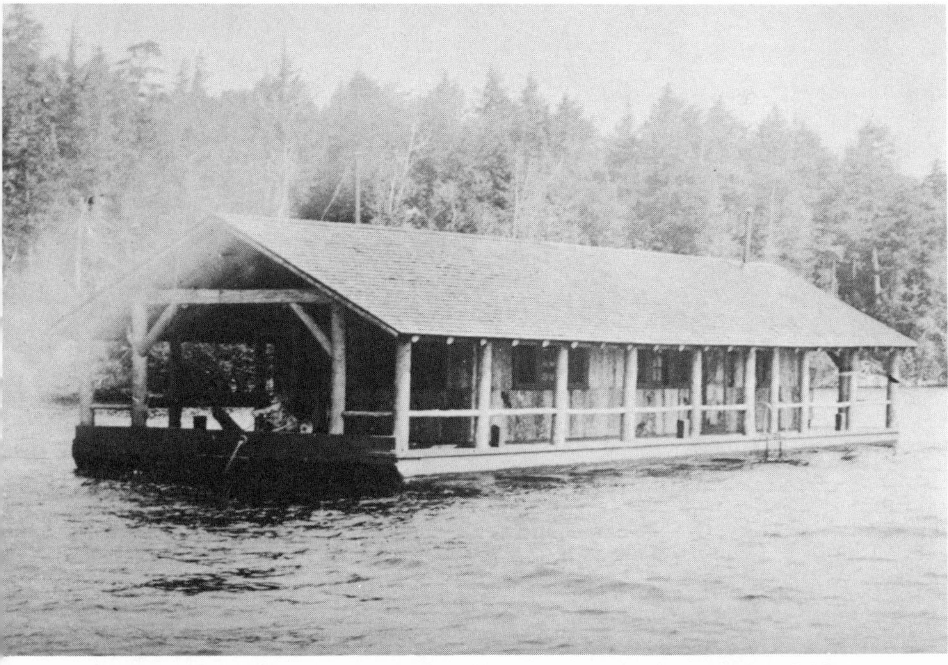

Courtesy Adirondack Museum

One of the unique buildings was an elaborate houseboat, the "Barque of Pine Knot." It contained four rooms including a kitchen and bath and had the luxury of running water.

Courtesy Thomas Norris

Kamp Kill Kare. Circa 1899.

Courtesy Helen Collins

In 1914, Alfred G. Vanderbilt deeded Kill Kare to Mr. and Mrs. Francis P. Garvan. A year later the main complex was destroyed by fire.

Courtesy Thomas Norris

Kamp Kill Kare after the main building was rebuilt.

Courtesy Mabel P. Garvin

After the fire, extensive expansion was undertaken under the supervision of John Russell Pope. Included was a reproduction of a Norman Chapel completed by 1921.

Courtesy Mabel Garvin

During the rebuilding of Kill Kare, a boat house, which included an upstairs guest house used by Mr. Garvan, was built.

Courtesy T. Norris

Construction worker's cottage at Kill Kare. Circa 1920's.

Author's Collection

The main complex at Uncas, often referred to as The Manor House, built in 1892. Circa 1950's.

Author's Collection

The dining room, a separate building overlooking the lake, is dominated by the huge fireplace providing a hunting lodge atmosphere. Circa 1950's.

Author's Collection

Sitting corner of Morgan's bedroom. Circa 1950's.

Courtesy Buster Bird

J. P. Morgan and friends on way to Camp Uncas via Mohegan Road, later known as Uncas Road. Circa late 1890's.

Author's Collection
Main lodge of Camp Sagamore completed in 1897. It is said to be the most impressive of the Great Camp buildings. Circa 1980's.

Author's Collection
The Playhouse built in 1911, attached to the bowling alley (right). Circa 1980's.

Courtesy Helen Collins

Richard Collins, with unidentified passenger in rear. Wife Margaret (Callahan) and children Margaret and Tom standing.

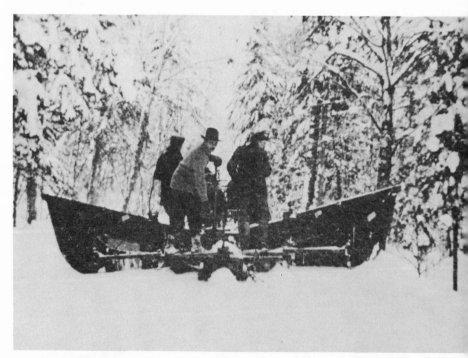

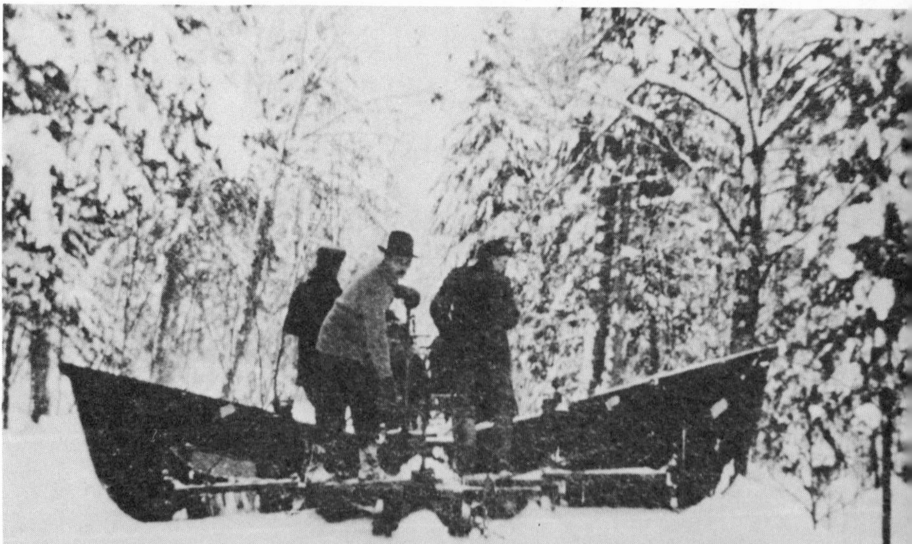

Courtesy Helen Collins

Richard Collins and two employees plowing the grounds at Sagamore. The plow, drawn by two horses, required Collins to guide the team, while a man steered the large blade on each side. Circa 1900's.

Facing financial difficulties, Durant was forced to sell Camp Uncas when J. Pierpont Morgan offered to purchase it. The sale was finalized in 1896, a year after the disposition of Pine Knot to Huntington.

It has been said Morgan agreed to the sale only if the Callahans would remain. Durant reluctantly agreed. In addition to Uncas, John Callahan had also supervised Durant's properties at Shedd and Sumner Lakes. For at least three years after the sale of Uncas, Callahan continued to assist Durant when Uncas was unoccupied.

John and Mary Callahan raised three children: Mary (who later married Judge Dillon), Dan and Tom. In 1920, Tom assumed the position of superintendent assisting his father.

While living at Uncas, Tom married Mildred Cox of LaFargeville, New York. The couple had a daughter, Mary Louise. In 1924 Tom left Uncas, moving to Sagamore to replace superintendent Richard Collins.

John Callahan served three generations of the Morgan family remaining at Uncas until his death in 1939 at age 84.

One of the problems encountered by Durant when he owned Uncas was the difficulty in reaching it. To transport supplies and guests Durant had a wagon road constructed from South Inlet Falls to connect with the steamboat landing on Raquette Lake. In 1896 an extension of the road was built from Uncas to Eagle Bay on Fourth Lake making it possible to ride the train from Utica to Old Forge, embark on a Fulton Chain steamboat and continue the trip by carriage. It was named Mohegan Road after the lake. Later it became known as Uncas Road.

Tom Callahan, who claimed to have worked on the road as a boy of nine, gave this description of its construction:

> "Construction started at Mohegan Lake with three separate crews each from our camp. There were 100 men employed, paid $1.25 each for a ten hour day, plus room and board.
>
> Road building equipment consisted of horse-drawn scrapers (small, two-wheeled dump wagons and mammoth plows). The bulk of the work was done by manpower.
>
> First was the crew of choppers with their razor-sharp axes felling trees as the first step. They were followed by crosscut sawmen who cut the trees in lengths to be drawn by teams of horses. Stumps were

> then blown out with dynamite and great iron plows were run through the debris to remove the roots. The plows were so heavy and large it required two teams to pull them while three men kept them on course.
>
> The roadbed was then leveled and filled by scraping and hand shoveling. In especially low places a corduroy section was installed by placing large trees close together crossways of the road and covering them with dirt. Several bridges were built along the way.
>
> Since work was not possible during the winter months, the Uncas Road was completed the second summer and parts have been in use ever since."

When the elder Morgan died, his family continued to maintain the camp. Anne Morgan, who used the camp more than other members of the family was an ardent trout fisherman and excelled with a rifle. She enjoyed the solitude Uncas afforded her.

In 1947, Uncas was sold to Mrs. Margaret Emerson, wife of Alfred G. Vanderbilt. Uncas received great publicity throughout the world in 1949 when the camp was host to General and Mrs. George Marshall, who entertained General Chiang Kai-shek and his wife. Shortly after this Mrs. Emerson turned the camp over to the Damon Runyon Cancer Fund.

An article in an unidentified paper, possibly the *Arrow*, dated February 13 (no year), stated that the Runyon Retreat at Raquette Lake known as Camp Uncas was purchased by Herbert A. Birrell, an attorney from Blue Mountain Lake and Fred J. Rosenau, a Philadelphia, Pennsylvania businessman. The sale price was not disclosed. Also noted was the property included eight buildings and a private lake.

The article continued, "The aim of these historically-minded persons is to preserve the beautiful estate for future generations and make it available to the public's view."

The camp was open for public tours for several years, but proved too costly to maintain.

Early in 1967 the camp was purchased by the Rockland County Council Boy Scouts of America for $240,000 and renamed "Camp Bulowa."

During their ownership the camp was stripped of its contents.

About 1974 or 1975, the state contracted to purchase the 1,500 or so acres and buildings of Uncas from the Scouts.

Shortly after, due to financial problems, the state declared a moratorium on land purchase. The Boy Scouts were advised to seek a buyer for the buildings as the state planned to purchase the acreage when it became feasible.

Dr. Howard and Barbara Glaser Kirschenbaum, founders and directors of the National Humanistic Education Center (an organization dedicated to the examination of contemporary issues for adults and professionals) purchased sixteen acres and approximately twenty buildings from the Scouts in May 1976.

The following year the state consummated its purchase of the remaining acreage from the Scouts.

The property remains in private hands with the Kirschenbaums occupying one house. Sagamore Institute staff members reside in two others. Sagamore's childrens camp uses part of the property for its summer program.

CAMP SAGAMORE

While living at Camp Uncas, Durant planned the development of a lodge and camp on Shedd Lake. He chose a point of high flat ground on a peninsula jutting from the southwest shore of the lake on which to build the future "Camp Sagamore." With the thought in mind that it would eventually be his permanent home, it was to be the most elaborate and luxurious lodge of all he had previously built. His fondest wish was to invite his influential friends to spend Christmas in the "isolated winter wonderland" in quarters as comfortable as those anywhere in a city. This goal, when achieved, would "prove him to be the greatest host in the Adirondacks."

When Durant sold Uncas to J.P. Morgan, Sr. in 1896, he moved with his family to the Shedd Lake Camp, which he immediately named Sagamore (another Cooper Indian character).

The main lodge of Sagamore is said to be the most impressive of the Great Camp buildings. The huge building which rises three stories over a raised basement and stone piers was erected in the style of a Swiss Chalet. Three flights of stairs rising from a circular drive in front lead to the main entrance double door with its wrought iron hinges. The lodge was constructed of unpeeled spruce logs cut on the site. Special windows with frames and sills were carried six miles through the woods by tandem from Raquette Lake. Each room contains a stone fireplace made of native stone, complete with wrought iron andirons and hardware forged at the camp. Other buildings were built with logs forming the frame and the outside walls were panelled in cedar bark. The bark was stripped from trees, soaked in the lake and nailed on. It has begun to fall away in places and the unique siding is difficult to replace. The service quarters are located about a half mile from the main complex.

Durant, obsessed with having Sagamore no less than perfect, went to great expense changing things with which he was displeased. Legend has it, he was unhappy with the main fireplace and ordered the stone mason to take apart the massive structure and turn each stone around, so the "backs" of the stone faced outward. It is said he had the front porch of the lodge built twice, because the first time it had been slightly out of line. He also spared no expense with his innovations of a year-round water supply and sanitary sewage disposal. He installed central heating and gas illumination, had hot running water and flush toilets.

Durant and his mother moved into the main lodge when it was completed in 1897. This was about the time he filed for divorce from his wife, Janet.

Between 1898 and 1901, a small boathouse, a floating observation post in the lake, a small stable, laundry and dining room were added.

While Durant reluctantly allowed the Callahans to remain at Uncas, Richard Collins who had worked for him at Pine Knot since 1895, arrived at Sagamore to assume the position of caretaker.

In 1901, Collins married Margaret Callahan, half-sister of John Callahan from Uncas. During their employment at Sagamore they had five children: Richard, John, Patrick, Margaret and Tom.

Janet Collins, widow of Patrick, said, "Patrick was the only baby born at Sagamore. His mother couldn't make it to the hospital and he was born in the kitchen."

In 1901, Sagamore was sold to Alfred G. Vanderbilt for $162,000. Durant claimed the cost to build the main lodge itself had been $250,000. Vanderbilt, who had married Elsie French, the same year, honeymooned at the newly acquired Camp Sagamore.

One of the first improvements Vanderbilt made was "the construction of a modern sewage and water supply system. This included a brick pump house, a series of spring houses, a concrete and steel reservoir, and an elaborate conduit system. This installation was far superior to that in operation in American cities and has never had any major repairs, and it was overhauled only once in its over sixty years of service."

The Vanderbilts added several buildings to their estate. In 1901 the building referred to as Lakeside was erected. The building originally planned as a nursery, became the home of the children and their friends under the guardianship of their nurses.

Sagamore was seldom used between the years 1903 and 1911. Elsie Vanderbilt had obtained a divorce and on one of Alfred Vanderbilt's many trips abroad, he met Mrs. Margaret Emerson McKim of Baltimore who had been separated from her husband. When the McKim's divorce was finalized in 1911, Vanderbilt and Margaret Emerson were married in England. Sagamore was used as "one of their American retreats."

Of the three camps - Sagamore, Uncas and Kill Kare - Sagamore is noted as having the largest staff of employees. Contrary to Durant's impression that Sagamore could be run with a minimum number of servants, the Vanderbilts were said to have maintained a resident staff of about twenty in addition to their personal entourage of servants usually numbering about fifteen, including a secretary, valet, chef and assistant chef, laundress, hairdresser and so on. When guests were expected, an additional ten to thirty persons were employed.

"The Playhouse" (now called the Recreation Hall) was built in 1911. Originally intended for a children's playroom, it was used once a year by the Callahans for their daughter's birthday party. "My classmate Mary Louise celebrated her birthday in January," recalled Kay Beals Garlipp. "We were invited to the party which was held in the Vanderbilt's playhouse. There was a victrola and we played ping pong and had a good time."

Later, indoor sports equipment and games of chance were installed in the Playhouse and it was nicknamed the Casino. There was also an exhibit hall for family hunting and fishing trophies. The rear of the building housed a staff taxidermist's work room. A bowling alley was attached where scores were kept in "innings" instead of "frames," recorded on the blackboard nearby.

The same year (1911) the Wigwam, a two-story house overlooking the trout stream was built. This was considered one of the most elegant guest lodges in the Adirondacks. It featured fireplaces in seven of its nine bedrooms. Originally there was no electricity in the room, gas fixtures made of brass supplied the lighting.

In 1915 Vanderbilt had the foundation built for two major buildings, the laundry (now the Conference building) and a barn on the site of the present superintendent's house. The barn was never finished, but a caretaker's house was erected in the latter part of 1915 along with the laundry. Servants were quartered over the laundry, which provided sleeping accommodations for twenty-two employees, while also using the living rooms on the first floor. The staff often outnumbered the guests three to one.

During this period Vanderbilt purchased his private railroad coach, the "Wayfarer," which included modern heaters in the coaches and had separate compartments in addition to an observation room. Local craftsmen were hired to make two elaborate carriages and two matched teams of four horses were chosen from the stables to draw them. These were used to pick up guests at the railroad depot.

"I remember," said Henry Carlin, "Vanderbilt's team of horses would come to the station for the five p.m. and the harnesses on the horses had little lights attached so the driver could see better. The footman and the driver rode in front while the guests sat bundled up in furs in the back seat."

In the spring of 1915, Vanderbilt sailed to England to inspect a stagecoach line he owned and to offer a fleet of wagons to the British Red Cross. An ariticle in the *New York Times* detailed the incident.

When boarding his ship, the Cunard Line's *Lusitania*, reporters questioned whether he thought the enemy might attack the ship. His reply was, "The Germans would not dare attack the ship." The impossible happened off the coast of Ireland. Torpedoes hit the vessel and the ship sank within twenty minutes. Vanderbilt's order given to his valet, "Find all the kiddies you can, boy," was editorialized as a statement that "gave expression to the whole idea of modern civilization."

Vanderbilt and four friends were credited with remaining on ship, giving aid to women and children, offering their own life preservers to some. It is said the "five men locked hands and waited for their watery grave." Vanderbilt was later described by a survivor as the "personification of sportsmanlike coolness. He was the figure of a gentleman waiting for a train."

Vanderbilt's widow, Margaret, later married R.T. Baker, Director of the United States Mint. A daughter, Gloria, was born of this union in the early 1920's.

Mrs. Baker maintained a year-round staff at Sagamore. In 1924, Collins left employment at the camp, moving to Blue Mountain Lake. Thomas Callahan, son of John Callahan of Uncas, replaced him.

In 1928, after ten years of marriage, the Bakers were divorced. Margaret Vanderbilt Baker resumed use of her maiden name, Margaret Emerson. Following her divorce she had two additional buildings constructed and another remodeled. The old laundry room was renovated into a cottage for her daughter Gloria and her nurse. Cottages were built for her sons, Alfred and George, on the lakeshore between the main lodge and the Wigwam.

Margaret Emerson began to spend more time at Sagamore during the summers and Christmas holidays. She became one of the "great social hostesses," entertaining many famous guests including Bobo Rockefeller, Gene Tierney, Gary Cooper, Eddy Duchin, Jean Arthur and Gene Tunney. Stories have been told of Hoagy Carmichael driving on the dirt road to Sagamore in his Model "A" Ford, composing his famous song, "Stardust."

General Pershing, Lord Mountbatten and General George Marshall ranked among the many statesmen and government officials she hosted. During the Truman administration, several high-level discussions on atomic energy were held at Sagamore attended by such men as Bernard Baruch and David Lilienthal.

Margaret Collins Cunningham of North Creek offered the following comments about life at the Vanderbilt estate when she was a child:

> There were five of us kids who lived up over the kitchen area. The Town of Arietta provided a school for us on the grounds. There would be maybe six of us, at the most it would be eight, and they hired a teacher.
>
> As kids at Sagamore we had a marvelous time. In spring my father would make maple syrup. The Vanderbilts shipped it all over the world to their other homes.
>
> When the Vanderbilts had birthday parties, we were included. At Christmas time we received gifts from them."

She remembers it "as an idyllic life for a child, catching fish in a mountain stream and cooking it over an open fire, or skiing behind a horse-drawn sleigh along road cut in to the wilderness around the 1,500-acre estate."

In the summer of 1939, Tom Callahan abruptly terminated his employment with Margaret Emerson, moving to Eagle Bay where he died December 10, 1965. Tom's wife, Mildred, had a widowed sister, Bertha Baltz, who had a son, Gerald. Bertha took as her second husband Lawrence Henry Lamb, who had been hired by Vanderbilt to care for his stable of horses. Bertha and Gerald moved to Sagamore where Bertha assisted with the cooking during the winter months and Gerald assisted with the horses. Gerald Baltz met and married Marian Erb, a music teacher at the Raquette Lake School.

When Callahan left, Lamb was asked to fill the vacancy.

During World War II, Mrs. Emerson served as assistant commissioner of the American Red Cross, on Guam and Saipan, shortly after the capture of those islands. She was awarded the Medal of Freedom Award in 1942. After the war Mrs. Emerson seldom visited the camp.

The Lambs left Sagamore in 1943 and were replaced by Hod Bird, who had been employed at Antlers. Bob Moore and Gerald Feistamel joined Bird caring for the property. The trio left Sagamore in 1948 moving to Kill Kare. Arthur and Mary Patrick were then hired as caretakers of the estate.

In 1956, having learned of Syracuse University's adult education programs at Pinebrook and Minnowbrook, Margaret Emerson deeded Sagamore to the University. The Patricks left and Bruce and Mary Darling from Tupper Lake became year-round caretakers in residence for the University.

Mary and Bruce Darling were active in Raquette Lake community affairs. Their children Wilma, Eugene and George attended the local school. Eugene (Gene) still resides in Raquette Lake working for the town and living with his wife, Carol Cleaveland, who is employed at Sagamore Institute. Their children, Eugene, Joanna and John and granddaughter, Stephanie, also reside at Raquette.

On September 19, 1976, the townspeople gave a surprise farewell party to the Darlings at Camp Sagamore, where they had lived for twenty years. On September 30th they were transferred to Camp Meadowbrook, Syracuse Conference Center in Blue

Mountain Lake to serve as caretakers.

In 1975 the University, hard pressed for money to maintain Sagamore, decided to dispose of it. In 1976 the forest was cut by a jobber, many of the furnishings were auctioned, and the bulk of lands, including the farm complex with its buildings sold for $550,000 to New York State. State law mandates the removal of man-made structures from lands acquired by the Forest Preserve. As a result the approximate seven acres of land containing the three-story lodge, a collection of cottages and service buildings overlooking the mile-long lake, nine other buildings and a partially enclosed bowling alley (the complex housed a total of forty-three bedrooms, twenty-three bathrooms and twenty-six stone fireplaces) was not sold to the state. The Preservation League of New York State, interested in preserving the historical buildings, purchased them, immediately reselling them to Dr. Howard and Barbara Glaser Kirschenbaum who had purchased the Uncas buildings. The Kirschenbaums, representatives for the National Humanistic Education Center, a nonprofit group, paid the sum of $100,000. While the League held the title, a convenant was inserted in the deed protecting the buildings and allowing access to the public. Sagamore Lodge and Conference Center was listed in the National Register of Historic Places upon purchase.

In 1980 the organization's name was changed to Sagamore Institute.

In an article in the *New York Times*, September 5, 1983, Diana Waite, executive director of the Preservation League, said that "under the stress of the moment," the service buildings were excluded from the transaction, and that in "hindsight it was a mistake." The Coalition to Save Camp Sagamore was organized by the Preservation League with United States Senators Daniel Patrick Moynihan (D-NY) and Alfonse D'Amato (R-NY) serving as co-chairmen. The Coalition, a statewide, grassroots network of organizations and individuals worked diligently to educate voters about the Sagamore referendum which appeared on the statewide ballot November 1983. The Sagamore ballot proposal would amend the state Constitution to protect the eleven historic buildings known as the "caretaking complex" from decay or destruction.

The amendment would authorize a land exchange between the state, which owned the caretaking complex, and the not-for-profit Sagamore Institute which owned the main buildings at

Sagamore. In exchange for the eleven endangered buildings and ten acres of land, the Sagamore Institute would donate to the state a 200-acre parcel of land to be added to the Adirondack Forest Preserve. Since the parcel for the exchange would be purchased by the Sagamore Institute there would be no cost involved to the state or to New York State taxpayers. The parcel involved in the transaction contains approximately 218 acres located in the Town of Arietta in Hamilton County.

During the final hours of the 208th legislative session, the State Legislature voted unanimously to approve the Sagamore Land Exchange legislation. Sponsors in the Senate were Senator Hugh Farley and Senator John Dunne; in the Assembly, the sponsor was Maurice D. Hinchey. The vote in the Senate was 60-0 and 140-0 in the Assembly.

On November 8, 1983, over 1,550,000 New Yorkers voted yes on Ballot Proposal 6, the Sagamore Land Exchange, which amended Article 14 of the State Constitution allowing the exchange.

> In the Spring of 1986 in the Adirondack exhibit of the State Museum in Albany, the eleven buildings were conveyed to Sagamore Institute which owns the remainder of the twenty-nine building rustic wilderness estate. Environmental Commissioner Henry Williams called it "an historical occasion . . . the first time in New York State's history when the constitution was amended to save historic buildings.
>
> Simultaneously, Sagamore Institute conveyed 218 acres of wild forest land to the state for inclusion in the Adirondack Forest Preserve.
>
> Although required to be available at least one day a week, the owner announced that for the first time in its 90-year history, Sagamore will now be open daily for public tours during summer and fall seasons."

In the future, Sagamore Institute plans on operating a living museum at the site, with all the original workshops in full operation, producing rustic furniture, Adirondack guideboats, artistic blacksmith work and other crafts that have come to be associated with the New York Adirondack region.

In August of 1986 it was announced that Dr. Howard Kirschenbaum, Executive Director of Sagamore Institute, received an $8,500 grant from the New York State Council on the Arts to conduct a major oral history project.

In order to accurately restore the buildings, furnish the exhibits and equip the workshops, the Institute has arranged under the grant to hire professional folklorist, Karen Lux, to interview people who worked and lived at Sagamore earlier in the century as well as talk to descendants of Sagamore caretakers and their families who have stories or photos to share.

On Sunday, October 19, 1986, "I Remember Sagamore Day" was held at the camp, the beginning of the restoration project.

CHAPTER VII

RELIGION AT RAQUETTE LAKE

THE CHURCH OF THE GOOD SHEPHERD

In 1880, when the Adirondack Mountains were a summer mecca for the rich, the Episcopal Church of the Good Shepherd was built through the generosity of William West Durant. It was designed to fit naturally into its woodland setting on Bluff Island. At that time it was the only place of worship within twenty-five miles, and the only Episcopal Church in Hamilton County.

William R. Mead of Philadelphia gave Bluff Island to the Diocese of Albany and the island was immediately renamed "St. Hubert's Isle" in honor of the patron saint of hunters. The church, built on a bluff of rocks on the north shore of the island, was consecrated as a summer chapel on September 12, 1880 by Bishop Doane of Albany and the Reverend Montgomery H. Throop was installed as priest-in-charge.

Each Sunday morning, one of the Stott sisters who lived on nearby Bluff Point, walked outside their lodge, loaded a small cannon and fired it, calling the congregation to church and alerting them the "church boats" were coming. The boats discharged Episcopalians and other Protestants at St. Hubert's Isle. After St. William's Catholic was built directly across the bay, the boat would continue there.

Durant, who later married Janet Stott, donated the stained glass windows in memory of Cora A. and Laurie B. Stott. The organ, built in 1873, was transported by Durant in time for the dedication. The lectern Bible was donated in 1880 in memory of

Captain Gideon Lathrop, formerly of Lake Champlain. The bell was built by the famous Meneely Bell Company of Troy, New York. Date of placement is unknown as is the origin of the baptismal font. In 1882, Durant built the rectory.

In 1885 another Episcopal Church, the Church of the Transfiguration, was consecrated on the east shore of Blue Mountain Lake, just north of the steamboat landing.

In 1889 Reverend Edward Octavius Flagg, rector of Grace Church, New York City was placed in charge of Good Shepherd as well as the Church in Blue Mountain Lake.

The Reverend William Brown-Serman, from Michigan, was installed by the Diocese of Albany as priest-in-charge of the Island Church in 1894. He held that position until 1941.

In 1914, the rectory was destroyed by fire. Several years later, the Brown-Sermans assisted by friends, built the guest cottage. A year later, in 1918, the present house was built.

Dr. Brown-Serman's children were raised on St. Hubert's Isle where the family resided during the summer months. A daughter, Muriel, was married in the Church of the Good Shepherd to the Reverend Asygell Carrington who assisted with the services for a short time. Two other daughters, Mary Walke and Betty Hayes, both have cottages on the lake.

A son, William, became a Professor of the New Testament at the Virginia Theological Seminary in Alexandria and took charge of the services in the 1930's. William often brought along seminarians to enjoy the lake while assisting with camp chores. Another son was killed during Air Force training in 1941. Rev. Brown-Serman left Raquette Lake that year.

The little church on St. Hubert's Isle fell into disuse. In 1946 Bishop Frederick J. Barry, assistant to Bishop Oldham of the Diocese of Albany, saw St. Hubert's Isle for the first time and immediately decided to use it as a retreat, reviving Sunday services. He was unsuccessful. The island remained uninhabited from 1953 until 1959.

At that time, Bishop Barry approached Reverend Ralph M. Carmichael, rector of St. Andrew's, Albany, requesting he live at the island while serving the Church of the Transfiguration in Blue Mountain Lake. Reverend Carmichael held the first public service in eighteen years on the island with over one hundred people in attendance, including the Echo Camp Choir who provided the music.

In 1960, the Diocese decided to sell the island to Father Carmichael, who used it as his summer home while directing services at the Church in Blue Mountain Lake. The yearly service is held at the Church of the Good Shepherd, usually the first week in August, with worshippers being transported by boat as in the early days. Prayers and psalms are read from the Book of Common Prayers dated 1889. The hymnals used date back to 1892, and the Echo Camp Choir provides the music, with Father Carmichael accompanying them on the 1873 organ.

By 1968, the need for repairs to the church had become critical and Rev. Carmichael's announcement of the situation at the annual service brought an unexpected response. Boy Scout Troop 400 (not one Episcopalian in the group), while camping on the north shore of Raquette Lake at Stillman Bay, decided their new project would be to renovate the church and salvage the historical structure. Led by Scoutmaster, Jack Eklund, and a strong committee which included two professional carpenters, Chet Armstrong, institutional representative and John Bacola, committee chairman, the scouts worked weekends until the snows came. At times they were assisted by Troop 134. Before the ice was fully out, they were back.

Although the inside was in fair shape, the outside was badly deteriorated. The scouts ripped out and replaced much of the stone foundation, re-cementing the solid blocks of limestone. The boys replaced the main beam under the sacristy, repaired two porches that were rotted out and some outside walls, which they painted to match the original paint.

One year and four months later, the church was back in use. The church was re-dedicated as a historic center of worship for all people by the Right Reverend Allen Brown, Bishop of Albany, Sunday, August 17, 1969. The scouts were presented with the Historic Trails award.

Since then, each year the scouts have continued repairing the church during the summer months with assistance of friends and Carmichael family members. Funds toward the projects are from private donations and money collected at the annual service.

In the fall of 1977, the tower of the church was shingled with cedar shingles completing the restoration of the roof.

In time for the Centennial Celebration, the church was painted in its original colors, extensive work was done on the chimney and a new carpet was donated. The first service of the Centennial year was held Sunday, July 20, 1980. Reverend Canon Robert E. Merry of Duxbury, Massachusetts, was celebrant. Worshippers were invited to dress in 19th century clothing, bringing picnic lunches to enjoy on the grounds after the service. Those who did not have their own guideboats or canoes to transport them, took advantage of the "church boat" provided from the town dock.

Several weddings have taken place within the past few years at the Church of the Good Shepherd. On July 17, 1983 Susan Ellen Folk of Somerville, New Jersey who attended the Church since she was a child, married Mark Gilkey of Berkley Heights, New Jersey. Valerie Lee Martino, another early worshipper married Richard Joseph O'Brien on September 1, 1985. Both are from Danville, Virginia.

In both instances guests were transported to and from the island by pontoon boats and private craft.

On June 1, 1986, a freak storm, labeled a micro burst, swept across Raquette Lake destroying many areas in its path including St. Hubert's Isle. Some seventy trees on the island were destroyed, may of them quite old. One was estimated to be about 140 years old. Many trees uprooted, exposing the bare granite stone on which they had grown.

Reverend Carmichael expressed relief that the church suffered minimal damage. "I couldn't believe the wind didn't tear off the roof," he said. "Probably because the trees were leaning on it."

The Church of the Good Shepherd, now over 100 years old, remains an Episcopal Church restored and cared for by Methodists, Catholics, Unitarians, Presbyterians and Baptists. Father Carmichael declared at the re-dedication ceremony in 1969, its doors will be open to "all the people who love the Adirondacks" and who want to "join in thanking the Creator."

The little church on St. Hubert's Isle has been preserved forever on canvas by artist J. W. Ehninger. His oil painting "Mission of the Good Shepherd" dated 1881 is owned by the Adirondack Museum in Blue Mountain Lake.

ST. WILLIAM'S CATHOLIC CHURCH

After building the Church of the Good Shepherd, Durant, although not Catholic, felt an urgency to help the Catholics of

Raquette Lake.

He and Reverend James A. Kelley met at the dedication of the Catholic Church in North Creek. In 1875 Durant invited the priest to visit Pine Knot to celebrate Mass. In July 19 1878, Reverend Kelley said Mass again at Pine Knot, and from that time continued to administer to Catholics during the summer months. This was the foundation of St. William's Parish.

Reverend Kelley was transferred to Baldwinsville, New York in October 1881 and the Reverend Michael F. Gallivan succeeded him.

In September 1890, Durant arranged with J.C. Cady and Co. of New York City to draw up plans for a church to be built on Long Point near what was the original Post Office. He then arranged with Hammond and Mosher of Saratoga Springs to build the church and to supply some of the building materials. Durant's mills were to supply the rest. The windows had semi-precious stones from the area imbedded within and were glazed with a double thickness of glass, and were said to have cost $1,600.

Durant donated the church and property to the Catholics of Raquette Lake. The offer was accepted and notes of appreciation were sent him on behalf of the faithful by Charles H. Bennett, John McLaughlin and E.F. Sheenhy. Others were sent from Bishop Edgar P. Wadhams and Father J.B. LeGrand.

On June 28, 1890, St. William's Church was incorporated by the Right Reverend Edgar P. Wadhams, Bishop of the Diocese of Ogdensburg, and the Very Reverend Thomas E. Walsh, Vicar General of the Diocese. They selected Charles H. Bennett and John McLaughlin to act with them as trustees. The church was dedicated in honor of St. William.

The first marriage recorded in 1891 was between Thomas McSimon and Nell Sheehan. In June of 1892, John and Rebecca McLaughlin's third child, Hubert, received the Sacrament of Baptism conferred by Father Gallivan. Legend has it the water used during the ceremony was donated by W.W. Durant who had brought it from the River Jordan.

Father Gallivan continued to administer to the Catholics of Raquette Lake until he was transferred to Gouverneur, New York in 1896. The Reverend John Fitzgerald, living in Old Forge, served the community of Raquette from December 1896 until July 1911.

A program from "The Annual Regatta and Water Sports," Raquette Lake, New York dated Saturday, August 20, 1910, indicates fund raising events were in operation at that time and regatta activities were enjoyed by all.

The program stated the affair was for "the benefit of St. William's Chapel and the various missions conducted by the Reverend J. Fitzgerald." Entries for the numerous competitive events were to be sent to "Chas. Bennett, Esq., the Antlers or to Robert Collier, Esq. Bluff Point Camp." Tickets of admission, 25 cents, were on sale at the Post Office, the Antlers and the Raquette Lake Hotel.

Engraved plaques and some cash prizes were awarded for fifteen events which included a five-mile sailing race with a Silver Cup valued at $25 as the prize. Other events included children's rowing races, double paddling race for canoes, fifty-yard tub race, one hundred-yard swimming race, canoe upset race, guides' open rowing championship, canoe tilting contest, visitors' open cup rowing race (amateurs only), climbing the greased pole and catching the greased pig (the pig was the prize). Depending on time and interest the potato, egg and spoon, three-legged, sack and, last but not least, shoe races were held.

In is unknown how many years the regatta took place. Eventually it was changed to a regular bazaar or fair where people took the "church boat" to the Point and joined in the games, enjoying food and companionship as well as having an opportunity to purchase the many handmade items and baked goods for sale. After the discontinuance of the event in the 1960's, regret was expressed not only by locals, but by vacationers who planned their vacation time around "The Event of the Year," held at St. William's on the Point.

Rowena Bird and Edna Colligan remember the fairs "as one of the biggest affairs in the area." Rowena remembers, "A group of the girls got some candy cigarettes in the grab bag, and did we think we were smart! We put those candy cigarettes in our mouths and pretended they were real."

"Mary Bryere was sitting on the church steps, and she thought they were real. Maybe she couldn't see well. Did she give us the devil! We tried to tell her that it was only candy, saying 'See, Mrs. Bryere, it's only candy. Try one!' We didn't hear the end of that one for a long time."

"We each had one dollar to spend on the grab bag and all. We had a big old time with our ten dimes."

They both spoke enthusiastically, sometimes at the same time, about the box lunches. "You'd make a lunch and put your name inside of the box." Edna explained. "Nobody was supposed to know which was which, and the guys would bid on them. And your brother usually got yours. I know that!" Edna exclaimed. "He'd know which was yours because he saw how you packed it and that it was something he liked."

"That was fun," Rowena added, "and the fancy cakes and pies the ladies would make to sell! There was one who baked the fanciest ones with cream. They always brought the most money."

Kay Beals Garlipp remembered another affair sponsored by St. William's Church. "A unique event to which we looked forward every year in August was the Moonlight Excursion. Until I was old enough to go on it, I enjoyed the preparations, decorating the barge and so on, hearing the music floating over the water as the dance was in progress. For the dance, a barge used for ferrying cars across the lake was attached to either side of one of the steamboats and here people danced to the strains of the band as they steamed around the lake. It was not always a moonlight night, in fact it frequently was foggy, but it was a romantic way to spend an evening."

In 1911 the Most Reverend Henry Gabriels, Bishop of Ogdensburg, invited the Franciscan Fathers of the Order of Minor Conventual to minister for Raquette Lake, and the attached missions, St. Paul's in Blue Mountain Lake, Holy Rosary in Big Moose and St. Anthony's in Inlet. Two stations at Carter (now Clearwater) and Brandreth lumber camps were also included. The grant was approved by the Sacred Congregation of Religious on February 22, 1912.

The first resident priest of Raquette Lake in July 1911 was the Very Reverend "Henry" Thameling. Shortly after, Brother Ulrich joined him.

At Raquette Lake, Masses during the summer months were held on the point. During the winter, Mass was sometimes held in private homes. Henry Carlin recalls "Mass was held in the old hotel lobby at times. Even the bar was quiet for the service. It was perhaps the quietest bar ever!"

A small building, rented at $50 per year from Maurice Callahan, became a chapel. The structure was located behind the store on a site close to where the present church is located.

Father Henry was transferred in July 1912. He returned in August 1919. During this absence pastors included Reverend Gabriel Eilers (1912-1913), Reverend Alphonse Volmer (1913-1918) and Reverend Hilary Hemmer (1918-1919)

Father Henry has been described as a huge man with strong, large hands. He was admired and respected by all who knew him and was considered generous, hard working, extremely community-minded and a "real friend" to all.

In 1922, Father Henry purchased a cottage from George Fallon for $1500. The house, located on the hill above Mick Road, was used as his residence from the time the lake began to freeze over until the ice was firm enough to permit travel to and from Long Point. He would return again to the village just before the thaw. In 1927 when the village was destroyed by fire, the chapel and an adjoining building were spared.

On Saturday, January 26, 1929 a deep sadness enveloped the hamlet of Raquette Lake. Father Henry was returning from the village to Long Point and on the way he stopped at Echo Camp. Returning from Echo to his rectory, his car fell into an ice hole which had been cut earlier while harvesting ice. Father evidently did not see the last brush pile marking the hole and, mistaking the previous marker as the last, drove into the opening. When he had not returned at the appointed time, a search began. The car was discovered with the lights shining beneath the ice. It was brought to the surface, door open and filled with water, but without Father Henry. Sunday morning his body was found under the ice.

Father's body was laid in state in the winter chapel in the village, with a guard of honor in attendance from Sunday evening until Monday morning when it was taken to the Casino, where a Requiem Mass was sung by Father Thomas of St. Anthony's, Inlet.

Trustees for the church were said to have chosen the words placed on the memory card for Reverend Henry Thameling, born August 13, 1878 and ordained April 16, 1901: "We have loved him during life - let us not abandon him until we have conducted him by our prayers into the house of the Lord."

Following Father Henry's death, Reverend Thomas Grassman, pastor of St. Anthony's Church was named administrator of St. William's and in August 1929 was appointed pastor. Father Tom decided to remain in the village rectory during the winter months.

Some remodeling was done including a small room on the second floor in which an altar was placed where the Blessed Sacrament could be kept. Ott Lanphear and the superintendents of Sagamore, Uncas and Kill Kare provided men to assist in the carpentry and general work. The following year some internal repairs were done to the church on the point and the concrete piers under the church were reset. By 1932 commercial lighting had been brought to Long Point and a landing dock and floating dock were set in place. The Friar's boat *Omicron* was used in the underwater cable laying operation.

In September 1933 Father Dominic Kimmel was assigned as new pastor of St. William's replacing Father Tom Grassman. The Reverend Daniel Lutz assumed the pastorate in November 1937. His added responsibilities included serving the newly formed C.C.C. camp which had been established near Blue Mountain Lake. On January 18, 1938 while Father Daniel was at the camp, a fire completely destroyed the rectory in Raquette Lake and all the parish records as well. Father Daniel urged the community to build a new church for the village. Mrs. Francis Garvan, John Callahan and the elder J. P. Morgan were the main contributors. The Alt Brothers of Utica were commissioned to build from the designs of N. LaVante, a Syracuse architect. Provisions were made not to insert the cornerstone until the church was ready for the dedication. The small white building that had been used as the winter chapel was then moved next to Dillon's house on Dillon Road and used as a temporary rectory.

On December 3, 1939 the dedication of the new St. William's Church was conducted by Bishop Monaghan, Bishop of Ogdensburg who laid the cornerstone. The celebrant of the Solemn High Mass was Minister Provincial, Father Vincent Mayer, with Father Tom Grassman giving the sermon. That evening Father Lutz erected the Stations of the Cross.

Total cost of the land and building was $19,260.16. All expenses except $1,000 had been paid by the day of the dedication. Statues, windows and the altar rail were contributed by parishioners and friends of Father Lutz.

The parish of St. William's celebrated its Golden Jubilee in July 1940. That December the church received $500 from the estate of John Callahan. This amount added to other donations received was sufficient to cancel the balance of the debt.

Father Cuthbert Dittmeier was assigned as pastor in March

1942. He was temporarily replaced by Father Julian Hubal, who later became pastor in 1945. After serving ten years he was replaced by Father Roland Gross.

The first recorded Confirmation held in St. William's Church was in 1956 administered by Bishop Kellenburg. Children confirmed included eight from Raquette Lake, one from Inlet and four from Blue Mountain Lake. That same year released-time instruction was initiated. The parish outgrew the two Masses normally held and added a third.

In 1959 Father Roland was given approval to purchase the "Casino" adjacent to the church. The building included an auditorium and living space on the second floor which was used as residence for the pastor and assistants during the summer months. St. William's on the point became a summer retreat for the friars and visiting priests.

Father Roland was replaced by Reverend Jude Schmeider in September of 1960.

Reverend Gebhardt Braungart replaced Father Jude in 1966. Shortly after, he was reassigned due to ill health and Father Paul Knapp was appointed Pastor of St. William's, St. Paul's, Blue Mountain Lake, and, when Mrs. Garvan was in residence, Kamp Kill Kare. When the Boy Scouts purchased Camp Uncas in 1966 their camp came under his jurisdiction also.

The Reverend Marcian Kandrac relieved Father Paul of his pastoral duties in 1970. Father Marcian celebrated his 25th anniversary of the priesthood in June of 1974. The last recorded confirmation held in St. William's Church in Raquette Lake, was October 24, 1975 administered by Bishop Stanislaus J. Brzana, Bishop of Ogdensburg. Monica and Nora Burke and Kevin Norris received the Sacrament.

Father Marcian was transferred in 1976. His replacement was Father Leo Linder. By mid-October of that year he was assigned to be the temporary Administrator of St. Henry's Church at Long Lake along with the Mission Church of St. Paul's in Blue Mountain Lake. Father Leonard Unger, pastor of St. Anthony's in Inlet, was requested to take over the duties of St. William's in addition to his own parish.

When the temporary assignment of Father Leo ended, he returned to St. William's and St. Paul's was assigned permanently to St. Henry's in Long Lake.

In November 1978, Father Henry Gibeau received the appoint-

Author's Collection

The Episcopal Church of the Good Shepherd, built on St. Hubert's Isle (formerly Bluff's Island) by Durant in 1880, was renovated in 1968 to salvage the historical structure. Circa 1970's.

Author's Collection

Interior of the Chruch of the Good Shepherd.

Author's Collection
St. William's Catholic Church built in 1890 on Long Point. Circa 1960's.

Courtesy Marguerite Fuge
The organ with very ornate carvings, was shipped by Durant from the Packard Organ Company, Fort Wayne, Indiana. It is believed the organ has been at St. William's since 1890. Circa 1970's.

Author's Collection
St. William's Catholic Church, built in 1938. Circa 1970's.

Courtesy Doris and Glenn Martin
Before the Raquette Lake Chapel was built in 1928, services were held in the railroad station or in a railroad coach on the siding. The group pictured includes: Back row L-R: Earl Pulling, unidentified girl, Norton Bird Jr., Mrs. Ezra Norton, Kay Beals, John Goodrow, Marie Waldron, Edna Lanphear, Winfield Martin, Walter Manning, unidentified girl and Norton Bird Sr. Middle row: Two boys on either side of Martin are Jerry Lanphear and Charlie Bird. Bottom row L-R: C.H. Carlin, Joe Bird, Stanley Lanphear, three small children unidentified, June Pulling, Mary Bird and Harold Bird. Circa 1920's.

Courtesy Rowena Bird

Among the first caretakers, of the Raquette Lake Chapel were twins, Harry and Howard Waldron. Circa 1925.

Author's Collection

The Raquette Lake Chapel. Circa 1970's.

Author's Collection

The wrought iron chandeliers in this photo of the interior of the Raquette Lake Chapel, once hung in the dining room of Antlers Hotel. Circa 1970's.

ment as Administrator of St. William's. Upon his death in 1979, the Bishop placed St. William's under the jurisdiction of St. Anthony's.

Father Leonard was replaced by Father Armand Sorento, who in turn was replaced in 1981 by Father Robert Leahey. As of August 1986, Father Kirk Howland was administering the duties of Father Robert, who was on sick leave.

Father Paul, a former pastor of St. William's, has continued serving the needs of its parishioners since 1979 when it became apparent the church might have to be closed during the fall, winter and spring. When he retired he was assigned to assist at St. Anthony's.

"I retired as a Pastor," says Father Paul, gasping from his illness, "not as a Priest, and I will continue to serve St. William's as long as God is willing." Father Paul celebrated his 50th anniversary in the priesthood in 1986.

The last marriage performed in St. William's Church was that of Joel George Zillioux and Kristine Bachlet of Brooklyn on July 12, 1986 with Father Kirk officiating as Parish Administrator. On December 1, 1985, Lindsay Denise Dillon, daughter of John T. and Cari Pelton Dillon, was the last baby to receive Baptism. Heather Marie Timm was the last child to receive First Holy Communion in the Raquette Lake Church on May 19, 1983.

St. William's "the Mother Church of the Mountains" has undergone many changes through the years. What lies ahead is in the hands of God.

THE RAQUETTE LAKE CHAPEL

When the village of Raquette Lake was moved from Long Point to its present site in 1900, the Episcopal Church on St. Hubert's Isle was in operation for only two months in the summer. During the winter, services were held in private homes, when a minister was available.

Some of the Protestant parents, because they wished their children to have some formal spiritual guidance, sent them to the Catholic Church on Sundays.

Kay Beals Garlipp remembers attending St. William's with her sister, Fredrica, until Mrs. Ezra Norton, wife of the night watchman of the New York Central Railroad, started holding Sunday School classes in her home. Later Mrs. Hunt also gave instructions.

In early 1927, members of the Protestant Faith, approached Reverend Herbert Baird, then minister for the Church of the Lake, in Inlet, requesting services at Raquette Lake. Meetings were held on Tuesday evenings in either the waiting room of the railroad station or in a railroad coach on the siding. Music was supplied by a portable pump organ. Kay Garlipp remembers her brother Malcolm Douglas Beals being baptized in a railroad coach.

The congregation at Raquette Lake organized as the Chapel of the Church of the Lake with hopes of having their own church building. They chose as a possible site, a siding with a shed built by Collis P. Huntington for the storage of private coaches of camp owners while they were at Raquette. Mr. Andrew Nielson, a New York City real estate broker and summer resident of Inlet, volunteered to contact the Huntington heirs on behalf of the congregation, with thoughts of purchasing the then vacant property. The parcel was sold to the Church of the Lakes for the sum of one dollar with the deed dated September 10, 1927 and signed by Archer M. Huntington and his wife, Anna. A restrictive clause was included in the deed stating the property may be used for religious purposes only. However, there was also a clause stating, "The erection of a library upon the herein granted premises shall not be deemed a breach of the foregoing condition."

Upon acquiring the property, plans were formulated to construct the present Chapel. Edgar Lamphear believes "Dr. Sam Evans, then owner of Tioga, put up the money for the chapel and John Blanchard, Ott Lanphear and other members of the crew from Tioga built it."

Buster Bird's Model-T truck was used for hauling stone for the foundation, and it is believed Jack Dole did the masonry work. The uniquely shaped windows were designed by John Blanchard and his son, Paul. Other men believed to have worked on the construction included Clinton Harvey, Henry Burnham, Bill Pulling, Anthony Harper, Norton Bird and Darius Waldron.

In the winter of 1927-1928 the Chapel was dedicated. Reverend V.L. Mackey, executive of the Presbyterian Synod of New York and the Reverend Arthur Dean, the Associate Executive, were present. The first Chapel Committee was composed of Norton

Bird, Chairman and Elder, Wallace Manning, Trustee of the Church of the Lakes, Mrs. Orrin Lanphear, Mrs. Clinton Harvey, and Mrs. Clarence Beals, Treasurer.

Because of the increase in tourists in the summer, it was necessary to secure an assistant for that time of year. This practice was put in operation in 1927 continuing until 1970.

The first recorded congregational meeting was held on January, 1958 with Mrs. Orrin Lanphear the only active Church officer. She served as Treasurer from 1933 until January 1973 when Mrs. Jay Cummings assumed the position. Mrs. Harry Waldron has been clerk since 1958.

Sunday school has been an important part of the Chapel's activities. During the late 1940's, regular worship services were not held during the winter months in the Chapel. However, the Sunday School classes were continued in the Raquette Lake Hotel lobby supervised by Charlesetta Christy and Catherine Northrup Collins. Some of the early teachers included Edna Lanphear Colligan, Jane Van Kirk and Catherine Beals Garlipp.

There was always an annual Sunday School picnic. The early ones were held on Tioga Point at Dr. Evans' camp and everyone had to be transported by boat. Later they were held at Buttermilk Falls. At times when the spring brought a heavier supply of black flies than usual, the picnic was held indoors at the Antlers.

Annual bazaars, which date back to the beginning of the chapel, have been an added source of income. The early "fairs" were held on the church grounds and later they were held at the Raquette Lake Casino, possibly on the porch of the railroad station and more recently at the Raquette Lake fire hall.

Mrs. James Bird and Mrs. Harry Waldron were chosen to represent the Chapel in the newly formed Council of the Fulton Chain area in 1958. The council operated as a guiding body for the area churches until 1967 at which time it was disbanded.

The original chapel was remodeled once in 1959 by Smith and Barrows contractors from Thendara. In 1962 wrought iron chandeliers that once hung in the dining room of the Antlers were donated to the Chapel by Blanche amd Lee Krimsky of the Raquette Lake Girls Camp. They were installed by Carl Kammer, a summer resident. The side lights in the choir area are from an old Genesee Street home in Utica. They were a gift of Mary Waldron Henry in memory of two school friends who lost their lives in an auto accident in the area. The candelabras on the walls were purchased with money raised by the children attending the Friday release time classes. Fifty new hymnals were given in memory of Sharon Beckingham in 1963. The blue spruce trees by the front steps and the vase on the communion table were given in memory of Moses Leonard. A pulpit hymnal was dedicated in memory of Dr. Warrick, and an outside bulletin board was given in memory of Mrs. Ethel Hall and Mr. Harrison Linforth.

A portable organ used before the chapel was built was replaced by a regular organ and when it became inoperable, a piano was acquired. In July of 1965, Mrs. Frances Clough Havinga presented the chapel with an electric organ in memory of her husband, Carlton Clough, and her son, John.

Many of the parishioners have shared their musical talents playing the organ during services. In addition to Mrs. Orrin Lanphear, they include Mrs. Livingston Bentley, Mrs. Denes Tamas, Mrs. Edwin Wires, Mrs. Kenneth Cross and Mrs. Harry Suits.

In 1967 the Chapel was enlarged. Art Jenkins laid the new carpeting and three new pews, acquired from the Inlet Church in Ithaca, New York, were added. Fred Burke transported them and Ami Martin fitted them into the chapel, staining them to match the existing woodwork. Steps leading up to the chapel road were also added at this time.

Between December 1960 and August 1967, Reverend Livingston Bentley served the Chapel and Inlet. Congregation records show that his stay was longer than any of his predecessors.

In 1968 the dedication of the church spire took place. The steeple was erected in memory of Carol Marian Jones, a sailing instructor and cabin counselor at Echo Camp. In the same year, Sunday School was replaced by release-time classes, and the first Easter breakfast was served. Harry and Howard Waldron were co-chairmen for the event.

The Chapel and the Church of the Lakes continued as church and chapel until September 1970. Both Reverend Bentley and Reverend Tamas, his immediate predecessor, encouraged the Chapel to be recognized as an independent church. During a period when the chapel was without an installed minister, the step was taken. The Reverend Joseph C. Sayers (a summer minister in 1969 and 1970) was present for the ceremony. From 1970 until 1972, the Chapel and Church of the Lakes were without a minister and services were again conducted by supply ministers and lay preachers.

In February 1973, Reverend Kenneth Cross was installed as pastor, and the chapel and parishioners flourished under his spiritual and practical guidance.

At various times the chapel has suffered financial difficulties. In 1970 the Jane R. Bird (Mother Bird) Fund was initiated. It paid for new doors purchased and installed by Art Jenkins. In 1971 the fund made it possible to repair and paint the interior and in 1976 the outside was painted and a new roof put on.

In 1973, the first annual Christmas appeal letter was sent to year-round and summer parishioners and in 1974 a permanent memorial fund was established.

The chapel was recipient of a pulpit Bible given by Mr. and Mrs. Kenneth Wanamaker in 1975 and in 1976 the outside bulletin board was restored by Jay Cummings.

Through the years, parishioners have acted as janitor and all around caretakers. Among the first caretakers were the twins, Harry and Howard Waldron, who not only cleaned the chapel, but brought in the wood and started the fire so the congregation could worship in comfort.

On Sunday, July 30, 1978 the chapel held its 50th Anniversary Recognition Service with many members of the clergy who had served at one time or another in attendance. A reception followed at the Fire Hall. In honor of the celebration, a booklet *The Raquette Lake Chapel - The 1st Fifty Years* was prepared by the anniversary committee, Marguerite Fuge and Beatrice Waldron. It is from this booklet, that much of the Chapel's history has been obtained.

In October 1981 Reverend Cross, who had served the Raquette Lake Chapel for nine of his thirty years of ordained ministry, retired. From that date until May 1982, Supply Minister, Howard Butler from Vernon, New York served the church and chapel. Fred Castiglioni, a seminary intern from Princeton served the parishioners from June 1982 until May 1983 when Mary Robards began her internship at the Church of the Lakes and the Chapel. On May 14, 1984 she was ordained as Minister to Ministry of the Word in St. Anthony's Catholic Church in Inlet. In accordance with Presbyterian tradition, an intern serving more than one church is ordained in a neutral church.

Bishop Stanislaus Brzana, of the Catholic Diocese of Ogdensburg, in accord with the ecumenical guidelines of the Catholic

Church and to reinforce the close relationship the churches have shared throughout the years, granted special permission to hold the ordination in St. Anthony's Church. He also extended his best wishes to her for a fruitful ministry, promising to remember her in his prayers. The ordination was held by the Presbytery of Utica.

On Sunday, May 27, 1984, Reverend Mary Robards and Mark W. Clark of Inlet were joined in matrimony in the Church of the Lakes in Inlet. Reverend Kenneth Cross, a former Pastor officiated with the congregation as witnesses. The couple recited the vows they had prepared.

As of December 1986, Reverend Clark was still serving the Church of the Lake in Inlet and the Raquette Lake Chapel.

CHAPTER VIII

CAMPS IN THE LATE 1800's

HENDERSON, HASBROUCK AND WHITNEY

Many camps sprang up around Raquette Lake during the 1880's, including the Henderson and Hasbrouck Camps.

The Henderson camp built in 1880 by John B. Henderson, ex-senator from Missouri, was situated near Brightside on Indian Point. In 1900, Dr. Otto Kiliani of New York took possession and the property is now owned by Mrs. Mary Tucker.

The Hasbrouck camp was built about the same time on the mainland near Beecher's Island in Outlet Bay by Frederick Hasbrouck, a wine and liquor merchant from New York City. Upon the death of Hasbrouck's widow, the property was willed to her sister, Mrs. Charles Bouchier. The camp was later inherited by Sophia Bouchier and her brother, Charles.

Although a summer resident, Sophia Bouchier was extremely active in community affairs. She was instrumental in the building of the present library. Her interest in the youth of the area, led her to organize the first Boy Scout Troop in Raquette Lake.

Upon her death the property was willed to her brother, Charles, and after his death, the property was left to the state.

Honest Joe Whitney set up his Rush Point Camp on South Bay near South Inlet in 1881. The camp (near what is now Burke's Marina) consisted of a two-story building affording adequate accommodations for about a dozen people.

H. Robert Beguilin of New York City took possession of the camp in 1917. The estate consisted of the main lodge, a guest cottage, kitchen with servant quarters above, laundry, ice house, cooler building and boat house.

Billy Cornell, described as a bright, educated man, built a camp on the Beguilin property. A guide and boat builder by trade, he worked at the estate until he drowned off the shore of Echo camp.

In September 1937, Raymond and Barbara Burke purchased the property from the estate of Robert Beguilin. The guest house was torn down by Ray Burke and his son, Fred. The laundry and boat house were moved to serve as rental cottages. The main lodge, kitchen building and ice house were also used as rental units.

Margaret Burke, daughter of Raymond and Barbara Burke, acquired the property which she and her husband, Bruce Risley ran during the summer months.

It is unknown when the original buildings were built. However, owner Bruce Risley says that a *Brooklyn Gazette* dated 1894 was found as insulation between the walls of one of the buildings when it was dismantled.

NORTH POINT AND CAMP GREYLOCK

Another of the early camp owners in about 1878 was James Ten Eyck of Albany who chose to build his camp on the northern end of Raquette Lake at Outlet Bay. It is referred to as North Point. The camp, with a view of the lake to the south and mountains beyond, maintained buildings similar to those at Stott's Camp on Bluff Point.

John Boyd Thatcher, whose family owned a camp at Indian Lake, vacationed at North Point on several occasions.

In 1902, Ten Eyck sold the estate to Mrs. Lucy Carnegie, widow of Thomas Carnegie, whose brother was steel magnate, Andrew Carnegie. Legend has it that Mrs. Carnegie spent $200,000 renovating the camp. She changed the original structure to that of a Swiss chalet, with the main lodge consisting of a two-story building used as a living room and family quarters. A gallery over the living room looked down to a massive walk-in fireplace. The lodge, built of logs felled and milled on the site, was joined to a second two-story building by a covered walkway.

The second building housed the dining room and kitchen with servants quarters above. Both buildings have since become self-contained individual units.

A large two-story boat house was included as well as scattered guest sleeping cottages with fireplaces, constructed in the chalet style. During these years Almon "Allie" Hunt became caretaker.

In 1910 Mrs. Carnegie deeded the 65-acre tract adjacent to the point to her son, Andrew Carnegie, III. He erected several log buildings which later became the nucleus of Camp Greylock for Girls.

In 1921, Andrew sold his property to Mrs. Herman (Rae) Mason, then principal of a school in Buffalo. With financial as well as physical support, her brother-in-law, Dr. Gabriel R. Mason, a prominent educator in the New York School System assisted her in forming a camp for girls.

Dr. Mason, founder of the Greylock Camp for Boys (situated in the heart of the Berkshires at the base of Mt. Greylock, Center Lake), was most influential in determining the format for the girls camp, using the program of the boys camp as a guide.

Campers traveled to Raquette Lake village by sleepers, then by boat to Greylock. The camp consisted of eight cabins referred to as "bunks." Approximately six girls were housed on each side.

"Aunt Rae," as Mrs. Mason was known, was director for twenty-seven years. During the last five of those years, her daughter, Mrs. Bryna Lieberman and her daughter-in-law, Irma, ran the camp.

Mr. and Mrs. Leonard Levine purchased the camp in 1956. Asked why she, a prominent attorney and business woman, wanted to buy a camp, Mrs. Levine replied, "A colleague of mine invited me to visit a camp that was for sale in Rockland County. He was interested in buying a summer camp and wanted advice. For reasons I cannot explain," she continued, "the more camps we visited, the more the idea of having a camp of my own haunted and intrigued me."

In February 1955, Mrs. Levine received a call from her broker advising her a camp in the Adirondacks called "Greylock" was for sale. She had never been to the Adirondacks and drove to visit the camp with Rae Mason's son, Malcom.

"Our first sight of the camp was, for me at least, breathtaking," said Naomi. "The entire property was covered with snow whiter than any I had ever seen. The trees appeared silver and white and were breathtaking. If it is possible to fall in love with a place, it was love at first sight for me."

She and her husband spent the summer of 1955 at Greylock observing the operation and in 1956 they became the owners. Many changes were made and new tennis courts were added behind the bunk complex where outdoor plays were held.

In 1971, although the camp was flourishing, Naomi was urged to sell off the land for vacation homes. The first piece of property was sold to Mrs. Libby Raynes Adelman who had been a Greylock camper from 1927 to 1931, during the time of Rae Mason. Later, her daughter Naomi became a camper at Greylock for eight summers.

In the preface of a booklet, *Greylock Association 1971-1981*, Mrs. Adelman had this to say about her purchase:

"More than fifty years ago a little girl came to Camp Greylock for Girls, fell in love with Raquette Lake and dreamed that someday she might have a home such as she saw hidden amongst the pines along the lake. . . . It seemed an impossible dream but by dint of nagging, pleading, and a combination of happy circumstances the Levines in 1971 decided to close Camp Greylock for Girls and sold me Sandy beach, an off-bounds area when I was a camper at Greylock."

Several parcels were purchased by "Greylockers," former counselors and campers.

The Levines' home is composed of two of the original Camp Greylock cabins, one of which was always occupied by the owner of the camp, the other by visitors or by a married counselor. The home has been completely modernized and winterized. In addition, the Levines kept the boathouse, (the upper story is now the Greylock Museum containing memorabilia of Camp Greylock from its earliest days), the shower house, two of the camp tennis courts and a guest house which is one of the original Carnegie buildings.

The property, excluding that deeded to Andrew Carnegie, III, was deeded to Lucy Carnegie's heirs on May 17, 1913 and remained in the family until April 1924 when it was purchased by the Raquette Lake Supply Company and became North Point Inn.

North Point Inn was advertised with a logo depicting woodsy mountains with a cottage in the foreground and the caption: "Raquette Lake in the Wilderness." Accommodations were listed as: "Mountains, lake, health, golf, riding, tennis, water sports, superior food, club-like privacy, exclusive clientele, unobtrusive management. Isolated yet accessible. Season ends September 30. Rates $42 weekly and up. Send for illustrated circular NOW." Within a short time North Point Inn became a popular resort with many guests staying for the entire season.

On May 29, 1944 the property was sold to Herbert A. Birrell and Roy A. Hayward, partners d/b/a The Steamboat Landing. On January 5, 1954 the property was deeded from the Steamboat Landing to Herbert A. Birrell, who in turn deeded the property to Margaret K. Birrell on July 30, 1959.

On September 14, 1959, Margaret K. Birrell deeded eleven acres and the remainder of North Point Cottages Inc. to Robert W. Birrell.

In about 1961 nearly all of the 200 acres of North Point including all of the buildings, except the game lodge, main house and garage, and the cottages in the bay, was acquired by a North Point partnership.

From 1961 through the summer of 1969 the partnership operated a cottage colony. During that time, fourteen cottages were sold. Of those, eleven were purchased in 1966 by Donald Langham who also acquired an additional parcel. The cottages were used as rental units, eventually being sold to private camp owners.

After the 1969 season, the North Point partnerhsip sold the remaining property back to the Birrells, who in turn have been selling to individual land owners.

CAMP STOTT — BLUFF POINT

Frank H. Stott, of Stottsville, New York, visited Raquette Lake for the first time in 1875. Stott, referred to as "Commodore Stott," was described by Frank Carlin as a big man, weighing about 240 pounds and "a fine gentleman, the old Commodore!"

Stott was partners with William L. Strong in the textile business. Strong, who became mayor of New York City in 1895, had been an occasional visitor to the area. His son married May Yohe (Hope) whose former husband, Lord Francis Hope, was the owner of the famous Hope Diamond.

Courtesy Doris and Glenn Martin

Summer camp of Mrs. T.M. Carnegie. Circa 1900.

Author's Collection

Andrew Carnegie III's summer home. Circa 1915.

CAMPS ON RAQUETTE LAKE 1876-1899

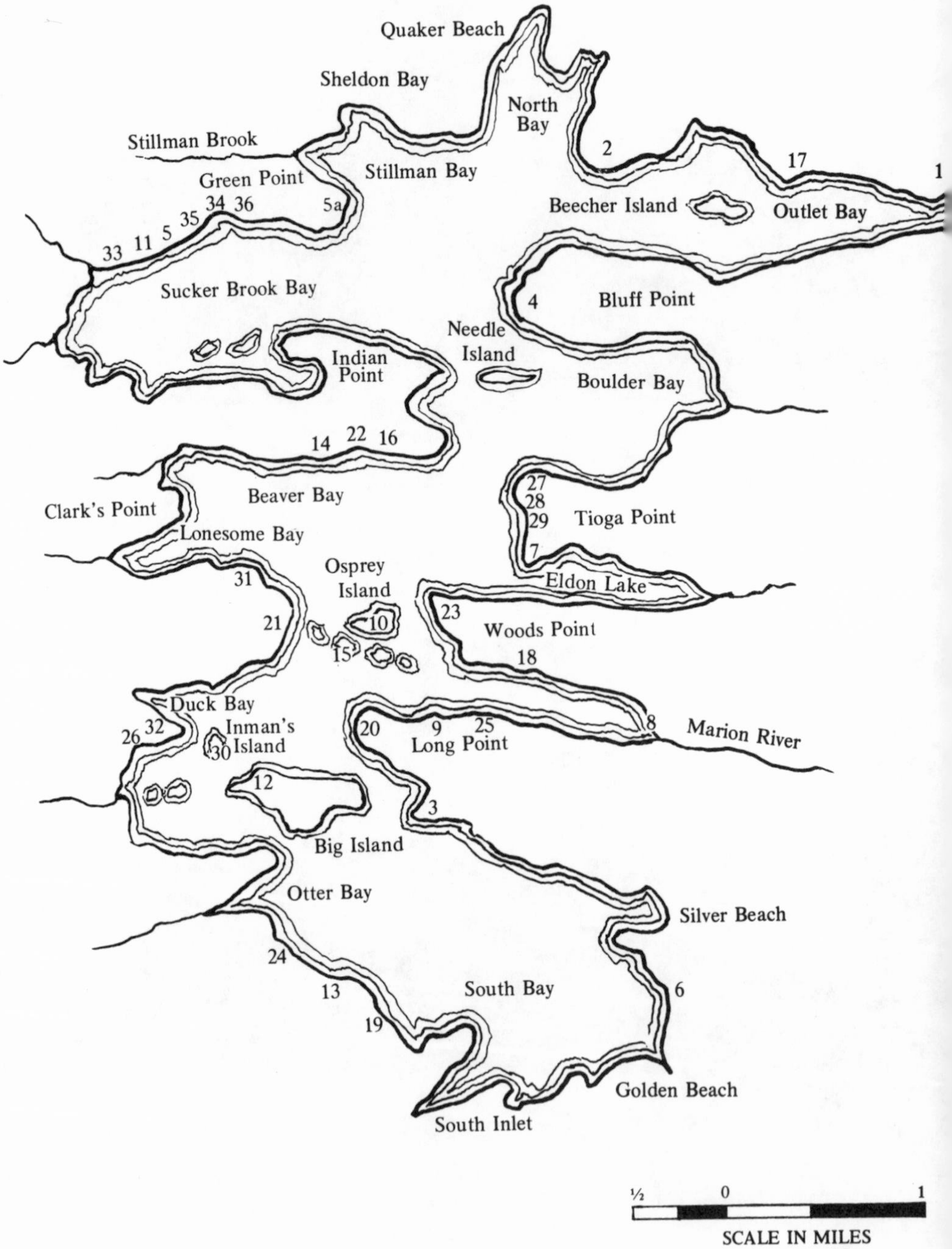

Quaker Beach
Sheldon Bay
North Bay
Stillman Brook
Green Point
Stillman Bay
2
17
1
Beecher Island
Outlet Bay
34 36
5a
35
5
11
33
Sucker Brook Bay
4
Bluff Point
Needle Island
Indian Point
Boulder Bay
14 22 16
27
28
29
7
Tioga Point
Clark's Point
Beaver Bay
Lonesome Bay
Osprey Island
Eldon Lake
31
21
10
23
Woods Point
15
18
Duck Bay
26
32
Inman's Island
30
20
9 25
Long Point
8
Marion River
12
3
Big Island
Otter Bay
Silver Beach
24
13
South Bay
6
19
Golden Beach
South Inlet
½ 0 1
SCALE IN MILES

LEGEND

(Locations approximate)

1. Frank Wood, 1870's
2. North Point - Ten Eyck, 1876
3. Camp Pine Knot - W.W. Durant, 1876
   Collis Huntington, 1895
4. Camp Stott, 1876
5. Charles Blanchard, 1876

5a. Charles Blanchard, The Wigwams, 1873

6. Chauncey Hathorne, Golden Beach, 1877
   W.W. Durant, 1891
   State, 1897
7. Seth Pierce, Sunset Grove, 1877
8. Camp Marion - Paul Tibbitts, 1878
   J. McLaughlin, 1880's
   Joe Grenon, 1892
9. Under the Hemlocks - Edward Bennett, 1879
   E.C. Finck, 1889
   Jack Daly, 1890
10. Camp Fairview - Charles Durant, 1879
    J. Harvey Ladew, 1891
11. William Payne, 1883
12. Camp Oteetiwi, Dr. Arpad Gerster, 1884
13. Henry Taylor, 1880
    James McGovern, 1893
14. John Jones, 1880
15. The Church of the Good Shepherd, 1880
16. Henderson Camp, 1880
17. Hasbrouck Camp, 1880
18. Sunset Camp, Richard Bennett, 1880
19. Rush Point Cottages, Joe Whitney, 1881
20. Camp Echo, Governor Lounsbury, 1885
21. Antlers, Charlie Bennett, 1885
22. Brightside on Raquette, J.O.A. Bryere, 1885
23. Tom Bennett, Big Island, 1886
24. Fred Maxim, 1887
25. St. William's Catholic Church, 1890
26. Frank Carlin's Marina, 1890
27. William Strange, 1890
28. Dennis McCarthy, 1890
29. Camp Deerhurst, Tom Platt, 1890
30. Inman's Camp, 1890
31. George Carlin's Hunter's Rest, 1894
32. Golding's Camp Osceola, 1895
33. Asa Payne, 1898
34. Lou Porter, 1899
35. Camp Furlough, late 1800's
36. Anderson Camp, late 1800's

Courtesy Naomi Levine

Mrs. Herman (Rae) Mason. Circa 1920's.

Courtesy Naomi Levine

The Camp Greylock boathouse. Circa 1950's.

Courtesy Madeline Fallon Case

The original Stott camp. Circa 1915.

Courtesy Madeline Fallon Case

George Fallon (right) posing with a friend and with a small cannon used to announce the coming of the church boats on Sunday mornings. The cannon is now on permanent display at the Adirondack Museum. Circa 1918.

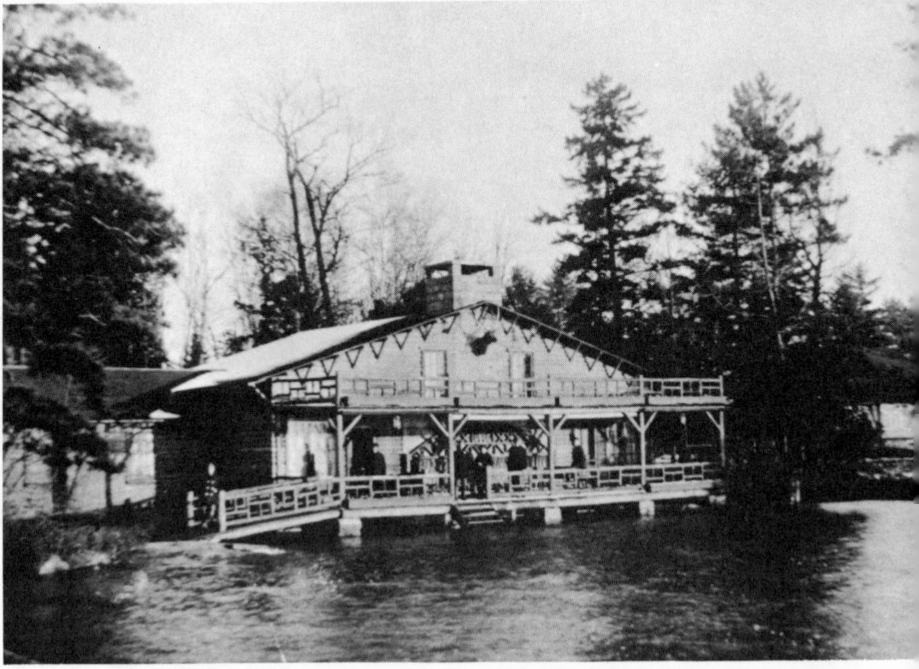

Courtesy Madeline Fallon Case

The plane hanger was convered to "The Playhouse." Circa 1913.

Author's Collection

The gazebo on the small island at Bluff Point. Circa 1970's.

In 1878, Stott settled on Bluff Point on land apparently claimed by William K. Mead and the State of New York. On June 6, 1884, by a special legislative decree (as shown as Item #1 of the Bluff Point abstract), the commissioners of the Land Office were permitted to lease up to 160 acres of land to Stott for thirty years at $20 per year with a provision to "preserve the timber thereon."

Stott's long time occupancy together with a deed from Mead to Stott (as shown as #2 of the Bluff Point abstract), led to his eventual ownership of the property.

The original Stott camp, built by Thomas Wallace, consisted of many one-story log buildings with simple fireplaces and were furnished in the "usual" camp manner.

Robb and Betty Tyler, present owners of the Bluff Point buildings have a copy of the original Stott Journal (with the first entry dated 1876) that is now the property of the Adirondack Museum. In it are several interesting notations.

A notation made during the summer of 1878 listed the following as guides for the Stott family: Charles and Wallie Hammer, Lorenzo Towne, William Cullen and Warren Cole. Under the year 1880, William West Durant in his own hand wrote "My first call!!!" On July 16, 1884 a notation was made: "Miss Janet Stott and Wm. W. Durant. Remained only a few hours. Returned to Blue Mountain Lake the same afternoon."

Further entries in the journal indicate a boat house was added and other construction was undertaken between the years 1884 and 1887. A notation on May 10, 1887 read: "Arrived at Camp Stott about six p.m., taking possession of the new house. . . ." It continued, "Guides for 1887 J.O.A. Bryere, Willard Locke, Frank Emerson, Dennis Mahan from Troy. August 30th, Sid Porter for Brown's Tract Camp. Sept. 20th, Jerome Wood for the hunt, John Ballard for the hunt, Ike Kenwell started dogs."

The journal entries also note Joe O. A. Bryere and family were caretakers in the early 1890's, Henry Brown in the mid-1890's and George Jenkins from Blue Mountain in the later 1890's.

The last entry September 19, 1900 brought to the end a chronicle of twenty-four years of joyful reunions, growing generations and reluctant separations at the close of each season. A feeling of sadness is imparted in the words, "All left for home . . . Party separated at Albany. A glorious day (?)." Not only was it the end of the journal, but it was also the end of the Stott regime. Robert

Collier, the magazine publisher, purchased the property in 1910 for $20,000.

ROBERT J. COLLIER

Robert J. Collier, a journalist, was born in 1876. He eventually inherited his father's weekly magazine and publishing business which he had helped build.

Upon acquiring Camp Stott he rebuilt the buildings to his preference. The fireplaces were rebuilt including a two-story brick fireplace in the main lodge. Other buildings were structurally changed, second floors were added to some, balconies to others and the total number was increased to about twenty.

In about 1910, George Fallon from Forestport and his wife, Agnes Ryan, from Olmsteadville moved to Raquette Lake to become caretakers at Collier's Camp.

In 1913, in order for the children to be closer to school during the winter, Fallon purchased the house built by Ezra Norton on property originally owned by Frank Carlin. The home is now owned by the Frank Lamphears.

Fallon traveled across the ice to Collier's by sled. Two years later he built another home on the side of the hill behind Carlin's Marina. He sold his first home to the Hunt family and in the mid-1920's, they in turn sold to Roscoe Carlin.

Madeline Fallon Case of Old Forge remembers Mrs. Collier always brought her maids with her when she went to camp. "She had her own hairdresser, manicurist and personal maid. She was rather pretty and seemed to know it. She spent a great deal of time on herself."

Collier, a boat enthusiast, launched *The Skeeter* in 1910. It had a sixty horsepower engine with a speed of about twenty-five miles per hour, and at the time was considered the fastest boat in the area. About 1913 he purchased another boat, the *Dixie II*, which was faster then the previous craft, with a speed of forty-five miles an hour. He later named her the *Stop Thief*. "I think he picked that name," wrote Frank Carlin, "because he stole every race from 'crazy Murphy.'" (Murphy was Collier's rival for the speed championship of Raquette Lake.) In 1914 he launched the ultimate in his collection of boats, a hydroplane called the

Skimmer. It was a raft driven by an airplane propeller and was rated at a speed of up to sixty miles per hour.

Stronger than his love of racing was his deep passion for flying. For many years Collier had been president of the Aero Club of America and was a pioneer aviator in his own right. In 1912 he had a hanger built on a bluff toward Boulder Bay, to house his sailboat and plane. He had a seaplane hauled to the village of Raquette Lake in a freight car. On July 1, 1912 he took the plane up over the lake. Hochschild mentions in his *Township 34*, "the flight was the first over the Adirondacks, antedating by three months that made on October 3, 1912, over Whiteface Mountain by George A. Gray."

In a diary of Maurice Callahan, which he maintained at the office of the Raquette Lake Transportation Co., there are several entries pertaining to Collier's short-lived adventures of flying over Raquette Lake. They are as follows:

> July 1, 1912: Collier up in his flying machine this p.m. near Golden Beach; did not go very high.
>
> July 3, 1912: Collier up to station in flying machine 2 p.m.
>
> July 13, 1912: Collier to station with flying machine after mail.
>
> July 28, 1912: Collier's flying machine fell 40 feet last night.
>
> Collier's sailboat capsized today.

After the accident, Collier salvaged the plane and shipped it back to New York. During the winter he had the hanger moved to the camp, pulled over the ice on wide wooden-runner sleds drawn by a team of horses. It was used as the shell of the playhouse which is still in existence. The playhouse eventually housed a bowling alley as well as a pool table and shuffleboard. Animal heads adorned the walls near the huge walk-in fireplace. Four large Frederick Remington paintings were the focal point of another wall.

A shooting gallery was added as was the structure which has become the landmark of Bluff Point - a gazebo located on the small island connected to the camp by a wooden bridge, one hundred feet in length.

In 1914 Collier became seriously ill while at Raquette Lake and for the next few years, visited the camp on a limited basis. Collier died in 1918 of a heart attack. His wife, who no longer wished to summer at Raquette, sold the camp to Anne and Belle Thomson of Yonkers in 1920. The property was sold with all the furnishings with the exception of the four Remington paintings.

George Fallon ceased being caretaker in 1922. After selling his house to St. William's Parish, he moved to Old Forge with his wife and six daughters.

The Thomsons opened a summer camp for girls, "Camp Collier in the Adirondacks—A School of Natural Development" with a description as "a school which stands for advanced and progressive ideals in the science of education." Tuition for the camp was $350 for the session from July 1st through August 31st. Campers met in New York City and traveled directly from New York to Raquette Lake via the New York Central and Herkimer Railroad express service.

In 1955 Belle Thomson donated a small cannon to the Adirondack Museum. It was the same cannon that had for years been shot by one of the Stott sisters to call the church boats on Sunday mornings. Arthur Howe, caretaker at Cortland, arranged to deliver it.

In 1956 the property was sold to Frederick Shephard from Texas who maintained it until it was sold to Jim and Marion Bird in 1969.

Robb Tyler had seen Bluff Point for the first time in 1932 and had tried to purchase it from the Thomsons, but they were unwilling to sell. He successfully completed the transaction with the Birds in 1971.

Between 1971 and 1980 the property was subdivided and sold to individual property owners. The main lodge (playhouse) with a one-half-mile waterfront, five small cottages, winter cabin and original Stott dining room, and a walkway from the house to the laundry, were purchased by Robb and Betty Tyler from Maryland in 1971. Mrs. Josephine Kent Worthington, grandmother of Mrs. Tyler, first came to Raquette Lake in 1896 staying at the Hemlocks.

The Worthingtons decided to build a cabin on the small island (near Osprey and Little Osprey Islands) referred to as "Wee Two." During the winter of 1896 they started the project, finishing for the 1897 season. The family has occupied the island every summer since.

Betty Tyler's parents honeymooned on "Wee Two" in 1908

and, during the summer of 1909, her father served as physician for Raquette Lake residents. Betty remembered her first trip to Raquette Lake was in 1919. Her father died in 1923, and her mother continued to summer there with her four daughters. Mrs. Kent Worthington died on the island in 1925.

INMAN CAMP

Horace Inman, a paper box manufacturer from Amsterdam, New York, purchased the small birch and pine covered island, (referred to as both Dog Island and Round Island) between Golding's Point and Big Island from Ed Martin and Bill Ballard in the 1890's.

During the early years, Jim Maloney was employed as caretaker, a position he held many years before he became a victim of the lake, drowning in what is referred to as Grave's Bay.

Inman's descendant, Jennifer Markworth, described him as "a bit of a gambler, adventurer, full-time manufacturer and inventor." Inman parlayed a natural inquisitiveness and mechanical skill into a small fortune. His most practical achievement was the creation of machines which made paper boxes and a system of manufacturing which utilized these devices "anticipating by eighty years the containerization revolution." For his ingenuity he was awarded top honors at the Columbian World Exposition of 1892, an international trade fair celebrating the achievements of the Victorian era.

The Orient fascinated Inman. He created his own Shangri La in the Adirondacks using mementos of his three trips around the world and thirty-five voyages to Europe. His company maintained branch offices in England and Germany and his trips were business mixed with pleasure. Crates of bamboo, exotic statuary and other materials were shipped from China and Japan to the Adirondacks. Inman used birch bark to decorate his summer and winter homes built on the island. Raw cork was imported from Portugal to insulate his winter home.

He had a passion for working with metal and for growing plants. There was a greenhouse on the premises and his tropical plants grew to lavish sizes with the help of piped-in steam. He fashioned highly ornamental chandeliers, door hinges and locks (which still work) in an iron foundry he built at one end of the island. When construction was at its peak, there were thirty-six buildings including two casinos and a dance hall.

David Inman (brother of Jennifer Markworth) recalled two of the several one-bedroom cottages which were included on the estate. One was known as the "Ace of Clubs," so named because of the club (taken from a deck of cards) fashioned out of wood, framing the entrance to the porch. Another, the "Bridal Chamber," contained inlaid floors. Decorative paper, enhanced with figures of Dutch boys and girls, was used as a border close to the ceiling. Three dimensional figures (possibly Egyptian) adorned the cabinets. In the 1950's, a wing was added to the original structure for kitchen and bath facilities.

Henry Carlin remembers that Inman referred to his summer house as the "Lodge." His dining room was attached to his radiator-heated winter house, the "Wigwam." The walls and ceiling of the dining room were covered with many different patterned plates.

"There were four bedrooms supplied with a hole in the roof to let the moonlight shine in. Several rooms had trees growing from soil through the roof and on each were mounted birds of all sizes and colors. He also had an aviary with real birds and peacocks."

"Inman had a floating Japanese pagoda, with a Japanese style roof with upturned corners over the water on the side toward the village," noted Carlin. "Mats were the furniture and one removed one's shoes before entering."

The structure, referred to as the "tea house," eventually wound up on Wood's Point. Harry Inman stated his father (William) "told Willy Wood if he could remove the teahouse - which had gone out on the ice - he (Wood) could have it for thirty-five dollars." The building was dragged across the ice to Big Island on wooden sled runners pulled by a team of horses.

Carlin enjoyed talking about the estate. "The grounds also contained floating gardens and a special round house with two rooms separated by a partition with a fireplace in the center and an open view toward Golding's Point. There was a bath house where one could change and slide into the water unnoticed."

Jennifer Markworth told how "the rustic haven which was Inman's home until his death included a well-stocked trout pool and layered fountain—a main one shaped like a lily with a dragon spouting water and three tiers of smaller ones."

David Inman recalled the family found Inman's initials on "everything in the house." Some items from the camp have been salvaged and are in possession of family members. Among them is a clock made from wood and birch bark. Replacing the numerals are the letters HORACE INMAN. Being one number short, a decoration has replaced the number six. A rifle and rug from Martin Van Buren, a friend and frequent guest at the camp, are among the family's acquisitions.

One of Inman's prized items was a cannon from the Spanish ship, *Santa Maria*, which had been sunk in the Spanish American War. During World War II, Inman's grandson William, donated the cannon for the scrap drive to support the war effort.

After battling a state litigation for more than twelve years. Horace Inman was finally granted title to his island. The island remained in the hands of his direct descendants for five generations. In 1979 the property was transferred from Harry Inman to his three children: William, Jennifer (Markworth) and David, with Harry Inman retaining life use.

Several buildings on the island remain in use and family members hope to do some rebuilding at the Inman camp. "Of what Horace Inman created," notes Markworth, "there are only the remnants of statues, fountains or foundries; all victims of time and vandals."

CAMP OSCEOLA AND WHELAN

John N. Golding, a New York real estate dealer, chose to build his Camp Osceola on a point of land between Antlers and the railroad station in 1895.

Golding maintained the camp until his death, after which the New York cigar store entrepreneur, George J. Whelan, purchased the property. The point later became known as Whelan's lower camp. Several small cabins were added. The main house was separate from the cluster of buildings, with numerous windows overlooking the lake.

The Whelan's owned a floating tea house which could be slowly towed around the lake while tied behind their boat, *Onondaga*. Mrs. Whelan often entertained her guests in this fashion, enjoying the view while escaping the black flies.

Harriet, Whelan's wife, had a reputation of being extravagant. Legend has it the tea house was built while she was away from Raquette Lake and upon her return the roof "didn't suit her." She supposedly had all the shingles removed and replaced with new ones.

George Whelan died in 1910 but Mrs. Whelan continued using the camp, entertaining guests including the Randolph Hearsts and Whitney Bourne.

"One summer, Irene Castle, a guest of Whelans, aquaplaned behind a speed boat," recalled Kay Beals Garlipp. "That was long before water skiing became popular. It looked like such fun that some of us were inpsired to try it behind Dillon's boat, but the boat proved too slow and the board too wide to work."

Kay Garlipp remembers her neighbors the Whelans very well. "The estate which started next door to us," recalls Kay, "covered several acres of woodland with many buildings . . . including a small one where Mrs. Whelan supposedly did some canning if the mood struck her. The entire estate was fenced in and each fence post had a wooden ball stuck on the top."

The Whelans had three caretakers during their ownership: George Reardon, Patrick Duffy and Scott Reid. Kay remembers the youngsters calling one of them "Old Red Beard" because they were afraid of him. This, however, did not deter them from playing pranks. "One day," said Kay, "my sister and I were annoyed by "Old Red Beard" so we removed most of the wooden balls from the fence posts and hid them. We lived in terror for days that he would find us out. Strangely enough we never heard a word about it."

Patrick Duffy is remembered as a "genial Irishman who owned the first station wagon in our area. Our day was made if we were invited to ride home in it after he picked up the mail at the Post Office."

Kay describes the Whelan home as a beautiful place. The main camp contained a large kitchen, butler's pantry, dining room, living room, sun porch and the forest room (a music or recreation room with walls paneled with barn boards to which the lichens still clung) on the ground floor. Upstairs were several bedrooms furnished with white French-style furniture, each complete with a bath and sleeping porch.

Mrs. Whelan is described as personifying the epitome of gracious living that was enjoyed by the affluent before the Crash of

1929.

Mrs. Whelan enjoyed spending part of the winter at her camp, recalls Henry Carlin. "She had a skating rink cleared in front of their property and provided lights so the locals could enjoy it. At Christmas she would invite the children in to see the huge tree and dollhouse which was furnished and electrified."

"I remember one Christmas party we were invited to by Mrs. Whelan," added Rowena Bird, "we played games and had refreshments. They had the big fireplace going -everything was just beautiful. When we were leaving she gave each of us a knitted stocking that had nuts, peanut brittle, ribbon candy, apples and oranges in it. Some of the stockings were so big the little kids could hardly carry them."

During the 1930's the Whelan property was leased to Arthur S. Roache. In 1941 it was acquired by the late Mary Dillon. Dillon family members seasonally occupied the main house and the lower cottages were used as rental units. The property remains in the ownership of the Dillon family.

ECHO CAMP

One of the most beautiful camps built on the picturesque islands of Raquette Lake was Echo Camp, so named for the multiple echoes which resounded from a call or shout.

The camp was built around 1883 on the south shore of Long Point by Ed Bennett for Phineas C. Lounsbury. Lounsbury was president of the Merchants Exchange National Bank in New York City and Governor of Connecticut during 1887-1889.

Its twin-tower main lodge is similar to that of Camp Fairview which was also built by Bennett. On the balcony railing, Echo Camp is spelled out in branches and twigs. Next to the entrance of the main cottage is a picture window, similar to a stained glass window, separated by lead mullions - rectangles of blue, pink and amber glass surround centers of colored globules. Another unique feature is that the fireplace is erected in a corner rather than having the usual flat placement against a wall.

The camp includes a complex of buildings once used for servant and guide quarters, a laundry, dining room and kitchen, carpenter and paint shops, ice house and other structures including wells and privies. The only winterized building on the premises was occupied by the caretaker. The original buildings, as with most of the camps built during that period, have withstood the ravages of time.

Governor and Mrs. Lounsbury occupied the camp, referred to by many as one of the great Adirondack camps, until his death in 1925 at which time it was willed to Mr. and Mrs. William Griffith. Upon Mr. Griffith's death in 1929, his wife, a niece of Lounsbury, remained at the camp until her death in 1940. The property was then inherited by her son, Maxwell Griffith of Connecticut and her daughter, Mrs. Margaret Blackard of North Carolina.

In 1946, Carlton and Frances Clough of Pleasantville, long time summer residents of Raquette Lake, rented the property, starting Echo Camp for Girls.

Fran Clough, affectionately called Skipper, paid her first visit to Raquette in 1922 while a high school student. She and her family drove in an electric automobile, "Old Magnetic" with the shift on the wheel handle, to North Point Inn where they vacationed for many years. In 1928 she married Carlton Clough. On a visit to Raquette during World War II, the couple stopped at the Echo Camp while canoeing. Almost immediately they decided they wanted to start a camp for girls. When asked why it had to be a girls camp, Skipper replied without hesitation, "The camp was so beautiful. It had to be a girls camp because girls take better care of things. Boys could be careless and destructive."

The Cloughs rented the camp for two years, during which time Carlton died. Skipper decided to purchase it herself and continued to run it as owner and director. A portion of the property, referred to as Re-Echo, was retained by the Griffith family.

From the inception of the camp, Skipper insisted on visiting potential camper families and interviewing them before accepting a child. Over the years, from a group of fifteen campers the first summer, it reached a capacity of about one hundred girls by 1977. By then the camp had attained international status representing thirteen states and eleven foreign countries.

As soon as the camp was purchased, a tennis court was built. From the beginning there was a music director. Jean Hoffman was the first, replaced by Evelyn Hallenbeck who served for many years. The Echo choir sang at the Raquette Lake Chapel from the time the camp opened and at the annual service at the

Author's Collection

One of the one-bedroom cottages on Inman's estate was known as the "Ace of Clubs," so named because of the "Club" shape fashioned out of wood, framing the entrance to the porch. The family on the porch in this photo is assumed to be Inman's grandchild William with his parents. Horace Inman is seated in the center of the lean-to flanked by two unidentified relatives. Circa 1895.

Courtesy Inman family

Inman's winter home, the "Wigwam." Circa 1960's.

Courtesy Inman family

The dining room at the 'Wigwam" covered with diverse patterned plates. Circa 1900's.

Courtesy Inman family

Japanese Pagoda on Woods Point. Circa 1900's.

Courtesy C. H. Carlin

Whelan's main camp with boat house to the left and the "floating tea house" to the right. Circa early 1900's.

Courtesy Buster Bird

Whalen's boat "Onondaga" with Buster Bird at the helm. Circa 1931.

Courtesy Doris and Glenn Martin

Echo Camp's twin-tower lodge built in 1883. Circa 1940's.

Courtesy F. Clough Havinga

Campers from Echo Camp.

Courtesy Frances Clough Havinga

The first campers at Echo Camp for Girls in 1946.

Courtesy Frances Clough Havinga

Camping out was always a treat using platform tents.

Courtesy Doris and Glenn Martin

Camp Oteetiwi. Circa 1920's.

Courtesy George and Lucille Loriot

Karl Bitter, sculptor, at Camp Oteetiwi. Circa early 1900's.

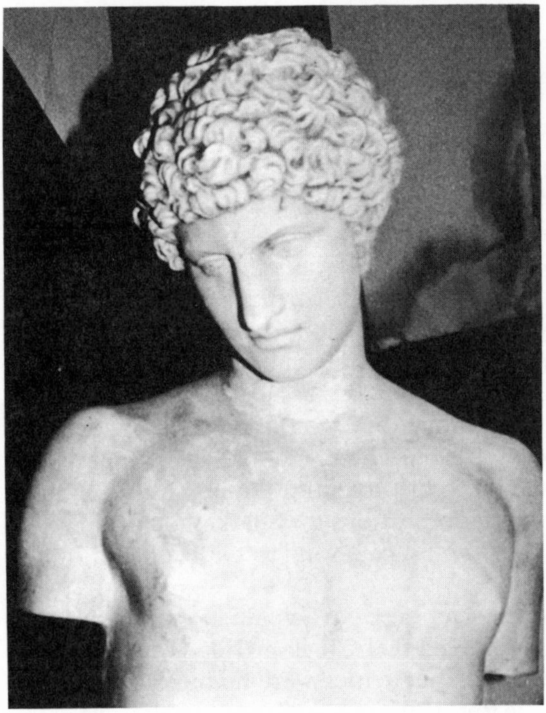

Courtesy George and Lucille Loriot

A bust sculpted by Karl Bitter. Circa early 1900's.

Courtesy George and Lucille Loriot

A plaster plaque of Bitter's wife. Circa early 1900's.

Church of the Good Shepherd since 1959.

Evelyn "Texas" Hubbard was the first drama coach, remaining for forty years in that capacity. Each year a music and drama festival was held. One special event which was started in the early years by Hallenbeck and Hubbard was "Christmas in July." It continued through the years as one of the most popular traditions. Christmas Day was always the Friday before the first four-week session ended. The week before, each camper was given the name of another camper to whom they would act as a "silent Santa." During the week a gift would be made for each camper. On Christmas Eve (Thursday), a live tree and the hall would be decorated by the campers with decorations they had made during their stay. After supper, there would be a song fest and stockings hung.

On Christmas morning, the campers participated in a pajama breakfast where each child received their stocking filled with gifts and fruit. During the day special activities were featured rather than the regular events. After Christmas dinner, a play was presented by the youngest campers. The highlight of the evening would be the arrival of Santa Claus, most often arriving astride his "Reindorse" (would you believe a horse with antlers?). With much joviality, he presented each camper with the gifts made during the week and the identity of the silent Santas would be revealed.

Camping out was always a treat. Platform tents were often used and the canoe camping trips were high on the priority list of activities for the girls from the beginning. Horseback riding was added during the first ten years of operation with horses being transported over the back road to Long Point via Silver and Golden Beach - a most difficult trip. One year when the route was impassable, it was necessary to blindfold the horses and transport them via barge from the mainland.

Throughout the years, Echo Camp maintained three bells. When the camp first opened, Clough acquired the original Raquette Lake School bell which was used for "morning get up call" as well as to alert campers to the change of activities.

In the early 1960's Frances Clough brought back an old Chapel Bell from a Madrid flea market, which was used to call the campers to vespers.

The third, an Austrian Turm and Bell, was engraved and brought back to camp from Kitzbuhl, Austria by Fran and Tod

Havinga. The bell was placed atop the dining hall and became the official dinner bell.

On the tenth anniversary of the camp, a plaque was placed in the main house and dedicated to Carlton W. Clough. It reads: "For whose wisdom, vision and faith, the family of Echo Camp for Girls expresses gratitude on this the tenth anniversary of its founding."

Skipper married Hendrik J. Havinga in 1971. After thirty-six years of dedication to Camp Echo, Skipper decided to retire in 1981. The Havingas sold the camp to Mr. and Mrs. Theodore Pope of Spencer, New York and their daughter, Gingie, of Saratoga.

Ms. Pope was not new to Camp Echo. She first attended camp in 1968, then worked as counselor and tennis instructor for many years, eventually becoming assistant director. When the camping season began in 1982, she assumed the role of director which she held until the close of the 1986 season when the Popes ceased camp operation.

Hendrik Havinga died at Raquette Lake on May 30, 1983. Skipper still summers at her home in Lonesome Bay overlooking West Mountain. When asked how she felt about the camp being closed she replied, "When I sold the camp and turned it over to younger hands I never dreamed it would be anything but Echo Camp for Girls. I was very disappointed and disheartened to learn it is no longer going to be operated as a camp and has reversed to private ownership."

CAMP OTEETIWI

Dr. Arpad G. Gerster, an eminent Hungarian-born surgeon, visited Raquette Lake for the first time in 1863. He came from his home in New York City for a brief visit staying at the Hemlocks on Long Point. Arrangements were made with Ed Bennett for Gerster and his family to vacation the following summer in a cabin situated next to the hotel. His wife, renowned vocalist Madame Gerster, found the area not to her liking. It lacked the privacy she sought and that fall the family moved into a two-story camp on Big Island, off Long Point. The camp, purchased from Jack Daly, was named "Oteetiwi," Iroquois for "ever ready," nickname of Red Jacket the Iroquois chief and rival of Joseph Brant. There the Gerster's enjoyed twenty summers living in semi-solitude.

Frank Carlin remembered Dr. Gerster as "a rough cuss with a strong accent who wore wooden shoes. However, there was many a time he took care of the locals and never charged them a penny 'cause they couldn't afford it."

Dr. Gerster and William Durant became fast friends. At Durant's urging, Gerster became one of the incorporators of the Raquette Lake Railway and although he assisted Durant in some of his projects, he never invested much of his money. When Durant found himself in financial trouble, Gerster was one of the first to offer him help.

The Gersters were not extremely sociable. They were known to entertain friends from the city on occasion but they enjoyed their privacy, accepting a limited number of invitations at Raquette to which they were compelled to reciprocate. Madame Gerster had her music to occupy her time, and the doctor enjoyed sketching the area and its people.

In 1905 Dr. Gerster sold the camp to Karl Bitter, and moved to the west shore of Long Lake. "He really loved the woods, the lake, the whole area," recalled Carlin. "When he died he was cremated and his ashes were spread over Long Lake."

KARL BITTER

Karl Bitter came from Bavaria when he was about twenty years old. A self-taught artist, he originally worked in wood. He became known when he was awarded a $10,000 prize for winning a contest to design areas of Trinity Church, one of the largest cathedrals in New York City. His wrought iron gates and art work around the church and its cemetery are still in existence. Subsequently, he was commissioned to work on numerous other projects, including monuments in many large cities and for two world fairs.

In the beginning he worked with a group of other sculptors. He eventually owned his own studios, one in Manhattan and the other in Hoboken, New Jersey. When he purchased Oteetiwi, it became his third studio. There he worked long summers creating his works of art.

In July 1907 the main building at the camp burned to the ground. When the maid was taking one of the children upstairs to bed, the open flame of the candle she was carrying set fire to the curtains. Bitter immediately "went to the drawing board to plan a new building."

Other structures added by Bitter included the artist cottage with its huge skylight and a studio for his assistant. In 1911 he added a boat house with an apartment above.

The Bitters had three children. Their son, John, became Vice President of Miami University. Their other son, Francis, served as a European diplomat. Marietta their daughter, a concert harpist, married Hollywood actor Walter Abel.

Karl Bitter's distinguished career came to an end when he was fifty years old and his daughter Marietta inherited the property.

In 1951, George and Lucille Loriot of Kearny, New Jersey purchased the property and all its contents from Marietta Bitter Abel.

"We trespassed, camping on this property in about 1947," recalled Loriot. "I used to camp this area but Lucille had never camped anywhere. We had our two- and four-year-old boys with us at the time. We rowed in the rain until we reached this point then, since it was too difficult to travel further, we took a chance and made camp until it cleared. It rained the whole week."

"Little did we realize," interjected Lucille, "we would own it someday."

Loriot, Dean of Instructors in the Kearny School System, and his wife gained possession of many treasures with the property. A bust, a plaster portrait of Bitter's wife and a plaque in the 1880 baroque style were among them, all sculptured by Bitter.

The Loriots have made some renovations, striving to maintain the original buildings as much as possible. One of the sheds has been converted into a laundry room which houses a gas-driven Maytag washing machine shipped from Kansas. A generator is used for electricity in the laundry building only and the other buildings will be electrified soon. The couple obtain drinking water from the well, but utility water is drawn from the lake. Another shed, also built on the property, is Lucille's pride since she helped build it.

The main house consisted of two buildings joined by a covered walkway, which has been closed to form a room between the buildings. The smaller building is used as a summer kitchen. The other building contains a regular kitchen, dining-living room with fireplace, porch, upstairs bedroom and a master bedroom on the main floor.

Evidence of Bitter's fine craftsmanship is displayed in many of his furniture pieces. Two of the beds are unique. The one in the master bedroom's back bedstead almost reaches the ceiling. Attached within it near the top, is what appears to be an open box the full width of the bed. In reality it is a crib. The bed in the other room, which is quite small, has drawers built into the structure, affording storage not available elsewhere in the room.

Heat is supplied with portable Aladdin stoves. Near the kitchen is a single hot water radiator which heats the back four rooms. There is also a wood-burning stove in addition to the fireplace. The artist's cottage, now a guest cottage, is also heated by an Aladdin heater in addition to the fireplace.

The main building is arranged so the grounds may be viewed on three sides with the front porch overlooking the lake. In the late spring of 1986, a storm caused much damage to trees at the camp with several crushing the front roof and porch. Arrangements have been made for the repair of the roof.

". . . but these things take time here in the north woods."

"There is still so much to be done," observes Lucille.

"Little by little . . . ," adds George.

CHAPTER IX

THE GROWTH OF A VILLAGE

THE RAQUETTE LAKE POST OFFICE

In 1889, W. W. Durant decided it was time Raquette Lake had a Post Office. At the time the closest post offices were located at Blue Mountain Lake, twelve miles distant, Minerva about forty miles, and Boonville about fifty miles distant.

On February 2, 1889 Durant presented a formal application to the office of the First Assistant Postmaster General in Washington D.C. The form asked what the proposed office would be called; Raquette Lake was written in W. W. Durant's hand. Description of the location read, Hamilton County, New York, twelve miles west of route No. 6292. A "special office" was requested with mail routed from Indian Lake to Long Lake, three times per week and daily during the summer.

In the 1889 record book of the Raquette Lake Post Office, kept by Mrs. W. W. Durant, the first entry was recorded as follows:

> This post office was established under the Administration of President Grover Cleveland. Dow M. Dickinson being the Post-Master General. William West Durant petitioned for the office and was appointed Post Master on February 11, 1889 and received his commission February 25th in the same year. He appointed John McLaughlin Assistant Post Master and built a little Post Office on Long Point at Raquette Lake near the hotel.

On November 1, 1889 a new application was presented moving the office "about one-third of a mile southwesterly" and stating mail was not possible during the winter months. John McLaughlin served as postmaster from June 1891 until February 1898 when John E. Tillson replaced him.

On July 19, 1900 the location of the Post Office was changed to 300 feet from the railroad track, the name was changed to "Durant" and C. McCoy was named postmaster. The Post Office building was attached to one side of the machine shop at Carlin's Marina with a small annex placed at Hunter's Rest.

In 1901 the Post Office's name was changed back to Raquette Lake. McCoy continued as postmaster until 1903 when he was replaced by John Moynehan. By this time the Post Office had been moved to the railroad station.

On June 21, 1904 the annex at Hunter's Rest was moved to the Antlers with Mervin Lines in charge. Later he was replaced by Margaret Bennett. Service at the Antlers annex was discontinued on August 14, 1920. Herbert Harrington was appointed postmaster February 1907, followed by Elizabeth Farrington, who was appointed February 1911. On November 15, 1913 Dennis Dillon became postmaster later assisted by George Denny as postal clerk.

In 1932 Charles Scanlon, an easy going gent full of goodwill and humor, was appointed and served as postal clerk for many years. Considered the town poet, his favorite pastime was writing jingles for greeting cards and about the locals. Unfortunately, his book of original poems was destroyed in the fire of 1927. Scanlon is credited with writing the words for the Raquette Lake School Alma Mater.

Dennis Dillon Jr. assumed the position of postmaster on June 1933. By then the Post Office had been moved from the railroad station to the present location behind the Raquette Lake Supply store. During Dillon's service in the armed forces, 1942-1946, he was temporarily relieved by Francis O'Connell.

At present mail is delivered and dispatched twice daily, once on Saturday. Cleo Aldous handles rural delivery. Bird's Marine has the contract for summer delivery by boat to the camps on the lake. Shirley Forsell and Peg Norris are part time employees at the Post Office.

After serving as Post Master for forty-three years, Dennis Dillon Jr. retired July 15, 1976. He was succeeded by Millie

Dillon who had been employed by the Postal Service for twenty years.

The following September, a retirement testimonial dinner was given Dillon at Rocky Point Inn. Marion Bird, Kris Cummings and Marguerite Fuge, long time neighbors and friends were hostesses for the evening. In addition to several awards and gifts given to Dillon, a framed scroll, shaped like an envelope with Dillon's picture as the stamp, was presented to him by local artist, Margaret Carrol.

Dillon's final remarks, after thanking his assistants for their efforts through the years they had worked together were: "I plan to spend my retirement playing with my first of many, I hope, grandchildren to be born in December to my son Tim and his wife Debbie."

THE RAQUETTE LAKE UNION FREE SCHOOL

In 1891 the residents of Durant (as Raquette Lake was then known) decided something should be done about educating their children. The first school was a small building behind John McLaughlin's general store on Long Point.

It appears that Julia McCarthy was the first school teacher with registered students including Harry Simms, Nellie, Edith, Madge and Lulu Bennett, Theresa and Grace McLaughlin and Tom and Mary Callahan.

Other teachers in later years included Annie McGinn, Mrs. Burroughs, Harvey Egan, Dennis Dillon Sr., Frank Hurley, Arthur Martin and Francis Haischer.

Dennis Dillon Sr., born in Hartford, Washington County, New York on October 20, 1876, came to Raquette Lake after completing his education at Fort Edward Academy. When he first arrived he spent almost a year working for room and board at Island Camp on Big Island. He then taught at the school on Long Point for a year while residing at Bryere's Brightside. Feeling that business afforded more opportunity for gaining financial independence he left the teaching profession. In 1899 he became a clerk in John Wheeler's (formerly McLaughlin's) store. When the store moved from Long Point to the present village, Dillon moved with it. Eventually Dillon became a prominent figure in the mercantile life of the community.

Arthur S. Martin came to Raquette Lake in 1904 to teach at the little school on Long Point. Martin was born in 1870 in Turin, New York and began his teaching career in his hometown. His teaching contract with the Turin School District, dated November 11, 1893, showed his salary at $6.50 per week.

Martin took up residence at Bryere's Brightside, transporting students to the Raquette Lake school at Long Point each day in his guide boat. While living at Brightside he met Mina Reynolds who was employed by the Bryeres. Mina was very proud of her famous ancestor, Major General Frederick Wilhelm Baron Von Steuben, who helped train the Revolutionary forces, and to whom a memorial exists in Utica. Arthur Martin and Mina married and had two sons, Winfield (b. 1907) and Glenn (b. 1909).

Arthur Martin died in 1913 of diabetes. His family continued to reside at the homestead where Mina Martin took in boarders, and did laundry and baking at the large camps to support her sons.

Glenn and his brother attended Raquette Lake School, traveling by boat or across the ice until 1926. Glenn remembers walking to school on the ice, "when it was so cold that a plant a friend had given me for my mother, and which I had carefully placed inside my heavy jacket, froze before I could get home." During Glenn's later years of schooling, he would start school at Raquette in the fall, transfer to a school in Utica in the winter, having to enroll again at Raquette in the spring.

After moving from Raquette Lake, Glenn and his mother continued vacationing at the family homestead. His brother Winfield never returned.

In 1939, Glenn met Doris Baker who was employed at the Raquette Lake Hotel. The couple married the following year, and returned to the lake each summer with their family. Mina Martin died of a stroke in 1961 at Glenn's home in Rochester.

Since his retirement, "Glenn has returned to his first and only home . . . Raquette Lake," says his wife Doris. While summering at his family homestead, Glenn "continues working to keep his boyhood home intact, as a heritage to his children."

Francis Haischer is believed to have been one of the first teachers at the school in the village. He married Florence Blanchard, daughter of Charles William and Harriet Baty Blanchard. The couple settled on a parcel of land originally owned by Frank

Carlin, next to what is now the residence of Bob Skiba.

After the death of his first wife, he married Helen Griffith whose father ran the Station Restaurant. His son Donald married Helen Wood of Island Camp on Big Island.

Between 1911 and 1929, Haischer served as agent for the Raquette Lake Transportation Company. The Haischer property is now partially owned by Richard Lauterbach, with the remaining portion in possession of Eva Humphrey.

THE VILLAGE SCHOOL

When the village was moved to its present location in 1900, it was still necessary to transport students to school on Long Point by boat. Residents who attended school at that time reminisce about their school days.

"The livery boated the kids from around the lake for all the years I can remember," said Henry Carlin. "Dad would shovel the snow from the boat when necessary and he or George Payne, Larry Grenon or Joe Pelletier would proceed to pick up the children and return them to their homes after school."

"There was no road," explained Edna Colligan. "In winter, children would snowshoe or skate across the ice. Some had to travel considerable distances walking many miles around South Bay and the South Inlet to get to school. There was no bridge at the Inlet. Children from Pine Knot and Long Point had to walk through Silver Beach swamp, then Golden Beach swamp, way down by Sagamore, and then around to the village."

"You could walk on the ice early when it started to freeze, but in the spring you couldn't risk crossing as it was ready to go out. Some of the kids just didn't go to school unless the ice was frozen solid. The only difference with the school being in the village was the direction of travel and of course the size of the school."

"I remember one day the kids were all excited when they got off the school boat," recalled Rowena Bird. "They told me there was a bad leak and the driver just pulled hard for shore and landed. They got some scraps and patched the hole with a pen knife and then they were off again."

Clara Bryere later reported "the boatman used a piece of his shirttail and together with some balsam (tree) pitch was able to make a waterproof patch."

In 1911 a new one-story school was erected on the site of the present school (on Route 28 and the corner leading into the village).

THE PELLETIER FAMILY

In 1913 Bart Pelletier was appointed truant officer at $8 per month. Since most of the students were transported by boat and he was one of the men transporting them, there seemed little need for his services in that capacity.

John Barclay "Bart" Pelletier, brother of Frank Carlin's wife, Mary, came to Raquette Lake with his wife, Ella Elizabeth Waters from Warren County. Bart's son Joseph was born on Big Island in 1907. Another son James Barclay (b. 1909) may also have been born on the island.

Henry Carlin remembers his uncle "ran a taxi service from Forked to Long Lake at one time and he and his family camped just beyond the outlet." In the 1915 census, Pelletier was listed as working as a mechanic for Frank Carlin. Later he strung snowshoes and did some carpentry.

The family lived down from the railroad on what is now Dillon Road. Joseph attended Raquette Lake School for several years while his father transported children from around the lake to school in one or another of Carlin's school boats, *Clyde*, *Balsam*, *Minnie* or *Will-Do*.

Bart's son Joseph, who visited Raquette Lake in 1986 with some of his family, recalled throwing his new glasses in the lake on his way to school one day, "because the kids made fun of me." He also talked of how the family piled their furniture near the tracks when they were moving to Old Forge in 1918. "It was all but demolished when it was hit by the train, but we salvaged some."

While living in Old Forge, Bart operated a sporting goods store. His children continued their education in the Town of Webb School. For a time Bart made "doodle-bugs," a fishing fly which he had hoped would make him rich. When his ventures failed he left the area.

Bart's brother Joseph is said to have also resided in Raquette

Lake in the 1920's transporting children to school and working for Carlin's marina as a mechanic. He also did carpentry. Not much else is known of him except that he drowned at Raquette in the early 1940's.

MEMORIES

By 1915, the original one-story building had to be expanded. Denny Dillon, who started school in 1916 believed there were about 82 children enrolled when he attended. "It took two school boats to pick them up. Families were much larger at that time."

"Students were separated into three classes," he explained, "grades one through four met in one room with one teacher. Grades five through eight met in another room with a different teacher, and then there was the high school, with three rooms and three teachers. There had to be discipline with four classes in one room," continued Dillon. "However, I was more scared of my mother than the teachers. She told me if I was bad and got whipped by the teacher, when I came home I'd get another one."

"School hours were from 9 a.m. until 4 p.m.," recalled Rowena Bird. "The huge bell, which sometimes one of us was privileged to ring, summoned us. The first ring was to tell us to get moving. The second meant we had better be in the school yard. I remember," said Rowena, "since I was within walking distance, I'd have to go home at noon during the lunch break, do the dishes, and then go back. The kids that had to be transported by boat were lucky since they could bring their lunch."

"Professor O'Donnell was the principal. His wife worked at the checkout for the Raquette Lake Supply Co. He taught math also, but he didn't have much control over us," she added laughing. "He was the janitor, too. In those days O'Donnell did just about everything—sort of a jack-of-all trades."

Carlin remembered the school was surrounded by trees within twenty-five feet all the way around on state land. "It didn't allow much room for a playground. Over the years the play area grew larger until we finally ended up with a full-sized baseball diamond," added Kay Beals Garlipp. "The boys and girls, large and small, carried on a ball game every noon hour in spring and fall. Prof was usually the umpire . . . unless he was needed to balance out the teams by playing on one of them. He often forgot to watch the time and we had extra playing time most days."

The one school sport during the winter was basketball. Boys and girls of all ages combined in order to have enough players for two teams - a boys and a girls - although they played by boys rules. "There was no gymnasium at the school," stated Rowena Bird. "The children used to go to the casino next to the store in the village to play basketball."

"There was no heat in there (the casino), it was colder than the dickens! I'd have to remember to put on a big heavy coat after we played, or I'd catch cold and get the devil for it."

In the mid-1920's the teams traveled to Indian Lake to compete. In the days prior to the building of Route 28 (1929), the trip meant a day-long journey in horse-drawn sleighs across the ice (now it is a mere forty minute drive).

"Everyone would go," Edna explained. "We'd bundle up in furs and big robes in the sleds and follow the old logging roads around to Blue Mountain Lake. The trip took all day, and the team would play that night. Indian Lake didn't have a school then so we played ball in the Town Hall."

Carlin continued the scenario. "The group would stay overnight with relatives and friends in Indian Lake, then return the following day traveling through the woods and across the lakes. Collins from Sagamore and sometimes the teamsters from the other large camps would furnish the transportation. The drivers and townspeople usually attended the affairs as well as the teams, so we had quite a safari."

"The team played at Old Forge as well as at Indian Lake. When the Old Forge team came to Raquette Lake to play, they came by train and stayed overnight at the homes of the Raquette players. The same courtesy was extended to Raquette Lakers while visiting Old Forge."

School proms were as important then as they are now. Junior Proms were in the late spring. "They were held in the casino which was elaborately decorated," described Rowena. "There'd be big orchestras from Boonville, and everyone's relatives from Indian Lake and North Creek would come. People would come to the dance whether they could dance or not. There were square dances and round dances and everything."

Dances were also held in the Casino during the winter. Usually the Senior class (two to four people) would "put them on," mainly to get enough money to buy class pins and rings. Young and old attended to listen to or dance to the music.

The school library was located in a small hallway between the classrooms. The study hall also contained shelves with books. Despite the small size of the institution, it offered a full curriculum including Latin, French and English. History, science, math, physical geography, economics and later business courses were also taught. Music and art were included whenever a teacher was available. Regents exams were taken as a matter of course.

Some of the teachers remembered include: Mildred Mick, Francis Haischer, Quida Girard, Edna Parr, Mrs. Reilly, Miss Costello, Miss Albanese, Lala Dewey, Dorothy Ettinger, Dorothy Taggert (who later became Mrs. Paul Owens), Miss Dale, Laurine Gardner and Marian Keane. Principals were the Messers. Kelly, Earley, Ordano, Taylor and O'Donnell.

Commencement exercises from the twelfth grade were formal affairs. Students dressed in their best and greeted parents and guests with printed booklets commemorating the event.

One such booklet with a printed ribbon as a marker, has been retained as a memento by the Egenhofer family. On the cover was printed, "Annual Commencement - Raquette Lake High School on Tuesday evening June the twenty-seventh Nineteen twenty-two: Casino."

The first page listed class officers: Richard J. Collins, Jr., Class President; Alfred A. Egenhofer, Vice President and Patrick F. Collins, Secretary-Treasurer. Also mentioned were faculty members Carl L. Earley, Principal, Myrtle E. Hough, Stella Olmstead, Catherine A. Carey and Margaret M. Collins. Board of Education members at the time included Mary C. Dillon, President, C. S. Beals, Secretary, W. A. Pulling, R. J. Collins, Sr. and William Rogers.

The class motto was "Build for Character, Not for Fame." Class colors were red and white and the class flower was the rose.

Father Henry of St. William's Church gave the invocation and benediction. The speech given by Salutatorian, Richard J. Collins Jr. was entitled "Our Modern Great Americans." An essay, "Conservation of Our Forests," was read by honor student Patrick F. Collins. Valedictorian, Alfred A. Egenhofer spoke on "The Spirit of Democracy."

In addition to the presentation of diplomas by Principal Earley, the program included the Class Day Program: Senior Charge was presented by Richard J. Collins Jr. with the Junior Response by C. Henry Carlin. Patrick F. Collins offered the Prophesy and Alfred A. Egenhofer the Last Will and Testament.

Later graduation ceremonies included the singing of the Raquette Lake Alma Mater. The words of the song were composed about 1925 by "poet" postal clerk Charlie Scanlon - the music is that of the old favorite, "Boola, Boola." The Alma Mater is as follows:

> "A-way up North in the forest lands where Raquette waters flow, the soft perfume from o'er the lea tells where the pine and popple grow. That's where my Alma Mater stands mid balsam scented hills. She's staunch and true the whole year through Alma Mater '86, '86. (The year of graduation is used here.) Raquette Lake School, Raquette Lake School, my Alma Mater staunch and true. When I leave my Alma Mater I pledge filial love to you."

Jean Lanphear Beckingham, who graduated in 1939, feels the education students received at that time was "the best offered anywhere in the state, and perhaps the country."

After graduation, if a student wished to expand their knowledge in a particular field or study subjects not taken during their school years, they were allowed to return for graduate work. This continuing education program was the result of a strong desire of the Board of Education to supply the best possible education for their students. Under the leadership of Mary Dillon (President of the Board for thirty-six years) this was accomplished.

THE SCHOOL AFTER 1949

The number of students declined after the railroad days. Families started moving to seek employment elsewhere. During World War II others moved out seeking employment in high-paying war industries and many left when they joined the service.

In about 1947 Dayton "Dayt" Cleaveland came to Raquette Lake from Rochester with his wife Rita Gibbs and their family, taking residence in the Maxam homestead on Route 28. Their son, Dayt, Jr. was three years of age at the time. The couple also had three daughters: Jan, Carol and Linda. All attended the Raquette Lake School.

In 1949, the school saw its last graduating class from grade twelve. There were two graduates: Peg Vogan Norris, still residing in Raquette Lake with her family and John Gauthier, who maintains a summer home at Raquette.

In 1954 the last graduating class from grade eight consisted of one student, Carol Cleaveland. Since that time classes have continued through the sixth grade. Children in grades seven through twelve attend the Indian Lake Central School.

With the decline in students, there was no need for a large number of teachers. Classes were broken into two groups, first through third grades (later Kindergarten was added) and fourth through sixth grades.

In about 1950 Cleaveland was hired as custodian, bus driver-truant officer of the Raquette Lake School, a position he maintained until 1976.

In 1963 Cleaveland, whose first wife Rita had passed away, married Ella Blanchard Gauvin. She and her daughter Holly moved to Raquette Lake. When Cleaveland retired in 1976, he and Ella wintered in Florida, and spent the summers in Blue Mountain. (Cleaveland died in Tupper Lake in 1983.) Louis Burke, who had married Cleaveland's stepdaughter Holly, replaced him in his position at the school.

In the last twenty years faculty members have included: David Curry, Beatrice Waldron who retired in 1975, Barbara Pope who served the Raquette Lake School System for thirteen years, Daniel Bronson, Nick and Luanne Moro, and Jean Risley.

Early in 1973, it was determined the community was in need of a new school. The old building was demolished and replaced with the present one on the same site, at a cost of $221,750. The original plaque which had been on the previous building was affixed to the front of the new school.

In 1977 a serious crisis arose which almost closed the Raquette Lake School. The Carey-Krupsak proposal to close all schools in New York State with less than the full K-12 curriculum was submitted.

On April 1, 1977 a letter to the editor of the *Adirondack Echo*, submitted by the parents, residents and board members of Raquette Lake was printed urging all to write to assemblymen and senators in Albany, including chairmen of the Education Committee and Finance Committee and Governor Hugh Carey, protesting the two bills. The letter explained the situation as follows:

Courtesy Doris and Glenn Martin

Arthur Martin transported students to and from school each day in his guide boat. Circa early 1900's.

Courtesy Doris and Glenn Martin

The school house on Long Point was built in 1891. Students pictured include the Simms, Bennetts, McLaughlins and Bryeres. Circa 1910.

Courtesy Rowena Bird

The village school built in 1911. Circa 1913.

Courtesy Nancy Madden

The village school after the 1915 expansion. Circa 1920.

Courtesy Helen Collins

Girls' basketball team: Back row: Mildred Mick. Bottom row L-R: Claire Fallon, Madeline Fallon, Margaret Collins, Martha Dillon, Margaret Rogers and Hilda Owens. Circa 1923.

Courtesy C. H. Carlin

Boys' basketball team. Back to front: Roscoe Carlin, Lawrence Grenon, C.H. Carlin, unidentified, Dick Collins, Arthur Mick, Paul Blanchard and Albert Egenhofer. Circa 1920.

Author's Collection

Present school built on site of original school in 1973. Circa 1980's.

Author's Collection

The Raquette Lake Library. Circa 1960's.

Author's Collection

Betty Dillon Schaufler served as librarian from 1945 until 1985. Circa 1960's.

Courtesy Cleo Aldous

Bing Aldous with his wife Cleo in front of their garage. Circa 1940's.

Courtesy Edna Colligan

Bert and Laurine Gardner. Circa 1970's.

Author's Collection

On July 1, 1952, the fire equipment was moved from Bing's Garage to the new fire hall. Circa 1960's.

Courtesy Theresa Cleaveland

Charter members of the Raquette Lake Fire Department and the Auxiliary celebrated the 30th anniversary of the Auxiliary in 1983. Members in attendance included: Back row L-R: Ann Lamphear, Edgar Lamphear, Buz Banta, Mary Lanphear, Gerald Lanphear, Shirley Forsell, Jean Beckingham, Bud Beckingham, Pat Gauthier, Frank Lamphear, Emma Lou Waldron, Ed Cleaveland, Helen Bird and Dayt Cleaveland Sr. Front row L-R: Doris Lamphear, Peg Norris, Jim Bird, Marion Bird, Cleo Aldous and Hubie Gauthier.

> "If the Raquette Lake Union Free School is closed, it will mean the small children (K thru Grade 6) will be forced to travel at least two hours each school day by bus to another school with already crowded classrooms. It will mean parents will lose all control over, and voice in, their children's education. It would also mean that our school taxes will triple (approximately) and the older citizens in the community will suffer an economic blow that a restricted income could not absorb. Busing over twenty-five or thirty miles of hazardous mountain roads in the winter is a real danger that our children should not have to experience. The quality of education in the Raquette Lake School has been, over the years, above state average. Students who went on to Indian Lake (7 thru 12 grades) have garnered far more honors, awards and scholarships than their percentage of the enrollment would indicate."
>
> "Our new school was built without one cent of state funds and we do not receive state aid, so the claim that this move is to save tax money is unfounded."

Public pressure brought about victory. The Raquette Lake Union Free School was not closed.

On opening day, September 8, 1981, students were greeted by two new teachers (replacing Mrs. Risley and Mrs. Pope), Principal John Joseph Leach III, a native of Old Forge, and Miss Deborah "Debbie" Fuge, a native of Raquette Lake.

Miss Fuge went through the Raquette Lake program, completed college and taught in Alaska for a year. She decided to return to Raquette Lake. "I did it all my life," she said, "I traveled to school (from Huntington Camp) on a boat, on skis, and I walked. I am home again!"

"This is really a very pleasant atmosphere to teach in," added Leach. "It's really challenging."

With the small number of students, classroom work is almost on a one to one basis. The faculty keeps abreast of all new procedures and techniques in education and advises the board members who demand a well-rounded education for the children.

For a number of years the children have had computer training. "Being in a small school," explained Debbie, "the students have more access to it, therefore they are better acquainted with its various applications. I think academically, these students may be better prepared for what's ahead, although they'll lack the socialization they'd get in a larger classroom," interjected Leach. "We try to make up for that in other ways. Visiting other schools, having other schools come here for gym, Little League, going on field trips, which is almost a mandate from the school board."

Field trips include outdoor activities such as camping, hiking and skiing, as well as cultural trips. Several times a year students are transported to Syracuse or elsewhere to visit museums and art galleries or to attend plays and musicals.

Keeping up with the space age, Principal John Leach and Miss Fuge introduced a space program, "Raquette Rockets" to the students in 1984 as part of a school science program.

Students build rockets from kits produced by the Estes Rocket Company. The large rockets are built from balsa and cardboard tubing, some having parachutes or streamers for recovery. Engines are fired by electric ignition (battery) and operated by a push-button handle that can be brought back about fifteen feet from the launching pad. "Like the *Columbia*, they can be reused by replacing the engine only. Both the body and the nose cones are attached to the parachute and can be retrieved."

John Leach had more than a passing interest in the National Space Program. He was one of the 80,000 applicants for the Teacher in Space Flight Program. When asked why he wanted to participate in the program, Leach replied, "I suppose it is an idea of being able to take part in an adventure of that scale and being able to share the experience with the students and other teachers."

Of the 80,000 applications filed, 10,000 were accepted for the first phase of elimination. Leach was one of them. Upon being bumped from the finals, Leach was disappointed. As it turned out, he was fortunate.

Leach remembers the day of the shuttle tragedy. At least a dozen calls came to the school that day. After he had the facts, and only then, did he try to explain to the children what had happened. He said the children were overwhelmed and he doesn't think they completely comprehended what had happened until they saw it on the news. "The full impact didn't even hit me," commented Leach, "until I saw the TV footage." Asked if he felt relieved he had not been chosen, Leach stated, "I don't think it ever went through my mind that it could have been me. I felt shock over the accident, sorrow over the losses, fearful people would react in such a way that the space program would be hurt irreparably. I wouldn't want that to happen."

In recent years there have been more children in the primary grades than the upper classes. In 1979 there were no graduates from the sixth grade. In 1984 there was one, Natalie Bird. In 1985 two, Robert Timm and Dieter Erdmann. In 1986, once again there were no graduates.

In the fall of 1986, there were three children registered in the upper classes (two of whom were sixth graders) and six in the lower grades.

In 1986-1987 the Board of Education members were A.G. Timm, president, Jim Dillon, vice president and members Gene Darling, Laurie Murdock and Sue Norris.

For a number of years, there was a decline in births at Raquette Lake. A new generation of young parents have chosen to remain or return to Raquette Lake and hopefully a new crop of children will eventually fill the classrooms once more.

RAQUETTE LAKE PHYSICIANS

In the early years, Raquette Lake was serviced by neighboring physicians from Long Lake. During the summer months the community was served by any doctor who may have been on the lake at the time.

Dr. Edward A. Hoffmann arrived at Brightside on Raquette in 1892 for a vacation. While in residence he attended to the needs of the ill.

"Obtaining medical assistance was difficult," recalled Louise Porter Payne who lived at Raquette Lake in Sucker Brook Bay in early 1900. "In the summer there would usually be a doctor on the lake . . . but in the winter, the doctor from Old Forge would get around and call on the houses. He would always come when summoned, no matter how bad the weather or difficult the trip. He would leap out of his buggy or sleigh and throw the reins to the men. It was understood that they would take care of the horse and rub him down after the hard ride, while the doctor would tend his patient."

"One time," she continued, "my father had to skirt the doctor around the edge of the newly frozen Raquette Lake, late at night. Real scary!"

On January 23, 1913, as part of the new public health program, it was resolved to employ a full-time resident physician for $500 per year. The physician chosen was Dr. H.J. Downey. By December the following year, Dr. Downey left and another doctor had to be found. Dr. John S. Parker accepted the position, while his wife became employed as a teacher at the local school.

In July 1916, a typhoid epidemic struck Kamp Kill Kare. At least ten persons were stricken, having to be transported by train to Utica.

After the Parkers left, Dr. Edward B. Kaple was hired in April 1917 with a change in compensation . . . $1,000 per year. Dr. Kaple resigned after two years being replaced by Dr. Hubert Carroll, a native of Indian Lake. Dr. Carroll's practice was short-lived when he decided to return to practice in Indian Lake. Dr. P.H. Huntington was then appointed, but left after six months. Finally, Dr. Clarence Beals accepted the position and chose to remain at Raquette. In 1930 his salary was raised to $1,500.

"Fortunately," said Kay Beals Garlipp, "Dad was paid a salary by the County, for people were too healthy to provide a large enough practice to feed and clothe us. When he did obtain a fee, sometimes it was tendered in venison or rabbit."

Kay recalls her time spent at Raquette Lake. "When I was about four and a half years old, my father decided to leave his practice in Salamanca, New York and move to Raquette Lake . . . that was in the spring of 1920. We, my father, mother, sister Frederica, and myself arrived on the Raquette Lake Railroad. Our household goods were deposited in due time at our back door and uncrated by my father, who was watched intently by the small fry of the neighborhood - the Fallon and Hunt girls and Rowena Roblee."

"The crate in which my mother's piano was shipped was put to good use for it became our playhouse. In it we kept the treasures we collected from various refuse piles and which were frequently subject to removal, without permission, to other playhouses by their owners. Eventually the playhouse became our chicken coop and was still in existence when we left thirteen years later."

"Our house had a fireplace made of native stone. It was said the fireplace was built first and the house built around it. . . .

Dad had a good-sized office, but it could only be used during the summers as it was not heated in winters; a downstairs bedroom was substituted during the cold months."

"Dad was the school physician and the children came to the house for their annual examination. This provided a welcome escape from school, albeit a brief one," she continued. "After protesting that it was not fair for me not to be allowed to get out of school for my exam, I too was allowed to go home for mine."

"Once or twice a year our living room became a dental office. My uncle, Dr. Foster Brown, who lived and practiced in Utica, came to visit us and brought along his tools of trade in case someone needed dental work done."

In 1936, Dr. Beals and his family left Raquette Lake, leaving the village without the services of a resident physician. In 1939, Dr. T.R. Travis Warrick settled in Raquette.

> "Dr. Warrick, a native of Glassboro, New Jersey, was the son of Woodward and Emma (Price) Warrick, who owned the entire town of Glassboro. By the time he was nine years old he had decided he wanted to be a doctor when he grew up.
>
> After graduating from the boys preparatory school at Lawrenceville, New Jersey, he entered the University of Pennsylvania where he received his medical and surgical degrees. His service as a physician and surgeon included twelve years in private practice in Richmond, Virginia, before he entered the U.S. Army. He served at the Mexican border before going overseas with the regimental headquarters of the 111th Field Artillery in France. Upon leaving the Army he served as diagnostician and chief resident at Northeast Hospital, Philadelphia, Pennsylvania, a post he held for ten years. When Dr. Warrick decided to retire to Raquette Lake in 1937, he found the community in need of a doctor and renewed his practice."

His wife Beulah Paterson, a native of Richmond, Virginia, died in Raquette Lake in 1940.

In 1942 Warrick married Loretta Gokey, and moved to Inlet the following year. He served both villages, frequently walking many miles in subzero weather to treat patients.

A story is told of Dr. Warrick delivering a baby at Blue Mountain Lake, where he had walked in forty degrees below zero weather. To make an already bad situation worse, during the delivery there was a power failure forcing him to deliver by candlelight.

Jim Bird recalls a time when Dr. Warrick asked him to take him across the lake to Brightside during a period of time when safety was questionable. Joe Bryere's feet had developed gangrene. "Why do you want to go when you might have an accident or drown?" questioned Bird. "Let me ask you," replied Dr. Warrick, "if it was your father would you lead me across?" They crossed the lake.

In 1951 he was one of nine doctors honored in the Utica area by the New York State Medical Society for having completed more than a half century of service to the profession.

Dr. Warrick and his wife Loretta returned to Raquette Lake in 1959. They built their home on a parcel at Poplar Point they had acquired from Orrin Lanphear. Warrick continued to practice until his death on November 19, 1962.

After his death, his wife sold the property to Raquette Lake natives Jerry and Mary Lanphear.

Once again, Raquette Lake residents were without a resident physician. Since then they have to travel to the health stations at Old Forge or Indian Lake, both a distance of twenty-three miles each way.

During the summer months, however, the town has had a "good Samaritan" who has been at their call. Dr. Horace Morey who came to Raquette Lake in 1958 has generously offered his services to those who need it.

Dr. Morey was born in Utica October 26, 1908. After completing his education in the Utica School System he graduated from the Liberal Arts College of Syracuse University and the Syracuse Medical School in 1933. He served one year internship at St. Joseph's Hospital, Syracuse, then began his practice in Mohawk in 1934. The following year he married June M. Meech, and a year later, a daughter Dawn, was born to the couple.

Dr. Morey served in the Navy during World War II from July 1942 until November 1947 when he resigned as Lieutenant Commander. The following year he received his license to practice in Florida. While serving at Opa-Locka Hospital, he met Ethel Whitney, a nurse also employed at the hospital. A few years later they were married. In June of 1949 he opened a private practice in Miami.

Dr. Morey came to the Adirondacks in August 1958 to attend

the wedding of his daughter Dawn. Her husband, Gary Bartow had been her teacher when she was studying at Potsdam College in 1954. After the wedding, Dr. Morey and his wife Ethel, joined the Bartow family vacationing at Sunset Point where Horace (Grandpa Bart) Bartow, father of Gary, owned property. The Moreys continued to vacation at Sunset until 1964 when they purchased their home at the Antlers.

In October 1984, a testimonial dinner was held for Dr. Morey in honor of his twenty-five years of service to the community. The affair, held at the Fire Hall, was attended by Raquette Lake residents and "snowbird" friends and relatives. In addition to receiving a plaque, a donation in his honor was given to the Ambulance Fund.

For the past several years, although the doctor has not been in good health, he continues to be "The Good Samaritan" of Raquette Lake.

THE FIRE DEPARTMENT

After the village was destroyed by the fire in 1927, it became apparent that fire protection within the town was needed. Nevertheless, nothing was done for almost ten years. On August 4, 1934, officers of the Raquette Lake Supply Company filed the first application for a fire district with the State Comptroller. On petition of the company, a hearing was finally held March 17, 1936 in the lobby of the hotel and approval for Fire District #2 was given. William Pulling, Joseph Mulhull, William Egenhofer, Paul Owens and Dennis Dillon, Jr. were appointed fire district commissioners. However, there was never a record of any meetings being held or other commissioners being appointed.

No fire department was organized and the safety of the village remained in the hands of volunteers.

In about 1945, the first fire engine was allegedly built by William "Bing" Aldous from parts either used or donated.

Bing Aldous, son of Edward and Jessy Smith Aldous, was born in Indian Lake in 1905. In 1933 he married Cleo E. Grant (b. 1915) daughter of John and Emma Gilson Grant of Albany. The couple lived in Indian Lake, coming to Raquette in 1940 where they took up residence in the Brewster cottage (now occupied by

Peg Norris). They have operated Bing's Garage since 1942. After Bing's death November 1977, Cleo continued to run the business while working part time for the Postal Service. The couple had three children: Paul, George and Maxine. Of them, Paul is the only one residing in Raquette Lake, living with his wife Patty.

There is no record of further action being taken to provide adequate fire protection until a petition of May 24, 1947, signed by Dennis Dillon and R.F. Carlin, was presented, requesting District #2 be dissolved. Simultaneously, a second petition was sent to the Town Boards of Long Lake and Arietta to establish Raquette Lake Fire District #3 to cover a wider area than before. Signers included Lillian G. Carlin, R.F. Carlin, William Egenhofer, Barbara Burke, Raymond Burke, Mrs. Norton Bird. Mrs. Minnie Waldron, Orrin Lanphear, William Fenner, Clara O. Bryere, John and Grace Moore, Roy A. Howard, Mrs. Rowena R. Bird, E.J. Blanchard, James and Marion Bird, John H. Blanchard, Mary C. Dillon, Raquette Lake Supply Company by Dennis Dillon and Dennis Dillon Jr.

At a public hearing at the Casino on June 12, 1947, Fire District #2 was dissolved and District #3 was formed. The Town Boards of Long Lake and Arietta appointed fire commissioners on October 9, 1947. There were James Bird, A. Joseph Bird, William Egenhofer Sr., Dennis Dillon Jr. and Roscoe Carlin. Charles Bird was hired as Secretary-Treasurer. Upon his death in 1978, he was replaced by Eugene Darling.

The Raquette Lake Fire Company was organized November 10, 1947. Meetings were held either at Egenhofer's Legion Room, the lobby of the hotel, or the Spoon. There seems to be no record as to the exact date when the firehouse was built. The land was donated by Laurine and Bert Gardner. Materials and labor were by private contributions.

The first fire truck purchased by the Commissioners was in 1948. The building, fire tank truck and ambulance are owned by the Fire Department. The truck pumper is owned by the fire district (under the jurisdiction of the Commissioners) which also rents the building from the company to house the truck.

On July 1, 1952, the fire equipment was moved from Bing's Garage to the new fire hall. The first ambulance was purchased in 1954. Vehicles have been changed when necessary to meet legal requirements.

Charter members of the fire department are recorded as: Bill

Fenner (President), Orrin Lanphear (Vice President), Charles Egenhofer (Treasurer), Bill Egenhofer Sr. (Fire Chief), Hoddy Bird (1st Assistant Chief), Bud Beckingham (2nd Assistant Chief), Dayt Cleaveland Sr. (3rd Assistant Chief), Ray Burke (Secretary), Hubert Gauthier, Jerry Lanphear, Frank Lamphear, Edgar Lamphear, Joe Gauthier, Ed Cleaveland, Fred Burke, Ed Banta, Howard Waldron, Jim Bird, Joe Bird, Moses Leonard, Rock Carlin, Fitz Vogan, Bill Egenhofer Jr., William Aldous, Fred Thomas, Dennis Dillon Jr., John Blanchard, John Moore, Fran O'Connell, Charles Bird and Jim Roblee.

In 1953, the Ladies Auxiliary was organized with charter members, Marion Bird (President), Emma Lou Waldron (Secretary), Jean Beckingham (Corresponding Secretary), Helen Bird (Treasurer), Rita Cleaveland (Vice President), Pat Gauthier, Cleo Aldous, Doris Lamphear, Shirley Forsell, Rose Bird, Anne Lamphear, Peg Norris, Margaret Gauthier, Mary Lanphear, Gloria Burke and June Thomas.

The following served as commissioners: Orrin Lanphear, Edgar Lamphear, Roscoe Carlin, Bert Gardner, Dean Pohl, Joe Bird, Howard Waldron, Don Langham, William Egenhofer, Hubie Gauthier and Jim Dillon. In 1986, James Bird was the only original commissioner still serving after thirty-nine years.

In 1976 the first squad of EMT's were certified to serve Raquette Lake. They included Tom Norris, Greg Timm, Gene Darling and George Aldous.

On May 14, 1983, the Ladies Auxiliary celebrated their 30th anniversary with a party at the fire hall. Of the original sixteen charter members, eleven were present. Charter members of the Fire Department were represented by ten of the original thirty-one. In commemoration, a plaque listing names of the founders of both organizations has been placed on permanent display at the fire hall.

From the time it was built, in addition to housing the fire equipment, the fire hall has been used as a community center. Organizational meetings as well as social functions have been held there and since 1955, the voting machine has been housed there.

Following the building of the new school (with its large gymnasium) it has been possible to hold some functions at the school. This eliminates the necessity of removing the vehicles from the hall while activities are in progress.

THE RAQUETTE LAKE LIBRARY

In 1922, influenced by Mrs. Mary Dillon, the Raquette Lake Supply Company donated two rooms over what is known as the Casino (adjacent to St. William's Church). The area was converted into a large, well-equipped reading room—the first library in Raquette Lake. A provisional charter was issued to the Raquette Lake Library by the State of New York, May 25, 1922. Board members included Margaret C. Collins, William Ryan, William A. Pulling, Sophia Bouchier, Dennis Dillon Sr. and Reuben Mick. Mrs. Collins was later replaced by Mrs. Dillon who served as president of the library trustees.

During the fire of 1927, the library was damaged and the books and charter were burned. A room was then partitioned off in the New York Central railway depot where the library was reinstituted and restocked with a number of volumes. During the early days of the library, faculty members and high school students took turns as librarians.

On August 31, 1930 board member Sophia Bouchier died. In her will she left one-third of her estate, over $33,000 to the Raquette Lake Library, the other two-thirds going to Bryn Mawr College. Her brother Charles, administrator of the estate, determined to carry out his sister's wishes, arranged for a suitable library building (still in service) to be built as a memorial.

The building was erected in 1937; Edwin Jackson was the architect and Charles and Frank Alt the contractors.

The remainder of the bequeathed money was placed in a trust fund as an endowment to provide funds for maintenance of the library.

On May 14, 1931, an item in the *Adirondack Arrow* read, "At a recent meeting of the Board of Directors and officers of the Raquette Lake Library, Charles Bouchier of New York City was appointed trustee and treasurer. Mrs. Paul H. Owens was appointed secretary."

After the crash, funds left for maintenance were depleted. However, the library continued to function, and was registered with the Board of Regents on June 11, 1934. An Absolute Charter was granted February of 1939 and until 1967, Raquette Lake Library was the only chartered library in Hamilton County.

In 1945, Betty Dillon Schaufler became librarian, a position she held until November 1985 when she was replaced by Holly Gauvin Burke.

Past trustee members not previously mentioned include Alex Peetz, Milly Dillon, Bertha Conley, Bert Gardner, Laurine Gardner, Sarah Griffith and Dennis Dillon Jr.

On Memorial Day, May 28, 1973, residents celebrated the fiftieth anniversary of the Raquette Lake Free Library. Program hostesses Marguerite Fuge and Laurine Gardner chose students Tina Timm, Holly Cummings and Joseph Bird to present flowers to librarian, Betty Dillon Schaufler, as an introduction to the program. Dennis Dillon, Jr., library trustee, introduced the following speakers: John Collins, former President of the Indian Lake Central School Board; George Fuge, Cortland Camp Director and President of the Board of Education of the Raquette Lake School; Sheriff Arthur Parker of Hamilton County; Mr. P. Cross, Southern Adirondack Library System Representative; Reverend Cross, Minister of the Inlet and Raquette Lake Churches; Reverend Marcian Kandrac, Pastor of St. William's Church and Mr. Zimmerman, Principal of the Indian Lake School. The program was concluded with a vocal solo by Miss Melody Eckhart.

In the early 1980's, under the leadership of a new Board of Directors and with the help of volunteers, work was started to eliminate old and outdated library volumes. An up-to-date filing system was set up and arrangements for new acquisitions were made.

The board of trustees for 1985-1986 include Jim Dillon, Marguerite Fuge, Donna Pohl, Anna Grosselfinger and Howard Kirschenbaum. The system is arranged so that one term expires each year.

The library is supported by funds from the county, town, local school district, Southern Adirondack Library System, memberships and memorial funds.

The Raquette Lake Library remains an integral part of the community as well as a living memorial to its founders.

CHAPTER X

THE RAQUETTE LAKE SUPPLY COMPANY

Throughout its history, the mercantile life of the community of Raquette Lake has been dominated by the Raquette Lake Supply Company. Before becoming the supply company, it started as a small business venture initiated by John McLaughlin on Long Point.

John McLaughlin of Minerva and his wife Rebecca Sheedy of Adirondack, came to work for Durant after their marriage in 1881. Ten years later, Durant gave McLaughlin thirty acres on Long Point where he (McLaughlin) proceeded to build the first general store at Raquette Lake.

In addition to his duties at the store he became postmaster at "Durant" on Long Point from 1891 until 1893 when he was elected Supervisor at Long Lake.

Sometime prior to 1900 the store was taken over by John Wheeler of Blue Mountain Lake and the McLaughlins and their six children moved to Massena where McLaughlin became engaged in lumbering. On May 4, 1905 McLaughlin and a friend Frank Gleason were drowned while crossing the Black River at Carthage in a rowboat.

In the spring of 1900 Wheeler moved the business across the lake to the Raquette Lake Railroad Station on ground leased from the railroad. Before Wheeler died in 1901, he sold the business to Patrick Moynehan. Moynehan, born near North Creek in 1849, worked as a lumberjack in the Blue Mountain area, where he later became a successful logging jobber.

The new owner made a long-term lease with the Raquette Lake

Railway Company covering additional land near the station on which he built warehouses for his store and supply business. At the same time he obtained the concession for the station restaurant.

Dennis Dillon, his nephew, who in 1899 became manager of the store on Long Point, was made manager of the new store.

THE ORGANIZATION OF THE RAQUETTE LAKE SUPPLY COMPANY

Dennis Dillon, John and Maurice Callahan and Dennis Moynehan (nephew of Patrick Moynehan) organized the Raquette Lake Supply Company in 1908, taking over the operation of Pat Moynehan's enterprises including the Raquette Lake House and the concession for the station restaurant.

Henry Carlin remembered the store having a shoe department, a pharmacy, hardware department and soda fountain in addition to the general store. New items were added all the time until there was hardly room to walk. Pennants of Raquette Lake were hung on the walls and post cards were hung on racks near the souveniers.

According to Carlin there was a concrete sidewalk from the station to the hotel and on to the store. The hotel had a fenced yard and tennis court. One of the activities for visitors was to walk about three miles from the hotel to see the work of beavers. Sometimes visitors would ride into town on the train, just to take the nature walk.

On July 7, 1913, the Long Lake Telephone Company, Inc. extended its service to Raquette Lake, but at the time only to the Supply Company.

In 1921, the Supply Company was commissioned to install street lighting in Raquette Lake for $350. First in line was the dock at the village. In 1929 the application for the Inlet Utilities was approved to furnish light to the Raquette Lake area. The Long Lake Heat, Light and Power Company, which furnished electricity to Long Lake village was also prepared to extend the service to Raquette Lake. In November 1929, the school was wired for electricity. By the mid-1930's the Old Forge Electric Corporation was furnishing electricity in Raquette Lake. Niagara

Mohawk Power Corporation took over lighting facilities at Raquette on October 16, 1952.

In 1923, the families who had owned the Raquette Lake Transportation Company, sold it to their manager of twenty years, Maurice Callahan and his partners in the Raquette Lake Supply Company. The company, which was now in a position to purchase commodities by the carload, became the main supplier of coal, groceries, hay, grain and lumber.

The Raquette Lake Supply Company played a prominent role in the setting up of a water district in 1924. Dennis Dillon, Dennis Moynehan and John Callahan were appointed the first water commissioners. The district was established at North Point on July 5, 1924 in compliance with the petition of a majority of taxable owners.

Ted Aber's column, "The Way Things Were," noted that during the period of October 1-15, 1931, "The breakdown of the old water system, after thirty years, had caused the village of Raquette Lake to issue $23,000 in bonds for an earth and concrete dam and reservior on a spring-fed brook"

"Charles Scanlon and Mary Dillon were appointed commissioners on April 11, 1932. That June the town board met to raise $7,000 for a local water district. A town ruling on December 13, 1947 empowered Dennis Dillon as Assistant Superintendent of Water District #1 of Raquette Lake who instructed his authorized agent, William Egenhofer, to refuse water service to any consumer in arrears for six months or more water rent. On November 20, 1939 the town of Long Lake appointed Bart Kelly, superintendent of the town's water systems with Harry Stone as collector. The Board met with the Water Power Control Commission of Albany, January 9, 1952 requesting repair of a leak in the Raquette Lake reservoir."

In 1927 the village of Raquette Lake was destroyed by fire. It changed not only the physical appearance of the area, but placed a great financial burden upon the Supply Company.

The disaster was but the beginning of the end of an era in the changing times of Raquette Lake.

Local residents have continued to be employed by the Raquette Lake Supply Company as full or part time workers. Numbered among those not previously mentioned are Alex Peetz, Louie McGuiness, Mary O'Donnell, William Netherton, Joe and John Mulhall and William and Charles Egenhofer.

JUDGE AND MARY DILLON

Dennis Dillon married Mary Florence Callahan, daughter of Mary and John Callahan of Uncas. The ceremony took place at Camp Uncas with the permission of the Morgan family.

The couple settled in Raquette Lake raising five children. Dennis, Jr. eventually took over from his father as managing partner of the Raquette Lake Supply Company. Sister M. DeLourdes, R.S.H.M. was associated with the teaching faculty of Marymount College, Betty Dillon Schaufler still resides in Raquette Lake, John is an attorney of Chappaqua, New York and Thomas a physician of Greenwich, Connecticut.

Dennis Dillon, in addition to becoming a partner in the Raquette Lake Supply Company and later in the Raquette Lake Transportation Company was one of the founders, as well as vice president and director of the Old Forge National Bank. He was also one of the founders of the Hamilton County National Bank in Wells, New York.

Dillon maintained the distinction of being the only County Judge in the state who was not a lawyer. At the time of his appointment to the judgeship by Governor Franklin D. Roosevelt in 1931, there was no resident lawyer in Hamilton County. He served one year by appointment and was then elected to two six-year terms. In 1943 he was defeated by Lansing K. Tiffany in his run for re-election.

Judge Dillon was considered "a tough man to be reckoned with." A classic example told by Charlie Egenhofer is a story of a time when the Judge was sitting on the bench outside Raquette Lake. "The lawyer was a young man defending his first client. He learned Dillon had never been a lawyer and evidently decided he would show the Judge how things should work. In an extremely heated moment, the young man, shaking his fist at Dillon, shouted, 'You don't know what you're talking about! What do you know about the law? You don't even have jurisdiction over this case, it's not your territory.'"

"Standing, the Judge answered him, 'You forget sir I am the Judge here. I hereby transfer venue of this case to Raquette Lake.' Giving the desk a resounding smack of the gavel, he stormed out of the Court Room leaving the young lawyer standing with his mouth open."

Judge Dillon served his community and operated the Raquette Lake Supply Company until his death in 1948.

Mary Callahan Dillon was born on February 26, 1884 near Glens Falls. Her father had come to Raquette Lake in 1885 to work for W.W. Durant. Mary was carried in a pack-basket by her mother when the family moved to Raquette Lake to join her father.

Although listed as a student in the early days of the school on Long Point, rarely, if ever, did she attend . . . for several reasons. The Callahan family moved to Uncas in 1890. The school on Long Point was started in 1891. The trip from Camp Uncas to the lake was a difficult trip in itself, but it was then necessary to cross the lake to reach the school. Because of the large number of children living with their families who were employed at Camp Uncas and Sagamore, the Town of Arietta arranged for a school to be set up at Sagamore.

At what point in time Mary Dillon went to live with relatives during school sessions is unknown. However, she did attend school in the Corinth School System. Her daughter Betty relates, "In 1903 Mother graduated from Albany State Teachers College with a Ph.D. degree and the purple ribbon, signifying high honors. Before her marriage she taught art and German in Utica."

In the March 2, 1983 edition of the *Hamilton County News*, the following article was written when Mary Dillon celebrated her 99th birthday. It referred to Mrs. Dillon's life as "spanning the huge technological gap between the age of the horse and buggy and the space age with men on the moon."

It continued, "She has lived through nearly half the time since Britain recognized American independence in 1783. Chester Alan Arthur was president when Mary Dillon was born. Later that year Stephen Grover Cleveland was elected to his first term as head of the Republic. There were only fifty million people in the U.S. at the time. There were only thirty-eight states."

"Mrs. Dillon was fourteen when Teddy Roosevelt led the charge up San Juan Hill in the Spanish American War. She was seventeen when Queen Victoria died at the height of the British Empire. In her thirty-third year the reign of the czars ended and the U.S. entered World War I."

One of her major achievements was establishing and maintaining the Raquette Lake School system. She was a member of the

Courtesy Bruce Cole

Patrick Moynehan's store near the Raquette Lake Railroad Station. Circa 1920's.

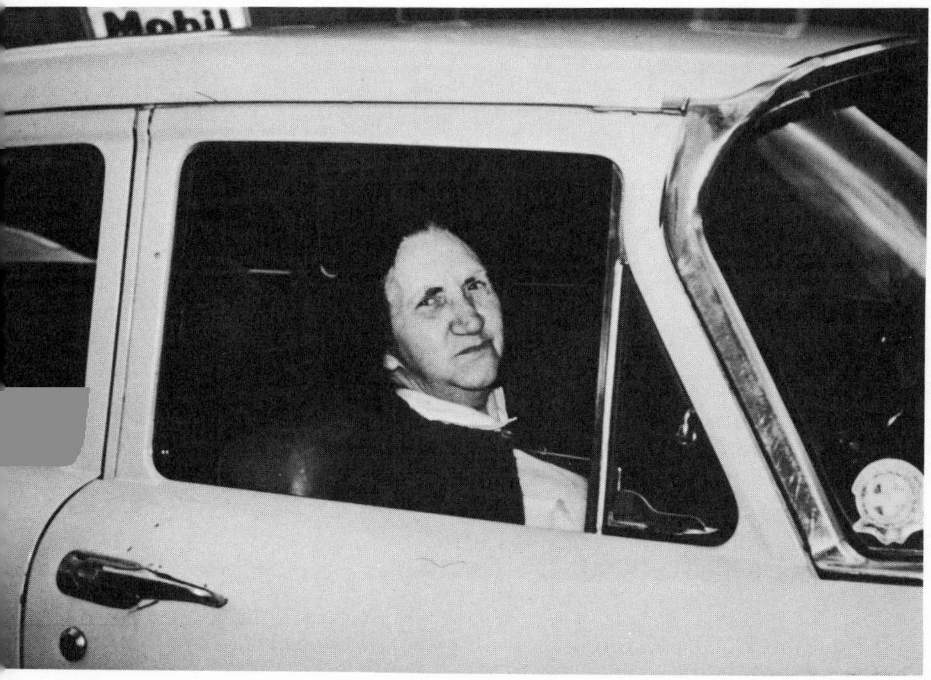

Author's Collection

Mary Dillon. Circa 1960's.

Courtesy Bruce Cole

The Raquette Lake Supply store. Circa early 1920's.

Courtesy Nancy Madden

People on the dock waiting to board one of the steamers at the Raquette Lake Supply Company. Circa 1920's.

Courtesy Rowena Bird

Ice field nearest the railroad spur was cut first during the ice harvesting. Horse-drawn plows containing teeth were used to cut the "key way" or channel. Circa 1930's.

Courtesy Bertha Conley

Gasoline rotary saw used to cut ice for harvesting. Circa 1920.

Courtesy Bertha Conley

Ice blocks moving up the conveyor ramp to the "shaver" at the top. Circa 1920's.

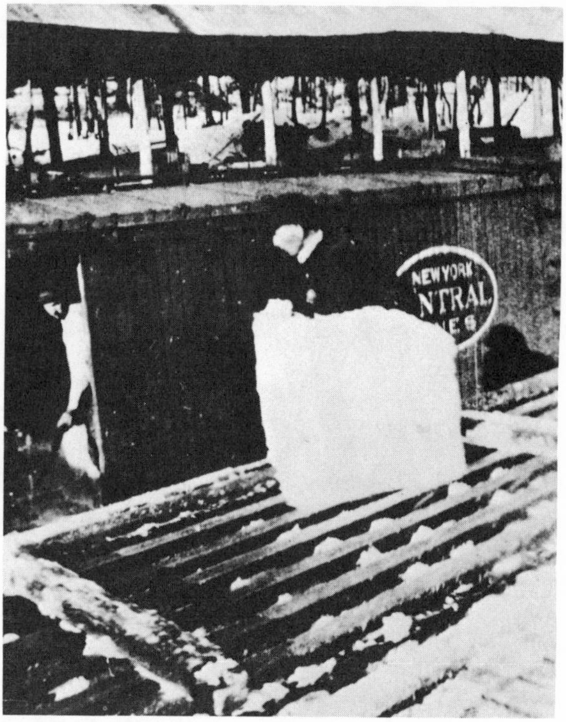

Courtesy Bertha Conley

he "switcher" pulls a cake om the conveyor onto a chute r loading into the car where ıe of the "loaders" swings the ock into place. Circa 1920's.

Courtesy Buster Bird

Ice cakes move along the conveyor loading five cars simultaneously. Circa 1920's.

Author's Collection

Tom Norris using the 1915 saw to cut the key way. Circa 1970's.

Author's Collection

After the blocks are moved up the key way, they are pushed onto the loader then onto a truck to be transported to the ice house. Circa 1970's.

Author's Collection

Denny Dillon Jr. supervised the ice operation from the early 1940's until his death in 1982. Circa 1970's.

Courtesy Seymour Craig

A logging train with steam powered crane loading logs on a flat car. Circa 1920's.

Courtesy Bruce Cole

Sawmill at Bassett's Carry on the Marion River. Circa 1890's.

Courtesy Thomas Norris

Logs being transported into town from Kamp Kill Kare during clean-up after the severe wind storm of 1950. Circa 1954.

Author's Collection

Artist's rendition of General Store, Dillon residence and Casino. Circa 1928.

Author's Collection

Bertha Conley in the kitchen behind the store where generations of young folks were drawn to her door by the aroma of her freshly baked bread and doughnuts. Circa 1960's.

Author's Collection

Horace Bartow at Grandpa Bart's, a caning repair shop. The building was originally a Raquette Lake Supply warehouse. Circa 1975.

Board of Education holding the position of President for thirty-six years, striving for the best education possible. For forty years she assisted the American Red Cross and was the driving force in the establishment of the Raquette Lake Library.

Mary Dillon, remembered as "the epitome of womanhood, a staunch supporter of her husband, understanding mother, and gracious hostess accepting her role as leader of the community with an air of majesty and dignity," died March 29, 1983, one month after her 99th birthday.

DENNIS DILLON, JR.

Dennis Dillon Jr. was born July 13, 1910. He was educated in local schools and was a graduate of Manlius Military Academy in 1928 and Fordham University in 1932. After serving in World War II he married Mildred "Millie" Foley in Ontario, New York.

The couple had three daughters, Molly, Maureen and Patricia and three sons, D. Timothy, James and John. The establishment remained a family business and as the children grew they worked at the store. Of the family, Jim and his mother still reside at Raquette Lake. Although the others have left the area, they return frequently with their spouses and children, remaining a part of the Raquette Lake community.

In addition to his responsibilities to Raquette Lake Supply, Denny followed in his parents' footsteps. He served many years as a member of the Board of Education and Parent-Teacher-Friend Association, as well as trustee for the library and St. William's Church. Denny held the position of Postmaster from 1933 until 1976 when he retired being replaced by his wife in that capacity.

After a long illness, Denny died November 4, 1982. Appreciation for his many years of service to the youth of the village was demonstrated June of 1983 when a scoreboard, built and erected by members of the community was placed on the baseball field as a permanent memorial to him.

James "Jim" Dillon replaced his father as overseer of the Raquette Lake Supply Company.

Jim, a graduate of Cornell with a B.S. degree in Civil Engineering has followed in his father's footsteps as an active member of the community. He is a member of the Board of Education, trustee for St. William's Church and the Raquette Library. In addition he is an active EMT in the Raquette Lake Ambulance Corp., as well as being a Fire Commissioner.

Since he has been in charge of the Raquette Lake Supply Company, the interior has had a face lift and several new services have been added.

Raquette Lake Supply Company was the driving force in the early development of the community and it remains an integral part of the history of Raquette Lake.

HARVESTING THE ICE

From 1906 until about 1922, ice harvesting became the major winter occupation at Raquette Lake. On January 29, 1906, Patrick Moynehan signed a contract with the New York Central Railroad to supply 20,000 tons of ice each winter. (Maurice Callahan and Dwight B. Sperry were named sub-contractors.) Later the quota was raised to 50,000 tons.

As soon as the ice on the lake reached a thickness of about fifteen inches, the work began. About seventy men and eight teams of horses were employed. They worked seven days a week until the job was completed.

The area nearest the railroad was cut first. The ice field was staked out then the cutting began. At first the ice was cut with a horse-drawn plow containing teeth that could cut ten inches deep. A straight line was scratched denoting the area to be cut. One man ran the plow while another guided it across the marked line, cutting the ice. Around 1915 a gasoline rotary saw replaced the plow. A key way (channel of water) had to be cut to float the ice blocks to the conveyor.

Buster Bird told how steam heat had to be kept going in a car hooked onto the train, where the men could take turns warming themselves. "At times the temperature was so low during harvesting nights, the men had to take turns shoving the ice blocks back and forth through the channel with a six-foot-long pike pole. That was the only way to keep it open until cutting resumed in the morning."

Strips of ice approximately four feet wide and thirty feet long were floated through the channel. These were then split into individual blocks (32 x 22 x 15 inches) as they were loaded up a ramp onto the conveyor. They then passed through a planer, which shaved them to a uniform height for loading and stacking in the freight cars. (Steam pipes were placed under the platform to keep the ice melted enough to move easily.)

Edgar Lamphear worked on the ice harvesting as a shaver while his father, Ott, was a switcher. Maurice Callahan was their boss.

After the ice was cut to fulfill the contract requirements, Raquette Lake Supply cut their own ice, storing it in their ice house to be used for refrigeration and sale.

Presently, Raquette Lake is the site of one of the last commercial ice cutting operations in the North Country. The ice that is cut is stored in the Supply Company ice house and sold to summer campers. An average harvest runs about 2,000 blocks, each weighing between 200 and 250 pounds.

For many years the ice house was located near the barber shop in one of the old warehouses; both were demolished in 1983. The ice is now stored on Dillon Road in a shed previously used as an ice house when the railroad was in operation.

In an interview with Denny Dillon in 1982, he said, "Harvesting the ice is part of a way of life in this little hamlet. We don't make any money at it. Originally it sold for a nickel a block then went up to a quarter. The kids (referring to his children) want to continue. They feel it is a tradition and the people seem to like the idea the ice was cut right here. Many folks try to take time to come and see us in operation. They are disappointed if they are too early or too late. We don't choose the time. Nature does that!"

LUMBERING IN RAQUETTE LAKE

Another source of employment, although not on as large a scale, was lumbering. From 1910 until 1930, Raquette Lake Supply Company had a mill in the village. The primary product they shipped was wood pulp.

Prior to that time lumbering in Raquette Lake was limited

because of the small amounts of acerage owned by individuals in and around the lake. There is evidence of several sawmills having been in operation on Raquette, but mostly for the convenience and use of the camp owners.

Old records indicate Samuel Payne had a sawmill on his property in 1858. In 1867, a sawmill was in operation at Constable Point later known as the Antlers.

When Durant arrived in Raquette Lake, his numerous ventures included some logging. While building Pine Knot, he found it advantageous to build a sawmill at Blue Mountain, which later was moved to Bassett's Carry at the Marion River. There it could be used easily for both Raquette Lake and Blue Mountain Lake.

Eventually, the large estates including North Point, Uncas and Sagamore as well as several others found it more feasible to erect mills on their property.

"In late November of 1950, a severe wind came about from the southeast, an unusual direction for an Adirondack storm," recounted Denny Dillon. "It reached a velocity of one hundred miles an hour. Thousands of acres of private land and 250,000 acres of state woods were affected by the blowdown."

"A state of emergency was called because of the danger of fire," he continued, "that storm and another smaller blow resulted in the largest amount of lumbering done in the Raquette Lake area. Cleanup lasted until about 1956.

THE GREAT FIRE

The headlines in a newspaper dated Monday, February 20, 1927 read: "Raquette Lake Village Swept by $350,000 Fire." Sub-head "Adirondack Hotel Area Is In Ruins." "Fire of unknown origin Sunday wiped out all holdings of the Raquette Lake Supply Company in this village at an estimated loss of between $350,000 and $400,000. Charred ruins are all that remains of the Raquette Lake Hotel, casino, store, post office, telegraph office, three dwellings and a fleet of three steamers and a ferry. Seventy-five persons were rendered homeless."

Several natives living in Raquette Lake at the time gave their recollection of the disaster; combined stories reveal the following incident.

A steady snow that had fallen all night had become a full-scale blizzard by morning. At about 10:30 a.m., Mrs. Daniel Lynn (wife of the Forest Ranger) left her office located in the store adjoining the Post Office to attend mass at the Catholic Church nearby. Before leaving she checked and banked the fire in the coal stove in the office.

A few minutes after she left, Frank Newton, the manager of the Raquette Lake Supply Company discovered a fire in the building. Fighting the heavy wind, he raced blindly to the neighboring church where most of the townspeople were worshipping. Service was interrupted while the men hastened back to the store to fight the flames.

Five families occupied quarters above the store, but all were at church with the exception of Slim Manning, his wife and two-year-old Tommy Dillon. The Mannings had offered to watch the little boy who was sleeping in the neighboring apartment while his mother attended services.

When the alarm was given Mary Dillon rushed out of the church and with the aid of a lumberjack forced entrance into the apartment. The child was found frightened but unharmed hiding under the dining room table. Meanwhile, Manning and his wife left the building by the rear stairs and escaped injury.

Fanned by a strong wind, the fire spread rapidly to the hotel (which was closed for the season) and to nearby dwellings, normally used to house hotel guests. At the time, however, lumberjacks working on a nearby job were living in them. The fire continued to spread to the supply store, post office and telegraph station.

Since Raquette Lake had no fire department, it was necessary to seek help from Inlet which had the closest fire apparatus. To do this, the alarm had to be telegraphed from the Raquette Lake Railroad Station to Utica, (seventy-five miles distant) back to Thendara (only twenty-seven miles from Raquette) then to Inlet (which is only thirteen miles away). For nearly two hours before help arrived, volunteers including the thirty-man crew who had been working in a nearby pulp mill owned by the Supply Company fought the blaze.

As the wind swept the flames through the raging blizzard, the steamers *Sagamore*, *Adirondack* and *Killoquah* which were lying in drydock for the winter, were completely burned. A ferry and part of the steamer dock were also destroyed. Three homes and a barn were devoured by the flames despite the efforts of the townspeople. Twenty or more horses which had been sheltered in the barn were set free. Since there was no available place to care for them, they were left to roam in the storm. Some who could not find shelter died of exposure.

Battling almost impassable snow drifts, fire apparatus (a gasoline pumping engine) arrived about noon. It was necessary for the firemen to push the equipment up a hilly embankment (caused by the drifting snow) to the village. Employees of the New York Central Railroad saved much of the adjoining property. Extra water was supplied by dropping a hose from a locomotive through a hole in the ice on the lake.

The railroad supplied shelter in the station for many left homeless. Others sought refuge in neighbors' homes. Because the Raquette Lake Supply Company was the principle source of foodstuffs for the town and surrounding areas, arrangements had to be made to rush supplies from Old Forge to the stricken village.

Because of the raging blizzard which forced them to remain at their homes, residents on the other side of the lake and on the islands were not aware of the fire.

Ernie Woods tells the story of Joe Bryere who had guests at Brightside. Several days after the fire, when the storm had subsided, he and one of the guests snowshoed across the lake to purchase tobacco at the store. Nearing the village the visitor inquired where the store was. Looking up Bryere pointed toward the village saying, "There it . . . Where the . . . did it go?"

After the fire, John Callahan sold his interests in the Raquette Lake Supply Company to his partners who rebuilt the hotel and store on the same site as the original. A two-story, stucco and cement building was constructed housing the store on the first floor with rooms on the second. The post office and Tap Room were built in the rear portion of the store with a small kitchen (later used as a bakery) adjoining the Post Office.

It was in this small kitchen that Bertha Conley worked serving breakfasts and lunches and baking for the store. Several generations of young folks visited her through the years, drawn to her door by the aroma of freshly baked bread and doughnuts.

Bertha and her husband Jack came to Raquette Lake shortly after the fire. At first they lived near the water across from Waldron's Grocery store. Bertha was the cook for the hotel and

Jack worked in the bar room. Later Bertha bacame the cook for the Dillon family. When Judge Dillon died, Jack and Bertha moved in with Mrs. Dillon and after Jack's death in the late 1950's, Bertha started baking in the store kitchen. Bertha became seriously ill and left Raquette Lake in the late 1970's. She died in 1980.

In 1976 Horace Bartow, long-time summer resident at Sunset Camp, opened "Grandpa Bart's" caning repair and antique shop in the old barber shop. In addition to cane repair, Bart sold old bottles, antiques and handmade apple head dolls as well as paintings created by local artist Margaret Carrol. Carrol, a Buffalo art teacher first visited Raquette Lake in 1921 becoming a permanent resident in 1958.

For four summers the shop was in operation but ill health caused Bartow to abandon the venture. In 1985, several buildings including the barber shop and the old ice storage shed were demolished.

CHAPTER XI

TRANSPORTATION

EARLY ROADS

Travel through the Adirondacks in the late 18th and early 19th centuries was mainly by old Indian trails or military roads. Swamp areas were made passable by using corduroys (logs placed sideways in rows). Water was crossed by rafts and later by guide boats.

There had been an old military road between Lake Pleasant and Raquette Lake, but after its original purpose of moving troops during the War of 1812, it fell into disrepair. A road "of a sort" went through the mountains from Glens Falls, through Indian Lake and into Blue Mountain Lake. Travel from Blue to Raquette Lake was by waterway.

On the Eddy map of 1818, another old military road was shown as having been constructed in 1812 between Sir William Johnson's Fish House Lodge on the Sacandaga River and Wells, New York. The road followed the old Indian trail from the Sacandaga to Raquette Lake. This was the route taken by Sir John Johnson and his band of Torries on their flight to Montreal in 1776. In 1837 the State Legislature authorized the route to be known as the Champlain to Carthage route. By 1901 the road was abandoned.

Another road, with Boonville as the main gateway to the Adirondacks, was the Browns Tract Road which extended from Old Forge via the tannery village of Moose River to the village of Boonville.This road was built in 1812 by Charles Herreshof, son-in-law of John Brown of Rhode Island, who originally tried to farm and settle the site that is today the Old Forge-Thendara section of the Adirondacks. The road thrived until 1892.

During later years, the Browns Tract Road was very nearly parallel to the "Wooden Legged Railroad" which ran on wooden wheels. One wishing to travel from Utica to Old Forge caught the early morning train to Boonville on the Utica and Black River Railroad. From Boonville a horse-drawn stage was taken to Moose River village where they boarded the wooden legged railroad. The rails ended at the Moose River just east of today's Route 28 between McKeever and Thendara. Transfer was made to a small steamer upstream to where the Thendara-Old Forge Road crosses the Moose River today. In 1892 when W. Seward Webb built a rail line through the Adirondacks from Utica to Malone via Thendara it was the beginning of the end for the old road. When the New York Central Railroad accepted the railroad as an Adirondack Division in 1912, the present Route 28 was opened up as a rough road from Utica to Old Forge and on north.

In November 1861, a private road was built from Josiah Wood's camp surveyed as "commencing at a maple bush on the north line of a lot in Township 40, now occupied and owned by Josiah Wood on the east side of Raquet (sic) Lake, and running north to the center of the Carthage Road, about six rods east of the bridge across the Raquet outlet, being a private road two rods wide."

By 1871, the railroad from Saratoga to North Creek was completed. Horse-drawn stage lines were established over difficult, uncomfortable roads that reached into the mountains.

Further development and repair of roads in service was pursued during the late 1800's.

Appropriations were made to Hamilton County in 1878 toward the repair of little-used roads. In 1881, $500 was appropriated to the town of Long Lake for work on the Raquette Lake Road.

In June of 1881, a private road was surveyed for W. W. Durant from Bassett's Carry westerly to the east line of the Long Point property of Janet Durant.

A resolution was accepted in 1883 to erect a road and highway from Long Lake to the highway at Blue Mountain. It was agreed a carry would be built from the outlet of Forked Lake to the head of Long Lake.

A road was built from Big Moose to Uncas in 1886, shortly before the railroad. This followed Big Moose Road east of Cascade Hill into Sucker Brook then to Eighth Lake campsite continuing south. Sucker Brook Road which ran from Eagle Bay to the Raquette Lake terminal on Sucker Brook Bay west of Raquette Lake was completed in 1887.

"On March 15, 1887, the town of Long Lake sought appropriations of "$500 for the Raquet Lake Road, $300 for the Carthage road between Long Lake and Raquet Lake and $200 for the road between Isaac Kenwell's and Carthage Road. $500 was appropriated to be used the following year for the road between North Bay of Raquet Lake and Brandreth Lake. On March 20, 1888, $300 was appropriated to construct a road between Ike Kenwell's and Bassett's Carry between Raquet Lake and Blue Mountain Lake."

Extension of the local transportation service was effected under the direction of Charles Bennett, proprietor of Antlers, to include the territory between upper Fourth Lake and lower Raquette Lakes. "The new service which he inaugurated in 1893 utilized small steamers on the upper lakes of the Fulton Chain and on Brown's Tract Inlet, a slim, tortuous stream that zigzagged a four-mile course between Eighth and Raquette Lakes. Horse-drawn wagons were employed to transport passengers and baggage over the carries between lakes and streams on the route."

An application was made in 1894 by John McLaughlin, storekeeper at Long Point for a highway from Sucker Brook on the west shore of Raquette Lake, through the town of Morehouse to the north shore of Fourth Lake, on through the town of Wilmurt, Herkimer County to the Mohawk and Malone Railroad Company tracks, south of Clearwater Station. The contract to build the road was given to Dennis Moynehan, Jr.

The town of Long Lake was given permission in 1895, to borrow $33,000 to construct two highways - one "from the westerly shore of Long Lake, westerly to the Mohawk and Malone Railroad and one from Sucker Brook Bay, Raquette Lake, westerly to the Mohawk and Malone Railroad, or so much thereof that lies in Long Lake." The contract to build the proposed road was again given to D. Moynehan, Jr.

William West Durant built a private carriage road in 1896 from Eagle Bay near the head of Fourth Lake to South Inlet, the head of the steamboat navigation point on the inlet of Raquette Lake. This made it possible to drive buckboards from the steamboat landing in Eagle Bay and South Inlet without making a change over. However, during the winter, steamships could not run on the lakes. The wagon road was then extended to be used as a winter road to Big Moose Station to connect Camp Uncas with the railroad. Later the township took over the road and graded it as a wagon road.

In 1897, a road was cut connecting Uncas, Sagamore and Kill Kare.

Wagon roads were, on the whole, not hard-surfaced before 1900. They were made of gravel or dirt and corduroys were common. When there was no snow, buckboards were the vehicles most commonly used. Sleighs drawn by horses were put into service during the winter months.

On July 7, 1902 the Town Board of Long Lake agreed to pay $350 to lay out a road from Bryere's Brightside to the Raquette Lake Railroad Station. In June of 1909, $500 was allotted for a road from Antlers.

Not only were the roads improved, but $300 was allotted to build a boardwalk from the station at Raquette Lake to the Raquette Lake Supply Company's store.

In June of 1911, $1,000 was approved for improvements on a highway from the Blue Mountain Lake road to the Raquette Lake outlet. Three years later repairs were authorized on the George Smith bridge and Pine Brook bridge on the Raquette Lake road.

In the 1920's there was only one road into Raquette Lake. It has been described as "a dirt one, subject to frequent holes as well as rocks which refused to stay covered. It had many curves, several little hills and a larger hill, quite hazardous to travel at times for it was steep, narrow and had a hairpin turn at the top."

In about 1925, after much dispute between the towns of Long Lake and Arietta and owners of Camps Kill Kare, Sagamore and Uncas, it was agreed that "the public highway leading from the junction of the road to Kamp Kill Kare with the road leading from Sagamore Lodge to Camp Uncas to the Railway station at Raquette Lake, should be laid out and open according to a survey by Wesley Barnes at the sole expense of the owners (J. Pierpont Morgan, Mabel B. Garvan and Margaret Baker). The completed road was then to be accepted by the town of Long

Lake." Meanwhile the school had been built on its present site allowing others to use the wooden structured road. Although only used occasionally by the owners, the road was maintained and repaired by them.

THE END OF AN ERA

In 1923 the heirs of the original organizers of the Raquette Lake Transportation Company sold it to Maurice Callahan, who had managed it for twenty years, and to his three associates, John Callahan, Dennis Dillon Sr. and Dennis B. Moynehan (who also purchased the Fulton Navigation Company).

A proposed highway was planned in 1925 with a road to be built between Seventh and Raquette Lakes with an extension to Blue Mountain Lake and north. When the state obtained approval from the voters for the hard-surfaced road, it was proposed it be built in two sections. One section was to be from Blue Mountain to Long Lake, the other from Eagle Bay to Blue Mountain, working toward the south shore of Raquette Lake.

Ironically the railroad and steamboat line assisted in bringing about their own demise.

When the actual surfacing began in the late summer of 1929, the asphalt was brought to Raquette Lake village by railroad car, which was run alongside the docks where the *Killoquah* provided steam to heat and liquify it. It was then taken by truck to be applied to the road.

With the opening of the new highway from Raquette Lake to Blue Mountain Lake, there was no longer need for the steamboats or the Carry railroad.

The Carry train made its last trip September 15, 1929 with James Proper at the throttle. The locomotive and passenger car were moved into the train shed at the lower terminal where they remained for twenty-six years. At first the Raquette Lake Transportation Company leased the land and buildings at its Blue Mountain Lake terminus to H. A. Birrell who later purchased them. Birrell had spent the summers of 1926 and 1927 at the terminus serving as company agent. He was replaced in 1928 by his brother Lowell M. Birrell.

The property in question was operated under the ownership of the Birrell family as a restaurant, store and filling station for many years.

The docks at the carry eventually became overgrown and collapsed. In about 1939, the rails went to a scrap dealer. The railroad was sold to Herbert Birrell.

In 1946, the Birrell family bought a tract of shorefront adjoining their land on Blue Mountain Lake from the Kirkham family and, in the same year, approximately 700 acres along the Marion River Carry from the Raquette Lake Supply Company and the Raquette Lake Transportation Company. A restaurant and cabins were built where this land fronts on Route 28.

In 1955 Birrell donated the Marion River car remains to the Adirondack Museum in Blue Mountain. One passenger car was put together from the remains of three and reconstruction of the wooden parts were made with the assistance of photographs.

The steamboats continued in use as public carriers until 1930. The railroad line operated from June 15 to September 15, 1933. "The total revenues were $5,600 and expenses not including maintenance were over $13,600 showing a deficit of $8,000."

In January 1934, the New York Central submitted a request to the Interstate Commerce Commission to cease operation of the line. Despite arguments of protest, the Commission issued a certificate permitting the Raquette Lake Railway Company to abandon the operation of the line February 27, 1934. This permitted discontinuance at the end of the 1933 season with the official date given by the Public Service Commission as of September 30, 1933.

Jim Bird recalls "a very sad day for the community in the early summer of 1934. On September 30th, the year before, the final run was made to end an operation of more than thirty years."

"Many of the town folks including myself," elaborated Bird, "had an idea that the Public Service Commission would reverse its decision and require the railroad to operate at least during the busy summer months. The rails and roadbed were in good repair and to crank up again would only mean to engage the crew and bring in the equipment from Utica."

"On the aforementioned day, the engineer, fireman and brakeman were recalled, but for a different reason. Instead of passenger cars and freight cars, it was a special work train designed to tear up the rails and ties. Starting where the roadbed ended at the large bulk gas tanks next to Carlin's Boat Livery, the train moved slowly but surely on a one-way trip taking with it the steel rails as it moved out of town. This certainly ended any doubt regarding the end of this rail line which had been in existence since 1901, and it was indeed a sad day!"

"The one thing we didn't understand until many years later," continued Bird, "was that the Raquette Lake Railroad lost money every year of operation. I guess we were lucky to have had the rail service as long as we did."

Most people were unaware of the following facts until they were brought to light by Henry Harter in his *Fairy Tale Railroad*.

> In 1906 the Railroad company reported the total operating income was over $28,000 but it left a deficit of nearly $4,000 and a total deficit had accumulated as of June 30, 1906 of over $42,000. This operating ratio was never to improve.
>
> . . . On March 14, 1917, the Public Service Commission of the Second District granted permission to the New York Central Railroad Company to acquire and hold the entire capital stock of the Raquette Lake Railway Company by assuming the indebtedness of the company. By 1921, *Poor's Manual of Railroads* was reporting that in 1920 the Raquette Lake Railway operated at a deficit of over $40,000.
>
> By 1928 the debt for deficit operations had accumulated to over $326,000, and the New York Central cancelled this indebtedness and among other things, obligated itself to assume all deficits from operation of the line in the future."

Denny Dillon had this to say about the end of the railroad: "Although railroad and steamboat workers lost their jobs, the impact on the hotels was just the opposite. They thrived since more people could come to the area because of the roads."

"The hard surfaced road was finished about the time of the crash. I think we should ask ourselves what changes the Great Depression would have brought about without road improvements."

"During the years 1929 through 1939," Denny continued, "it was easier to make a living at Raquette Lake than in the city. Due to the American plan hotels, the new campsites, the benefits of the State Game Laws and fish-stocking, people continued to come on vacation. There was plenty of kitchen and maintenance work at the hotels and restaurants. The store and livery prospered. Some Raquette Lakers could even afford to purchase small cottages."

"It may have been a depression, but despite low wages and some unemployment, Raquette Lake business was on an upswing."

"While still in the tail of depression, World War II broke out with gas, tire and other transportation rationing which resulted in a temporary standstill of Raquette's growth. However, even with many of the men gone, the hotels were still in operation. Even before the end of the war, tourist trade was back better than ever."

"As late as 1950," added Jim Bird, "six summer hotels were still in operation: the Antlers, Hunter's Rest, Brightside, North Point, Camp Marion and Tioga. The last hotel to close was Hunter's Rest at the end of the 1962 season."

The railroad brought to Raquette Lake in the early 1900's, a life that other progressive and more accessible areas had enjoyed during the late 1800's.

The highway brought more people to the area eager to purchase property. Hotels and large estates that limited ownership to the wealthy landowner or hotel proprietor, were split and sold to individual owners increasing the summer population. This presented more business opportunities, as seen by the establishment of two additional marinas, another grocery store and additional restaurant and bar facilities . . . all outside the original village area.

Through the years road construction and maintenance opened up a new avenue of employment for residents hired as permanent employees of the town, county or state.

Despite the bleak outlook brought about by the end of the steamboat and railroad era the situation proved to be a boon rather than a disaster. Raquette Lakers survived because of, or perhaps in spite of, the "changing times."

DURANT'S STEAMBOATS

In order to transport passengers from Blue Mountain to points on Raquette Lake, it was necessary to travel by water through the Eckford Lakes across Raquette. Dr. Thomas Durant established a rowboat service to accomplish this.

"Rowers had to wear uniforms while transporting customers," wrote Frank Carlin. "Everything had to be strictly first class with the Durants."

William West Durant established his line of small steamboats as a link between Raquette, Utowana, Eagle and Blue Mountain Lakes all of which were connected by the navigable Marion River.

Durant's fleet came into being in 1878 as the Blue Mountain and Raquette Lake Steamboat Line. The first of his vessels was the *Utowana* built the same year at Blue Mountain Lake. In the spring of 1879, Durant had the *Killoquah* built to join the *Utowana* in service between the two lakes.

In 1882, Durant acquired the *Maid of the Marion* to supplement the *Killoquah*. Two other steamboats joined the *Utowana*. They were the *Irocosia* and the *Toowarloondah*. Several years later, Durant moved the *Utowana* to Raquette for his personal use. The *Irocosia* served the Eckford Lakes until the line was taken over by the Raquette Lake Transportation Company in 1901. It was then used to serve both sides of the carry until 1910 when it was shipped to the Fulton Chain of Lakes. In 1909 the *Toowarloondah* was beached.

In 1891 the original *Killoquah* (Indian for lake) had to be replaced by a second *Killoquah*. The *Killoquah II* was destroyed by a fire at the Raquette Lake Station in 1927. A third *Killoquah* replaced it. That craft was originally a double-decker known as the *Daniel P*, built at Long Lake in 1900. The upper deck was removed and it was transported to Raquette Lake being placed into service until 1930 when the steamboat service was abandoned.

Mrs. Phillips, owner of the Raquette Lake Girls Camp at Antlers, purchased the *Killoquah III*. It was beached near the camp and used as the art studio. Finally, time and the elements took their toll and during the summer of 1984 the craft was destroyed.

Another boat, the *Sagamore*, built for the Raquette Lake Transportation Company to replace a steamer lost in the 1927 fire, was sold to the Whitney family in the 1930's. It was moved to Forked Lake and renamed *Killoquah IV*.

The Raquette Lake Boys and Girls Camps renamed one of their craft the *Killoquah V* in about 1985.

"Commodore" Henry Bradley was appointed superintendent of the steamboat line in 1879. His assistant J. George Thompson took over in about 1890 when Bradley changed employment to serve as land agent for Durant, a position he held until he retired in 1902.

The earliest crew members on record in 1878-1879 included Wesley Bates, Phelps, Cheney, Breeze and Barnard. Pilots in the 1880's included T.S. Murphy, Melanchthon Jones and Henry Mansfield. W.H. Sullivan, Tom Fogarty, William Mahar, John Hall Jr. and John Hammond (who was still working as a pilot in 1900) were listed as pursers. William Wyburn and William Roberts worked occasionally.

Of these, Melanchton Jones has descendents still residing at Raquette Lake.

THE JONESES

Melanchton Jones was born in 1829 in Vermont. He and his wife Jane Noble arrived at Indian Lake around 1880.

The couple had seven children. John was born in 1866. He later became a guide and raised a family on Raquette. Charles was born in 1868 and became a guide and caretaker. He married Katherine Kinnison, who was born in 1877 in Scotland; she died in 1935 and he in 1941; both are buried at Long Lake. One of their children Theresa married Kenneth Riley, a guide on Raquette Lake.

His daughter Mary was listed in the 1905 census as a waitress at Charlie Bennett's Antlers. His son, Freeland, remained in Raquette for many years. Nothing has been found on Melanchton Jones' other children, Jesse, Elsie and Allen who were listed as living at Raquette in the 1900 census.

Freeland Jones was born at Dresden, New York in 1874. He was working as a carpenter at Raquette Lake in the early 1900's, during which time he met Mary H. Hodgson, born in Sheffield, England.

Freeland, referred to as "Free" or the "Old Bear" married Mary Hodgson on March 16, 1902 taking up residence at Golden Beach in 1903. During the 1900's he worked as a member of the steamboat crew and on the early mailboat run.

The Jones children included Frederick, Constance, Everett, May, Roger and Shirley who apparently left the North Country. Their son Thomas (1904) and his wife Mary Cassidy of New York had three children, Martin Douglas, Dolores and Orpha.

Orpha Jones, a music teacher, married David G. Curry of Sabattis in 1955. For many years, Curry was principal at the Raquette Lake School. They currently reside in Blue Mountain Lake.

Ted Aber, county historian relates this story told by Orpha about her grandfather. "In about 1904 or 1905, Freeland Jones was declared legally dead. He had had an attack of some kind and at that time, if no heartbeat was found, the person was declared dead and, of course, there was no embalming. During the wake - a real old-fashioned Irish one - Freeland sat up and asked what was going on.

"You're dead," he was told, "and we're holding your wake."

"Good," replied Free grinning, "give me a beer!"

From 1903 until 1909 Jones lived at Golden Beach. In 1910 he moved to his home in South Bay between the Maxam and Blanchard homesteads. He and his family eventually moved to Blue Mountain where he died about 1959.

In the 1890's, steamboat engineers included George E. Snyder, Ed Fowler and George E. Scarritt. Scarritt later became engineer on the Marion River Carry locomotive.

Pilots were recorded as Dan Cunningham, George Pashley and Maurice Callahan. The latter became a prominient figure in the field of transportation in Raquette.

MAURICE CALLAHAN

Maurice Callahan became an integral part of Durant's ventures as well as an important individual in the growth of Raquette Lake.

Born July 18, 1870 in Mill Brook on Schroon Lake, he moved to Raquette Lake in 1895. He was the half-brother to John Callahan, superintendent of Camp Uncas.

When Maurice Callahan arrived at Raquette Lake he was engaged as a telegraph operator at Pine Knot. A year later he was offered the position as Senior Captain on Eckford Lakes for

Durant's Blue Mountain and Raquette Lake Steamboat Line. He maintained the position until 1901 when he was promoted as Assistant Superintendent of the line which was then incorporated as the Raquette Lake Transportation Company. For the following two years he also served as confidential assistant bookkeeper for Durant's Raquette Lake and Eckford affairs.

He was promoted as superintendent of the Transportation Company as well as Webbs Fulton Navigation Company and the Fulton Chain Railway. Subsequently he was elected a director of the three companies as well as the Raquette Lake Railway Company.

In 1903 he moved to Old Forge, where he helped organize the First National Bank, becoming the first president of the establishment.

THE RAQUETTE LAKE RAILWAY

Legend has it the building of the Raquette Lake Railway was the idea of Mrs. Collis P. Huntington, who strenuously objected to the inconvenience of traveling from Old Forge "through the Fulton Chain in those small steamboats, get out and travel to another boat with all the inconveniences and length of time it took." Furthermore she gave her husband an ultimatum that she would not visit Camp Pine Knot until he built a railroad. . . . "If he could build one from New Orleans to San Francisco, California, he could build that little short road for her."

Incorporators of the Raquette Lake Railway were no doubt among the wealthiest men in the country—each with their own reasons for wanting easier access to the territory. Most of the needed capital for the venture ($250,000) was put up by Collis P. Huntington, J. Pierpont Morgan, Dr. W. Seward Webb and ex-Secretary of the Navy, William C. Whitney who had large timber preserves in the vicinity. The remaining directors who put in smaller amounts included John A. Dix who owned lumber mills and timber land in the surrounding area, Robert Bacon, F.G. Smith, Harry R. Whitney, J. Harvey Ladew, Samuel Callaway (President of the New York Central), Chauncey M. Depew, Charles E. Snyder, Edward M. Burns, William W. Durant and Dr. Arpad Gerster.

Officers elected were Huntington as President, Edward M. Burns, Vice President, Huntington's assistant, J.E. Gates, Secretary and Charles H. Burnett, Webb's assistant, Treasurer.

The September 12, 1899 edition of the *Morning Herald* reported:

"Clearwater-Raquet Lake—The New Railroad Between These Two Points Practically Open - Raquette Lake, Sept. 11 (Special) —C.P. Huntington left New York City in his private car Saturday morning (September 9) for Raquet Lake, arriving here that evening over the new railroad from Clearwater. This is the first time anyone has ever made this through trip by rail from New York."

Huntington's enjoyment of the railroad was cut short by his death in August of 1900. Dr. W. Seward Webb was elected to replace him as president and on July 1, 1900 the Raquette Lake Railway was opened to the public.

The 1901 railroad inspector's report included station accommodations enroute. "At Clearwater there is a combination passenger and freight station of good design, new and properly equipped. At Eagle Bay . . . there is also a new and convenient freight and passenger station. At Raquette Lake, a commodious freight and passenger station with restaurant included, all new and of modern design, neatly and properly finished. The other stations are small about 12 x 12, with covered shed about the same dimensions and at these no agents are employed."

Some camp owners traveled in their own private railroad cars. Among them Vanderbilt's "Wayfarer," Whitney's "Wanderer" and Brady's "Adventurer." After disembarking in Raquette, the cars were parked under cover in Huntington's railroad barn, located on the property now occupied by the Raquette Lake Chapel.

J. Pierpont Morgan Sr. chartered a sleeping car from the Pullman Company when he visited Camp Uncas. His stays were rarely longer than a few days, and the locomotive was kept in preparation, day and night, for any business emergency in New York City.

Throughout the life of the railway, summer service between New York and Raquette Lake consisted of two trains daily in each direction. One, which included sleepers and coach, arrived at eight a.m. at Raquette, leaving Raquette at eight p.m. The other carrying coaches and freight left Raquette at one p.m. and arrived at Raquette at five p.m. During the winter there was one train three times a week, Monday, Wednesday and Saturday which left Raquette at one p.m., arriving at five p.m.

Special authorization had to be obtained from the State Legislature, to burn coal as fuel during the winter months when there was no danger of forest fire. From April 1st to December 1st, oil was used.

"The tracks of the railroad ended fifty feet from the livery," recalled Henry Carlin. "There were two rail breaks - one for circling to reset the train for take-off and another for freight cars destined to be shuttled onto the barge which carried freight cars to the Marion River Carry and later passengers and freight and supplies.

In an excerpt from Ted Aber's column, "The Way Things Were" in the *Hamilton County News* (1976), it states "In the Inlet-Raquette Lake area (between July 1-15, 1926), train officials reported the heaviest travel ever. Fifty-eight sleeping cars were used. The Raquette Lake Railway station took on the aspect of Grand Central Terminal on Friday, when forty-three Pullman sleepers arrived from New York carrying hundreds of children, with their leaders and counselors, who were to spend the summer months on the shores of Raquette Lake. The Raquette Lake Transportation Company reported that all records of past seasons were broken and that 105 automobiles as well as several hundred passengers were carried on the ferry to Forked Lake."

THE MARION RIVER CARRY

Emerging from Utowana Lake, the Marion River becomes very hazardous for a short distance. At this section, generations of campers and hunters found it necessary to carry their boats some 1,300 yards between the waters. The place (now known as the Marion River Carry) was called "Bassett's Carry," after Fred Bassett, a woodsman who lived there.

Bassett had come to Raquette Lake about the mid-1870's settling at the carry where he set up lodgings for travelers and those he guided. Joe Whitney, then a guide, lived at the carry also for a while in 1880.

Bassett left the carry in the fall of 1889. The following spring,

Durant built a small hotel on the hill near the lower end of the carry. This was owned by Durant until 1902, during which time Henry Brown served as proprietor.

For a while passengers, baggage and so forth were transported over the portage by means of a horse-drawn hay wagon, without springs. During the 1890's Ed Martin and Ed Fowler drove the wagon team. Many passengers preferred to walk while their baggage was transported. This soon became impractical and Durant concluded a railroad would do a better job. In the summer of 1899 the road was begun and by the spring of 1900, "the shortest standard gauge railroad in the world (approximately 7/8ths of a mile) was born," completing the route from the Raquette Lake Station to the Marion River Carry by steamboat, crossing the carry by railroad to reboard another steamer for the trip through the Eckford Chain of Lakes.

On the trips back and forth, the steamboat would stop at Antlers long enough for the passengers to have breakfast or supper. Durant and Charlie Bennett had an agreement. The passengers would stop for meals in return for allowing the steamboat to have baggage, freight and express business for the Antlers.

Frank Owens arrived at Raquette Lake from Minerva in 1899 to take over the Marion River Carry. Later he served as captain on several company boats.

The carry railroad was originally equipped with three horse-drawn street cars discarded by the Brooklyn Rapid Transit Company and bought by Durant for $25 each. One was a flat-bottomed job for carrying freight and baggage (canoeists, for the fee of $1, were happy to have their canoe carried). The other cars were open with seats placed crosswise and with a long step the entire length of each side. This permitted easy boarding and allowed the conductor to swing along as he collected fares.

The open cars, painted brown, contained red and white striped canvas awnings which served a dual purpose. They could be let down during stormy weather and prevented the cinders from the stack of the locomotive from blowing onto the passengers. The cars which seated about 125 passengers were in service for the life of the line.

The engine was a four-wheeler with a tender as part of the unit. It was originally coal-burning but was sent by Durant to the Schenectady Locomotive Works to be converted to burn oil. Until it was put into service, locomotion was achieved by one of the street cars being drawn by a horse. When it arrived in Raquette Lake, the locomotive was towed to the carry on a car float.

"Car floats" were long, flat, shallow draft barges with rails spiked to the decks. They were used to transport carloads of coal or other merchandise to Raquette or Blue Mountain after being pushed up the carry from one float to another. (During the 1920's, smaller auto floats were built so autos could be transported to the private roads on their owners' estates.)

The locomotive was found to be inadequate for hauling loaded freight cars and had to be replaced by a larger one rented from the New York Central at $5 per day. Unfortunately the car proved to be too heavy and too expensive to run, so another was purchased from the H. K. Porter Locomotive Works in Pittsburgh. This engine had no coal supply bin or tender. The boiler was hand-fired from a coal pocket on the dock at each end of the road, and a reserved supply was kept in a pile on the floor next to the firebox.

George E. "Rassie" Scarritt was one of the early engineers serving from 1902 to 1912. Others included W.H. Horton, Harrison Linforth, Claude J. Covey, Elmer D. Jones, A.W. Harris, Floyd C. Brown, Charles P. Ives, George Ripley, Frank Tiernan and James Proper who made the last run.

THE RAQUETTE LAKE TRANSPORTATION COMPANY

In 1901 the steamboat lines and the railroad were reorganized as the Raquette Lake Transportation Company with Dr. W. Seward Webb as president. Maurice Callahan, who had been appointed manager of the company and Thomas J. Regan, Adirondack representative for Whitney were elected to the board of directors in 1903.

Included in the transfer was the 105-acre right-of-way of the Marion River Carry Railroad (a strip of land bordering the river on both sides). Moynehan retained 600 acres which included Durant's Carry Inn and Sawmill. When the inn burned in 1911, Moynehan rebuilt it to serve as a boarding house for the employees of the mill and the crew of the Marion River Railroad. The boarding house was enlarged and improved and for a number of years, first Raymond Burke, then Charlie Egenhofer ran it as an inn.

Charlie Bennett placed his naphtha launch "Antlers" into service between the Antlers and the station hauling freight and baggage for the hotel. The Raquette Lake Transportation Company arranged for through passengers to stop at the station restaurant for their meals instead of at Antlers.

By the time of the reorganization, many of the wealthy landowners found their own motor boats were much cheaper and faster to transport their guests to camp. Among those in operation were Mrs. C.P. Huntington's pride *Oneonta*, Charles Durant Jr's. *Stella*, Frank H. Platt's *Ellen*, A.T. Strange's *Lorna Doone*.

Despite the loss of transporting local camp owners and their guests, additional boats were put in service on the steamboat line. The *Tuscarora*, known as the pride of the Eckford Lakes was built for Durant in 1900. It was abandoned in 1929. The *Adirondack*, a double-decker similar to the *Tuscarora* was put into service in 1902. Both of these had a capacity of 300 passengers and were used as excursion boats on heavy traffic days. The *Lillian* was purchased by Durant as a towboat for the car floats in 1901.

After the fire in 1927, the Raquette Lake Transportation Company purchased Hasbrouck's *Mohawk No. II* renaming her the *Utowana*. At times she carried some of the passengers and towed others on a scow.

Mrs. Freda Becker Westfall recalled one trip she made on a heavy traffic day and which she will never forget. "There was to be a barge attached somehow to the steamboat. We all sat on chairs on the barge and when we came to the narrow section of the Marion River, the boat went one way, the barge another. People flew in all directions; I don't know how many fell off the barge, but I remember I went into that slimy, dirty muck!"

In 1936 the *Utowana* was sold and moved to Indian Lake. Other vessels acquired and used included Mrs. Carnegie's forty-foot motorboat *Rambler*, the *Raquette* and the *Myra* obtained from Old Forge.

Courtesy Edna Colligan

The "Utowana," built in 1878, was the first of Durant's steamboats. It had a capacity of 300 passengers.

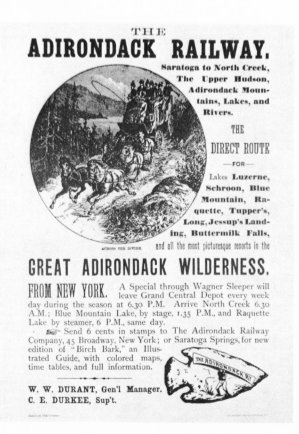

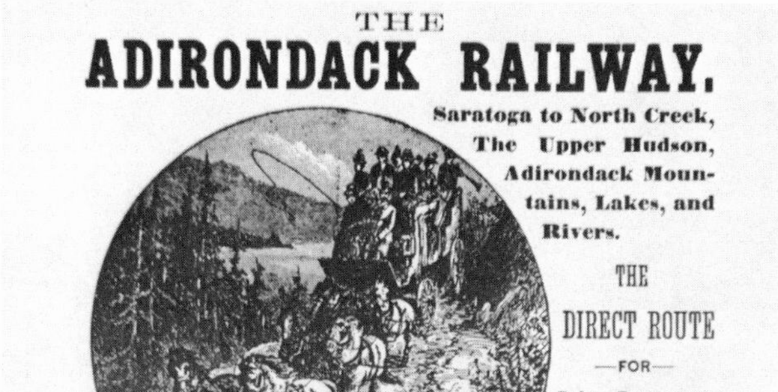

Author's Collection

Advertising circular for Adirondack Railway. Circa 1890's.

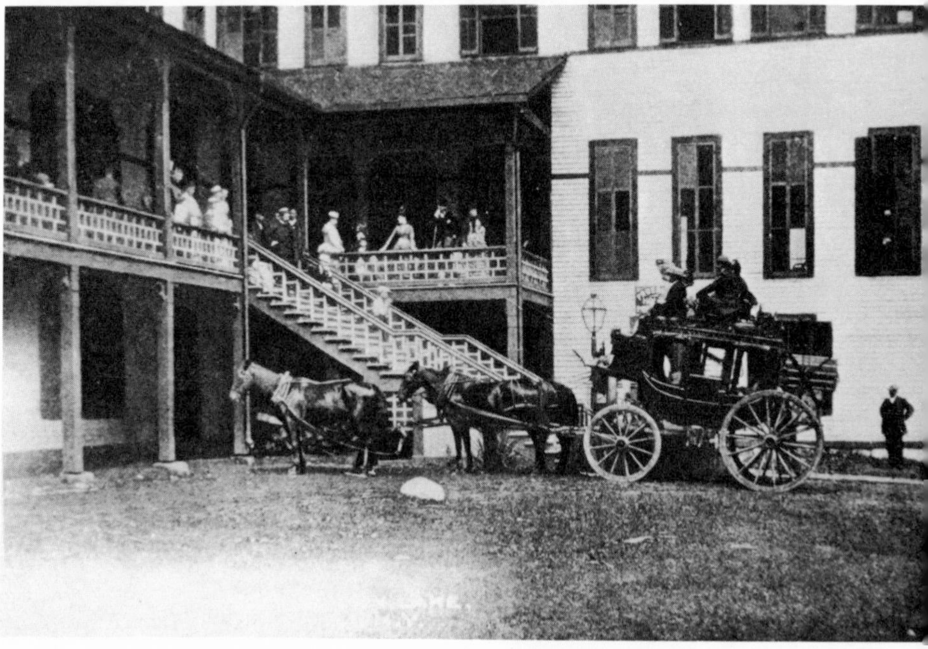

Courtesy Doris and Glenn Martin

A stage coach at the Prospect House in Blue Mountain. Circa 1870's.

Author's Collection

In the spring of 1879, Durant had the "Killoquah," shown here, built to join the "Utowana" in service between Blue Mountain and Raquette Lakes. Circa 1880's.

Courtesy Doris and Glenn Martin

The Raquette Lake Railway brought the era of prosperity to Raquette Lake. Concrete sidewalks were built joining the Raquette Lake Supply Store and the Raquette Lake House to the railroad station. Circa 1925.

Courtesy Doris and Glenn Martin

After completion of the Marion River Carry Railroad in 1900, passengers would disembark from the steamboats and take the rail car the 7/8 mile to reboard the other steamer. Circa early 1900's.

Author's Collection

The Carry Railroad with both freight and passenger cars. Circa 1900's.

Courtesy Rachel Phinney

Guests from Sucker Brook Bay ready for their journey on the Carry railroad. Circa 1920's.

Author's Collection

The steamer "Adirondack" pulling into Bassett's (later Marion River Carry) to disembark passengers from Raquette Lake Village. They would then portage to another steamboat to complete the trip across the Eckford Lakes to Blue Mountain Lake. Circa early 1900's.

Courtesy Nancy Madden

A "car float" leaving the docks complete with passengers, furniture (note the piano) and cars. Circa late 1920's.

Courtesy Ernest Wood

William Wood transporting his horse to Big Island. Circa 1930's.

Courtesy Edna Colligan

William Pulling became agent at Raquette Lake Station in 1906, serving in that capacity until 1933. Circa 1930's.

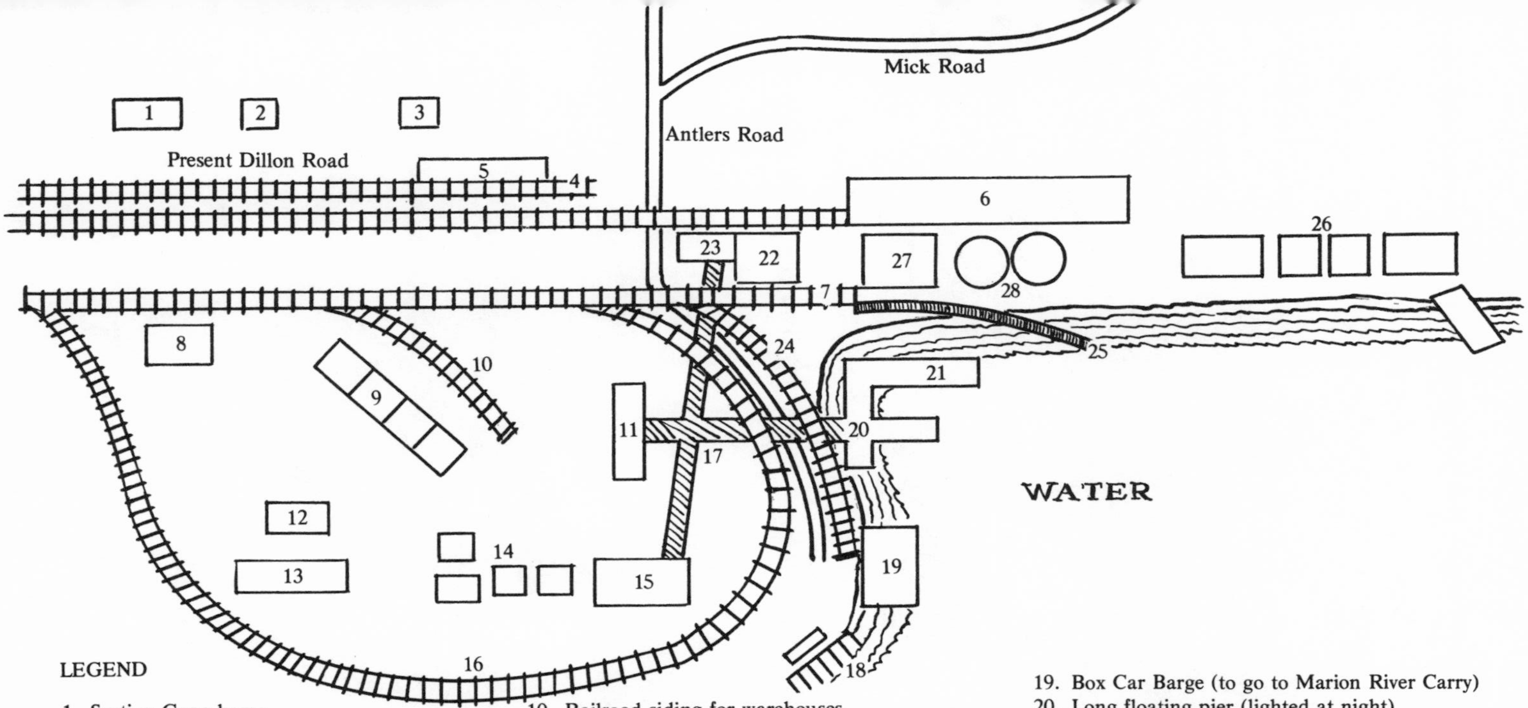

LEGEND

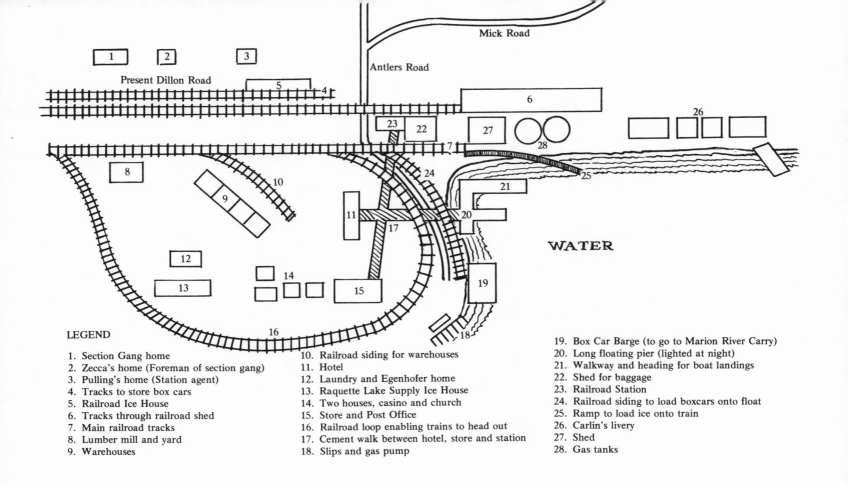

1. Section Gang home
2. Zecca's home (Foreman of section gang)
3. Pulling's home (Station agent)
4. Tracks to store box cars
5. Railroad Ice House
6. Tracks through railroad shed
7. Main railroad tracks
8. Lumber mill and yard
9. Warehouses
10. Railroad siding for warehouses
11. Hotel
12. Laundry and Egenhofer home
13. Raquette Lake Supply Ice House
14. Two houses, casino and church
15. Store and Post Office
16. Railroad loop enabling trains to head out
17. Cement walk between hotel, store and station
18. Slips and gas pump
19. Box Car Barge (to go to Marion River Carry)
20. Long floating pier (lighted at night)
21. Walkway and heading for boat landings
22. Shed for baggage
23. Railroad Station
24. Railroad siding to load boxcars onto float
25. Ramp to load ice onto train
26. Carlin's livery
27. Shed
28. Gas tanks

Courtesy Robert M. Evans from collection of Harold Vollrath

The Raquette Lake Railway Engine #1. Norton Bird Sr., engineer on right, Darius Waldron, fireman on left. Circa 1920's.

Courtesy Rowena Bird

The Raquette Lake Flying Club's Cessena 140. Circa 1946.

Courtesy James Proper's brother and Bruce Cole

The Marion River Carry train made its last trip on September 15, 1929 with James Proper at the throttle. Circa 1929.

Author's Collection

The Old Station of the Raquette Lake Railway. Circa 1960's.

SCHEDULES AND RATES

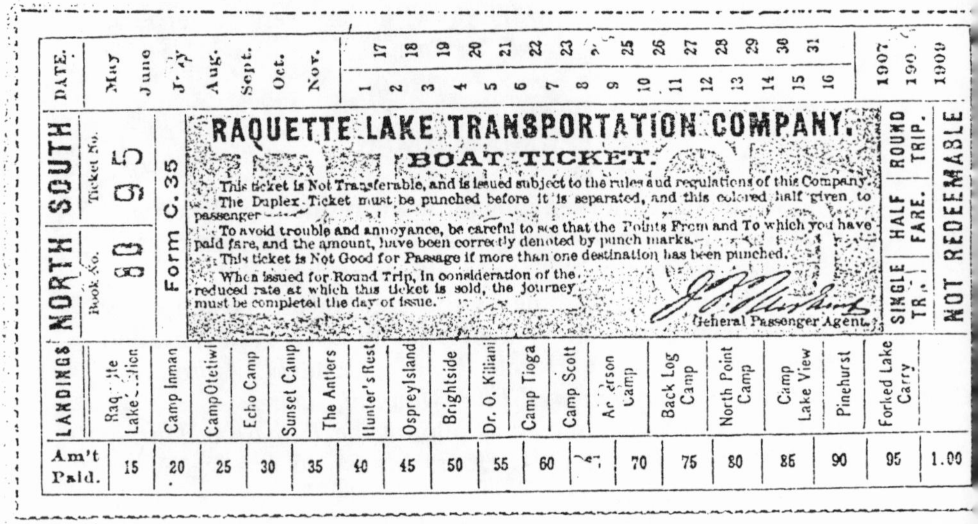

DATE. May June July Aug. Sept. Oct. Nov.

1 2 3 4 5 6 7 8 9 10 11 12 13 14 15 16

17 18 19 20 21 22 23 25 26 27 28 29 30 31

1907 190 1909

NORTH SOUTH

Book No. 80 Ticket No. 95

Form C. 35

RAQUETTE LAKE TRANSPORTATION COMPANY.

BOAT TICKET.

This ticket is Not Transferable, and is issued subject to the rules and regulations of this Company.

The Duplex Ticket must be punched before it is separated, and this colored half given to passenger.

To avoid trouble and annoyance, be careful to see that the Points From and To which you have paid fare, and the amount, have been correctly denoted by punch marks.

This ticket is Not Good for Passage if more than one destination has been punched.

When issued for Round Trip, in consideration of the reduced rate at which this ticket is sold, the journey must be completed the day of issue.

General Passenger Agent.

SINGLE TR. HALF FARE. ROUND TRIP.

NOT REDEEMABLE

LANDINGS	Raquette Lake Station	Camp Inman	Camp Otetiwi	Echo Camp	Sunset Camp	The Antlers	Hunter's Rest	Osprey Island	Brightside	Dr. O. Kiliani	Camp Tioga	Camp Scott	Anderson Camp	Back Log Camp	North Point Camp	Camp Lake View	Pinehurst	Forked Lake Carry	
Am't Paid.	15	20	25	30	35	40	45	50	55	60	[illegible]	70	75	80	85	90	95	1.00	

Steamboat ticket, 1907 - 1909

Rates for autos and passengers as noted in the 1928 schedule were: automobiles weighing under 2,000 pounds, $4.00 one way, same day round trip $7.00. Over 2,000 pounds one way was $5.00 with the round trip $8.00. Each passenger excluding the driver was $1.25 one way with $1.55 for round trip. Children under five free, between five and twelve years, half fare.

From May 15 to September 15 inclusive, there were three trips daily each way. From September 16 to October 31 two daily, and from November to the close of the season, trips were made on request, with a minimum charge of $10.00; "regular rates when two or more cars are carried." Time of a single trip was quoted as "about an hour."

One of the favorite pastimes for some of the youngsters was playing "steamboat." They would make many a trip along the shore in one of the family boats, "using leaves for tickets, taking on and dropping off passengers on large rocks along the way." The "Junior Boat" owned by the Dillon family was sometimes used. When this was the case, it followed that the Dillon children would be in command. Martha Dillon was usually captain, piloting the boat. Denny Dillon, engineer would run the motor and Betty Dillon and Kay Beals Garlipp shared the purser's duties of collecting fares and tying to the dock. Others were passengers.

STEAMBOAT MEN

The steamboats afforded jobs for many residents. The crew of a steamboat consisted of a pilot, an engineer and sometimes a purser. The purser was the senior officer of the vessel.

The following list of some of the crew members and other employees who served under the Raquette Lake Transportation Company was given in Harold K. Hochschild's, *Adirondack Steamboats on Raquette and Blue Mountain Lakes*.

In 1901, Norris Hale served as pilot of the *Tuscarora*. During 1902, 1903 and part of 1904, Henry Mansfield was in charge. Hale then returned and continued to pilot the *Tuscarora* until he retired in 1917. Later she was piloted by Maurice Callahan, head of the line. Occasionally Erwin Hanna or Winnie Treadwell, regular pilots on smaller boats, would take the helm. Other pilots during the present century were Dutch Leffler, Charlie Brewster, B.J. Brewster, Dan Malakie, Lester Stephens, Ed Conlin, J.E. Burns, Bert Richards, Dick McLaughlin, Arnold Hale and Arthur Mick.

Engineers included Robert F. Hanna, C.E. Ervin, Chauncey Covey, Fred Brown Jr., Peter White, Ed Martin, Rassie Scarritt, Orvis Locke, Harrison Linforth, A.A. Radell, Russell Merwin, E.N. Brown, Bert Brown, Fred Brown Sr. and Floyd Brown.

Dennis Dillon, Will Crapo, Ralph Springs, Walter Merwin, James Curry, Ed Churchill, W.A. Manning, E.E. Tuxill, Charles Mick and A.T. Claffee were listed as pursers.

Master mechanic in 1901 and 1902 was David C. Preacher who was succeeded by George R. Ernest, Charles Covey and Chauncey Covey.

Allie Leffler and Darius Waldron were listed in the 1915 census as steamboat captains and Raymond Burke a boat fireman.

Ships carpenters were listed as F.C. Marks, J. Bezenet Sr. and J. Bezenet Jr. Agents at Raquette Lake included A.T. Claffee from 1903 to 1908, George T. Burns from 1909-1918 and Francis

C. Haischer from 1919-1929.

Maintenance workers during 1900 and 1901 included painter Frank Little who had also worked at Pine Knot, Uncas and Sagamore, and his assistant Chester L. Stanton. Arthur O'Brien was hired as civil engineer and Jess Britton as chief dredge operator. John Asher was appointed head ship carpenter and George Fuller and Joe Potter Sr. of Blue Mountain were hired to do hauling. Han Wheelock and his son Will did masonry work and Tommy Blue was the cook for the crew.

RAILROAD MEN

The advent of the railroad afforded more job opportunities to the residents of Raquette Lake.

"At least ten or more year-round employees were needed," says Jim Bird. "For a town of this size, that's darn good."

"There were two men on the engine, a fireman, conductor to help the passengers, a brakeman, watchman, station agent and helper to unload the freight. The maintenance or section crew had a foreman and three crew members for the roadbed and track walker."

"Now, a wage of thirty-nine cents an hour for a maintenance man, and forty-two cents an hour for a track walker seems low," continued Bird, "but it was darn good at that time."

"From about the first of May until about the first of October, track walkers had to walk ahead of the train during all weather to be sure no trees or debris had fallen on the tracks that would cause an accident. One man walked from Raquette Lake to Eagle Bay while another walked the other route from Carter to Eagle Bay where they met.

Men serving the railroad from its inception to the time it was disbanded are recorded as follows:

From 1900 to 1903, Lee Stevens was engineer, Lester Stevens, fireman and William Clark, agent having succeeded E. B. Peckins. Lee and Lester Stevens were still serving between 1905 and 1914 with Arthur W. Jencks as brakeman, John J. Murray, conductor and Arthur H. Kennedy and Egbert W. Brown Jr. as baggage clerks.

Bill McGraw served as engineer before Benjamin Hall who was

followed by Frank Allen, William Walker and James Cummings.

Between 1914 and 1917, workers included John Babcock, engineer, William Pulling as station agent, Frank Owens brakeman, Norton Bird and Peter Dial firemen, John Rank conductor and Jimmy Zecca foreman of the section crew.

From 1917 until 1933, Norton Bird was engineer. Bill Lunforth worked as fireman from 1917 until 1920 when he was replaced by Darius Waldron who remained until 1933. Asa Norton and Fred Brown also worked in the mid-1920's as firemen with Frank Owens, A.J. Lashaway and Bertram Gardner as brakemen and Charlie Egenhofer as railroad clerk.

Names such as Pulling, Owens and Gardner are well remembered by locals.

THE PULLINGS

William Pulling was born December 1881 in Brushton, New York. His wife Ida was born July 19, 1888. Their home on Dillon Road is still occupied and owned by Leland DeMarsh. For years it was the only house in that area.

Pulling who had worked as agent in Tupper Lake Junction station and Eagle Bay in 1905 and 1905 became agent at Raquette Lake in 1906, a position he maintained until 1933.

Despite suffering severely from arthritis, Pulling served as "ticket seller, telegraph operator, report writer, janitor and general information dispenser," remembers Kay Beals Garlipp.

"He had a keen sense of humor and was well-liked by young and old. Many a cold, wintery afternoon he tolerated the small fry in his cozy office heated by a glowing pot bellied stove, so we could listen to the chatter of the telegraph as we warmed ourselves by the fire."

For a period, Pulling's sons Earl and Dick served as assistant station agents. When the railroad service ended, Pulling became an agent in Thendara for the New York Central Railroad.

THE OWENS

Frank M. Owens was born in Minerva in 1868 of James and

Rosann Ward Owens. After his marriage to Hester Little of North Creek he operated the Forest House, located between Indian and Blue Mountain Lakes.

Owens came to Raquette Lake in 1899 to accept employment taking over the Marion River Carry. Later he served as captain on several company boats. For a period he worked at Sagamore Lodge for the Vanderbilts. By 1915 he was employed as brakeman for the Raquette Lake Railroad, a position he maintained until he was forced to resign because of ill health in 1924. He died in Raquette Lake October 1926 at age 58 and was buried at North Creek.

Frank and Hester Owens had four children: Lee, Paul, Harry and Huldah. Little is known of Lee (b. 1903). Paul Owens (b. 1907) served as a conductor for the railroad from 1929 until 1933.

Harry Owens served as T/Sgt. with the 864th Engineers Aviation Battalion in the South Pacific during World War II. While on Biak Island in New Guinea, Owens was severly injured.

Huldah (b. 1905) remained in Raquette Lake marrying Bill Egenhofer who was employed by the Raquette Lake Supply Company.

THE GARDNERS

Bertrum "Bert" Gardner was born in Elmira on February 5, 1890, son of Nelson and Evelyn Roloson Gardner. As an adult he suffered from tuberculosis and was advised to move to Arizona. Instead he headed toward the Adirondacks—where he had never been before.

"He took a train north and got to Carter," said Edgar Lamphear, "when he became curious as to where the car went from there, he wound up at Raquette Lake. No one would speak to him because he was carrying a rifle and the locals thought he was a special game warden. Later he was liked by everybody."

While at Raquette, Bert met Laurine Kavanaugh who was working in Inlet. Laurine was born September 15, 1900 in Marion, Indiana and was educated in Toronto. She received her degrees at Cornell and the University of Indiana.

The couple were married in Niagara Falls in 1925. "When they came back to Raquette on the train," recalls Edgar, "the train whistle blew and blew. Norton Bird and Darius Waldron were on the railroad together then and they always did peculiar things looking for a good time."

Before his marriage, Gardner lived alone in the house now occupied by Pat Gauthier on Mick Road. When the couple married they continued to reside there.

"In the winter," Rowena Bird, a neighbor tells, "Laurine would skate night and day."

When they were first married, Bert and Laurine leased Scotty's Inn in Inlet. Shortly after, Bert went to work for the railroad as a conductor. He switched to being a brakeman in 1929, a position he held until the railroad ceased operation in 1933. He then worked as classified ad manager for the *Denver Post*. During 1927 and 1928, Laurine taught Latin and Ancient History at the Raquette Lake School. When Bert took the position of food manager for S.S. Kresge Company near Boston, Laurine remained at Raquette while her husband commuted weekends and summers.

"Laurine always worked at a gift shop of some type," relates Rowena. "She worked at the Antlers Casino gift shop and also sold ice cream. For about two or three years she worked for the Raquette Lake Supply Company selling souvenirs."

Around 1940, Laurine and Bert acquired the property on which the firehouse stands, adjacent to their home. They also acquired the property across Route 28 where, during the 1960's, Laurine operated her own gift shop.

In the early 1970's, Pres and Pauline Taylor operated the shop. During 1976 and 1977, Leland and Loretta DeMarsh ran it, adding a bakery.

Laurine Gardner died in Florida February 1980 and Bert in April 1981. On February 12, 1981, Laurine was honored by the townspeople for her years of service on "Mrs. Gardner Day." A plaque denoting the day is on permanent display in the library.

THE DeMARSH FAMILY

The DeMarshes, year-round residents of Raquette Lake for many years, raised five sons: Perry, Richard, Greg, Matthew and Patrick, all of whom were educated in the Raquette Lake School

System. Both Loretta and Leland are state employees. Of the children, only Patrick remains in Raquette.

THE KAVANAUGHS

Gerry Kavanaugh, Laurine's cousin, was a railroad worker near Chicago. After the war he settled in Raquette Lake and moved Bird's old gas station building across Route 28 onto property owned by the Gardners, adjacent to the gift shop building. Here he and his wife Lil started "Lil and Gerry's" bar and restaurant, later to be known as "The Spoon."

Gerry was employed by the state as caretaker for Limekiln and Eighth Lake campsites. His newspaper column written under the pseudonym "Mossy Granite" was quite controversial at times. In 1978 he filled the unexpired term of Charlie Bird as town justice. During this time his wife died. A year or so later Gerry was killed in a freak automobile accident. The Spoon, still in operation, was willed to his son Wayne.

THE EGENHOFERS

Charles Egenhofer Sr. was born in Wurtenberg, Germany and his wife Josephine in Baden. They migrated to Poughkeepsie, New York.

Suffering from tuberculosis, Charles decided in the early 1900's to retreat with his family to the mountains chosing to settle in Raquette Lake.

Egenhofer worked for the railroad, cleaning cars, until his death April 22, 1913. In the 1915 census, Josephine was listed as a houseworker with three sons, Charles age 15, William age 14 and Alfred age 12.

While the children attended Raquette Lake School, they lived over the laundry near the old ice house in the village. Josephine supported her family by taking in laundry and working at the hotel.

Charles "Charlie" Egenhofer, Jr. (b. 1899) operated the "Carry Inn Hotel" also known as the "Marion River Hotel" for years. He later became station manager for the Raquette Lake Railroad, then bookkeeper for Raquette Lake Supply.

In the November 28, 1929 edition of the *Adirondack Arrow* it was noted: "Charles Egenhofer, the genial assistant station agent, slipped one over on his friends by being quietly married to Ann Shields of Utica." The couple had no children. Ann died in 1966. Charlie remained in Raquette Lake, wintering in Englewood, Florida after his retirement. He died in Englewood in 1973.

William "Bill" Egenhofer (b. 1900), connected with the Raquette Lake Supply Company since he was big enough to work, was one of the most popular and respected men of the area.

An article in the October 1, 1927 edition of the *Adirondack Herald* read: "Pretty Wedding Party at Raquette Lake. On Wednesday at 8:30 a.m. at St. William's Church, Raquette Lake, Father Henry Thameling officiated at the wedding of William Egenhofer and Miss Hilda Owens. . . . Miss Owens is a daughter of Mrs. Frank Owens of Raquette Lake. . . . A large number attending the wedding were transported to the church from Raquette Lake Station by steamboat." (The ceremony was held at St. William's on Long Point accessible only by water.)

Two sons, William (b. 1929) and Robert (b. 1931), were raised in Raquette Lake.

In 1947 the Egenhofers bought the Sunrise Terrace (Feitz Camp) on Sixth Lake, where they operated a resort business. On November 2, 1957, Bill died unexpectedly at the camp. His son Robert and family reside in Inlet.

The youngest son Alfred (b. 1903) worked for the railroad summers while attending the Boston College of Accounting. After graduation in June 1927, he moved to New York.

In the June 25, 1945 edition of both the *Glens Falls Post Star* and the *Glens Falls Times*, it was reported that, "Alfred Egenhofer, while fishing alone in the Fish Pond Section of the Jenks Beaver Meadow in the Town of Johnsburg, was killed when he was shot. The rifle, a 30-20 repeater, was fired by Gilbert Henry Wells of Wevertown who claims he saw something move in the brush nearby and assuming it to be a fox fired his rifle in that direction. When he heard groans he rushed to the spot to find Egenhofer lying face down in the marsh. The bullet entered the body just above the heart." No further details were mentioned regarding disposition of the case.

THE BIRD FAMILY

Norton Bird who came to Raquette Lake in 1900, was one of the few who "stayed on for a lifetime." He found his wife—raised his family—and left descendants in Raquette. His contributions and those of his family have played an important part in the changing times of Raquette Lake.

Norton Bird was born in Blue Mountain Lake in 1883. His parents, Edward and Fanny Bird of Indian Lake, moved to Blue Mountain about three years previous. When Norton arrived at Raquette he worked in maintenance at the Antlers. In 1905 he met Jane Rollins from Buffalo, who was employed as a waitress at the hotel and later that same year, the couple were married.

Their first home was at the site of the present home of Helen Bird. In 1909 they purchased their permanent home from John Rank, located on the corner of Antlers and Mick Roads.

In the early years, Bird worked as a guide, steamboat engineer and was employed at the various hotels and camps on the lake. In 1913 he signed on as fireman for the Raquette Lake Railroad. He became engineer in 1917, a position he held until the railroad ceased operation in 1933.

After his employment terminated with the railroad, he worked at Echo Camp (which at the time was a private estate) until his demise in 1939 at age 56. His wife Jane left Echo returning to the Bird homestead in the village.

"Mother Bird," as she was affectionately called, led a quiet life with daily visits from her family and many friends, including the children who stopped on their way from school, her daughter-in-law Marion recalls. "She was one of the early members of the Raquette Lake Chapel who worked to obtain a charter. Church on Sunday was a vital part of her life. Gardening took much of her time as she grew older, and the flowers she grew echoed the beauty of her soul." Jane Bird died in 1969 at the age of 87.

Norton and Jane Bird's family consisted of three girls and six boys. The couple suffered two tragedies in their family life. Their daughter Helen, age two, drowned about one-half mile from the village and in 1920, they lost another, Dorothy, only six at the time. "While coming home from school one cold, snowy day in November, the child was crossing the Brown's Tract River on the old wooden bridge when she slipped and fell into the icy waters.

Although she was a good swimmer, her heavy clothing and the freezing water, made it impossible for her to save herself."

Norton "Buster" Bird Jr. was born in 1908. After attending the Raquette Lake High School, he held employment in various capacities at Antlers and other hotels and camps.

"I remember when my father was engineer on the Raquette Lake Railroad," recalls Buster, now of Old Forge. "He got his running experience on the two-mile run from Thendara (then the Fulton Chain) station to the Old Forge station during 1915 and 1916.

Buster himself, later served as part time watchman and fireman until 1933 when the railroad performed its last service. To his knowledge he is the only surviving employee of the line.

"It was at the Carry Railroad I received my nickname," declares Buster. "I was always hanging around and the engineer, Rassie Scarritt, used to tease me. He gave me the name and it stuck."

Although a young man at the time, Buster recalls the fatal accident on November 9, 1913 when three Raquette Lakers were killed. "A storm blew a tree across the track in the area opposite the present location of Foley's North Woods Inn. The engine plunged down the embankment and Benjamin Hall the engineer, John Case the fireman and A.G. Lashaway the brakeman were killed."

"The conductor John Rank, was obliged to walk one and a half miles in the fog to the Burnap home (where Roberts' Four Season Cottage Colony is now on Fourth Lake), and Don Burnap's father took him by boat in the heavy fog to the telegraph office to report it."

In 1932, Buster married Laura Ford of Inlet and about two years later moved to Syracuse where they had two sons, Robert and Donald. About 1942 the family moved to Inlet. Buster started flying about 1948, eventually starting "Bird's Flying Service." His son Donald has taken over the business, with Buster's assistance.

Allen Joseph Bird, known as "Joe" was born in 1910. He too held employment at various camps, including the Antlers. It was while there he met Helen Rapp, another employee. They married June 1938 and had two children, Carol who moved to Indian Lake and Richard "Dick" who resided in Raquette with his wife Diane and children Joe, Natalie and Mark Anthony.

In 1940 they leased the waterfront property (which is the site of the present marina on Route 28) from Bert and Laurine Gardner. At first they started with a gas station, selling candy and soda and renting boats and canoes. In 1942, Joe obtained the contract from the Postal Department to revive the mailboat run from his marina, delivering mail to the camps on the lake. The first runs were made using a Gar Wood speed boat. During Joe's tour of duty in World War II, the late Larry Payne assisted Joe's wife Helen by running the mailboat.

After the war, the old gas station building was purchased by Gerry Kavanaugh who moved it across the highway. Joe expanded the marine business, built a new boathouse and replaced the original mailboat with a Chris Craft named *Dickie*. In 1949 the Ownes Cruiser *Carol* was launched.

Upon Joe's death in 1956, the mail run was continued with Pres Taylor as operator for the following twelve years. (Pres and his wife Pauline both died in the 1980's.)

In 1982 the *Carol* was replaced by the *Kara* which was in turn replaced by the *Lucy*.

The mail run has become a popular tourist attraction. For a fee, passengers may ride along while the mail is delivered, affording them an opportunity to view the old and famous camps still in existence. The smaller mailboats have now been replaced by a pontoon boat with a much larger capacity.

In the early 1960's, their son Dick further expanded the marine facilities with additional structures across the highway from the original marina.

Charles "Charlie" Bird (b. 1912) took up aviation as a hobby after his graduation from high school. As did most locals, he held various positions with the camps and hotels. While employed at Antlers, he married a schoolmate and neighbor Rowena Roblee.

During World War II, Charlie was an aviation mechanic technician serving as Sergeant 1st Class on the aircraft carrier *Bunker Hill*. While in the Pacific, the carrier was hit and Charlie was among the injured. Because of severe smoke inhalation during the fire on the *Bunker Hill*, Charlie developed emphysema. He was discharged with a commendation.

About 1946 Charlie and seven others decided to start a flying club. Members included Charlie, his brother Hod, Denny Dillon, Edgar Lamphear, all of Raquette Lake, Al Brussels and Art Miller from Old Forge, Chuck Hansen from Eagle Bay and Archie

Del Marsh from Rocky Point.

Pooling their resources they purchased a Cessna 140 that utilized pontoons in the summer and skiis in the winter in order for it to land on the lake. When not in use it was docked in the bay behind the store.

At the time Charlie had his commercial license. Several of the other members took lessons from Ellsworth flying service in Big Moose. Art Miller did not have an active interest but the others took turns using the craft.

In *Up Old Forge Way* by David H. Beetle, there was a story about the Raquette Lake Flying Club. "Last winter (1948), Charles Hansen, an Eagle Bay garage owner pulled himself out of a tough spot. He and Harold Bird were flying from Raquette to Big Moose in a ski-equipped plane when clouds boiled up unexpectedly. First Big Moose disappeared; a moment later so did Raquette. Below him, through the last hole in the clouds, he saw a remote wilderness pond, Shallow Lake. He dove down and by the time he had taxied his plane to a halt he couldn't see twenty feet."

"Finding shore, the two short-circuited the plane battery to get a fire going. They were huddled around it wishing for snowshoes when a search party of fellow members of the Raquette Lake Flying Club came upon them. Next morning they flew on to Big Moose.

In the 1950's and 1960's, during Shepherd's ownership of Bluff Point, Charlie served as caretaker. He was later employed by the state on the highways. In 1968 he was elected Town Justice, a position he held until his death in 1978. During his last years, he piloted the Boys Camp boat on a part time basis.

Rowena and Charlie Bird had two children: Kathleen now resides in Rome, and a son Jim, resides in Indian Lake with his wife and daughters. Rowena has remained in Raquette Lake, living in the family homestead on Mick Road behind the Raquette Lake Chapel.

James "Jim" Bird (b. 1916) recalls his first job. "When I was about eight to ten years old, I used to shine shoes for ten cents at the barber shop when it was attached to Carlin's Boat Livery near the railroad. When the evening train brought in the papers I would sell them around town for a nickel."

Jim's next job was as a caddy at the Antlers Golf Club. "You were old enough to caddy," said Jim, "when you could put the bag on your shoulder and it didn't drag on the ground."

After he graduated from high school he worked at the Antler's year-round, then in 1935 he worked with George Carlin at Hunter's Rest. The following year he worked in Syracuse (at the Ford agency) where he met Marion Craner. The couple married a year later in 1938 moving back to Raquette Lake where they purchased Hunter's Rest camp.

Hunter's Rest was run as an American plan hotel from the summer of 1939 through the summer of 1962. During World War II, Jim served in the army and was awarded the Bronze Star. In the July 13, 1944 edition of the *Adirondack Arrow* it was noted "T/S James Bird and his brother T/3 Joe Bird recently were fortunate enough to meet in England and spend a short time together." Marion, with the help of her sister, Mae, and brother-in-law, Hubie Lee, continued to run the establishment while Jim completed his tour of duty.

The Birds sold Hunter's Rest in 1964. Jim continued his career as a contractor and construction worker gaining the reputation of being able to do almost anything with his "machine." He has moved huge buildings from one place to another—on land and across the ice. He has engineered what seemed "impossible feats" almost single-handedly. Among other projects, the two-story boathouse at North Point was cut in half and transformed into two houses with the help of his brother-in-law, Jerry Lanphear.

In 1971 the Adirondack Park Agency was formed for the purpose of protecting the land, rivers and lakes of the Adirondack park. James Bird was appointed by Governor Nelson Rockefeller to be one of the first members to serve on the agency. Bird, because of his interest in the welfare of the Adirondacks accepted the appointment serving for a period of four years. His term expired November 1975.

Jim and his wife Marion, reside in Charlie Bennett's homestead at Antlers (built by Joe Bryere in 1905) which they purchased in 1958.

Mary Bird (b. 1919) attended beauty culture school in Syracuse after graduating from the Raquette Lake High School. In 1940 she married Jerry Lanphear, a native Raquette Laker. The couple operated the Marion River Cabins and restaurant for several years, then from 1963 until 1969 they operated the North Point Cottages. After leaving North Point they moved to their permanent home on a parcel (part of Poplar Point) which they purchased from Mrs. Warrick, widow of Dr. Warrick.

Jerry and Mary have one daughter Marcia, who is married to James Roblee and one grandson Jamie.

Frederick Bird (b. 1925), after graduating from the Raquette Lake High School, was employed by Hunter's Rest, Antlers, Sunset Camp and Echo Camp. He then became involved in marine service and repairs at Carlin's Marina and Hunter's Rest.

During World War II he served as a corporal in the Marine Corps. After his discharge he married Janet Puffer of Inlet and returned to work in marine service. He left Raquette Lake to work with George Richards who maintained the Johnson dealership in Utica. Later he gained employment in West Virginia, Iowa and Florida.

In 1986 he was operating his own marine business on the west coast of Florida where he maintains a permanent residence with his wife. The couple have six children: Candice, Brenda, William, Mary Jane, Joseph and Edward.

Harold "Hod" Bird was first employed as a caddy at Antlers. This was followed by employment at several of the camps and hotels on Raquette. Later he worked at Carlin's Boat Livery and Echo Camp.

During the late 1940's, Hod was employed at Antlers, Sagamore and Kill Kare.

In 1941 Bird married Mary Louise "Rosie" Axtel of Old Forge. She had the distinction of being one of the first certified lifeguards in New York State. The couple had four children: Barbara, Dorothy, Janice and James.

In 1954, he and his wife Rosie moved from Kill Kare to California where he was employed as superintendent for the Shadow Valley Ranch owned by George Vanderbilt of Sagamore in Raquette Lake.

When the Birds moved to California, two associates from Kill Kare went with him. In 1962, one of them, Gerald Feistamel and Hod were involved in a fatal automobile accident. Hod's family remained in California where Rosie died September 7, 1986.

In 1972, Donna and Dean Pohl purchased the Bird homestead from the estate. They have renovated and enlarged it, using it as their permanent home. Both Donna and Dean (a private contractor) are employed at the Boys and Girls Camps in the summer. They have four children: Bill, Rachel, Jim and Rebecca.

THE WALDRONS

The last of the railroad men whose descendants still reside in Raquette Lake was Darius Waldron.

Darius (sometimes pronounced Drycy) Waldron was born in 1886 son of John and Nancy McCarthy Waldron of North Creek. As a young man he was employed as a stagecoach driver on the route from North Creek to Blue Mountain Lake (a round trip took three days).

On October 6, 1909 he married Marguerite "Minnie" Hunt who was born in 1887 of Charles T. Hunt and Myra Blanchard at Indian Lake. Charlie Hunt was a well-known craftsman who built the rustic furniture for J. P. Morgan's Camp Uncas. Minnie first visited Raquette Lake at the age of twelve when she stayed with her sister Lucy Blanchard on Green Point.

Darius and Minnie Waldron moved to Raquette Lake where he built their home on Pug Bay. He traveled across the bay in a naphtha launch daily to North Point where he worked as a carpenter for his brother-in-law, Almon (Allie) Hunt, who was Carnegie's caretaker at the time.

In the 1915 census Waldron was listed as a steamboat captain in Raquette. That year, the Waldrons had twin sons, Harry and Howard.

When Darius started working for the railroad in 1920, the family moved to the village living in an apartment over the railroad station. The young boys amused themselves by watching for the train to come into town so they could wave a greeting to their dad in the cab of the locomotive.

Later the Waldrons moved to an apartment over Carlin's machine shop. About 1922, they purchased the family homestead on Antlers Road on the hill leading to Mick Road.

Darius Waldron remained with the railroad until it ceased operation in 1933. He died January 1957. His wife, Minnie died December 1964 in Pompano Beach, Florida where she was spending the winter.

Harry Waldron, one of the twins, became a carpenter. He helped build housing at Pine Camp (Watertown), which is now Fort Drum, home of the 10th Mountain Division. He was also employed at the Tahawus location of the National Lead Company, building apartments for the personnel. When Cortland

State College acquired the Huntington property of Pine Knot, Harry worked refurbishing the buildings.

Waldron entered the U.S. Army in 1941 serving the European Theater. He was discharged as S/Sgt. in October of 1945.

Harry married Beatrice (Bea) Myers Townsend. Bea taught business for eight years at Mohawk Central School and three years at Herkimer High School. "In 1946," recalls Bea, "William Fenner, principal of Raquette Lake School was anxious to reinstate a business course which had previously been eliminated from the high school curriculum. I was hired to teach the course." Bea left Raquette Lake in 1947, returning in 1949 to start a family. That year the couple purchased property on South Bay. The house built by Andrew Sims in the 1890's still stands.

In 1965 Bea Waldron went back to Raquette Lake School as kindergarten teacher. On June 8, 1975, the Parent Teachers and Friends of the Raquette Lake Union Free School held a tea in honor of Bea's retirement after twenty-two years of teaching. Many of her old students attended the affair. A silver tray was presented to her as a sign of gratitude for her many years of service. Harry became caretaker at Baekeland Camp on Utowana Lake in 1951, a position he still maintains (1986).

The couple had one daughter Mary Henry who resides in Old Forge with her two daughters.

Howard Waldron, Harry's twin, also became a carpenter after completing his education. In 1939 he married Emma Lou Leonard of Raquette Lake, daughter of Moses and Inez Stevens Leonard. The couple have two children, Betty and Bob.

During World War II, Howard worked on the Alcan (now Alaska) Highway. In 1950 the couple and Howard's brother Maurice went to Alaska, staying from April to October. Emma Lou worked at the Post Office and ran a restaurant and the men did commercial fishing.

In 1954, Howard and Emma Lou opened Waldron's Grocery store on Route 28 which is still in operation.

Their son Bob, who left Raquette in 1965 to attend college, returned to the area permanently in 1978. He married Colette Reffay while in France. Colette was employed as a French teacher at Cornell. During the summer months, she and their son Matthew join Bob at Raquette. On December 5, 1986, Bob and Colette Waldron became the parents of twin girls, Camille and Clare.

The couple purchased the Marion River Cottages and restaurant which Bob turned into a cabinet shop. He now owns Waldron Carpentry, working throughout the North Country.

Emma and Howard's daughter Betty, married Jim Bennett from Indian Lake in 1959. They live in Chittenango with their family of two boys and two girls. Jim is a manager for United Parcel in Syracuse.

In addition to the twins, the Waldrons had two daughters. Marguerite who married Charles Windhausen settled in Pompano Beach, Florida. Marie married James Regan, only son of summer people James and Betty Regan, who worked for Ladew on Osprey Island and later at Antlers. Marie and James Regan purchased the Waldron homestead in 1968 from Howard and Emma Lou Waldron who had owned it for three years. James and Marie Waldron Regan had five children: Patricia, Jack, Joan, Carol Ann and Jim who married Maureen Dillon of Raquette Lake.

Another son of Darius and Minnie Waldron was Oliver who also settled in Pompano Beach, Florida.

Maurice (pronounced Morris) Waldron (b. 1925) was born in the Waldron homestead on Antlers Road. He served as an Air Corps Sgt. during World War II from March 1945 until October 1947, after which he worked for the state. In 1950 after returning from Alaska, Maurice became employed in maintenance at Cortland's Outdoor Education Center at Pine Knot, a position he held until 1985. Maurice now operates his own excavating contracting business in Raquette.

In September of 1953, Maurice married Elizabeth Grace "Betty" Dunay from Binghamton. At the time Betty and her brother were in business together at the Wood Hotel in Inlet.

The couple have three children: Nancy Ann, a horticulturist in interior design in Silver Spring, Maryland, Elizabeth Marie, a therapist aide working with the mentally retarded at the Syracuse Development Center and Joseph William, who lives in Raquette Lake employed as a ranger at the Golden Beach campsite during the summer.

THE END OF THE OLD STATION

The last remaining link between the railroad and Raquette Lake was the Old Station terminal and restaurant. During the early years it was used for meetings, church services and, in the back, a section was reserved for use by Judge Dillon for his office and court.

The upstairs apartment housed many native families at one time or another, and after the fire in 1927, it served as a library for a short period.

In 1936 the Raquette Lake Supply company purchased the nearby property of the abandoned Raquette Lake Railway including the Old Station. Until 1970, the Old Station had functioned intermittently as a restaurant and a bar.

In July 1971, Jim and Linda Cleaveland Rogers and Gene and Carol Cleaveland Darling reopened the Old Station. The group preserved the original atmosphere planning to maintain service on a year-round basis.

> On December 8, 1972 the Old Station was destroyed by fire. About 3:20 p.m. Tim Dillon saw flames leaping from the windows at the east end of the building. He immediately ran into the bar room and screamed, "The station is on fire!" Joined by Kurt Forsell, the two sped to the fire hall in Kurt's truck to sound the fire alarm and prepare the fire equipment.
>
> Dean Pohl, who was at the building at the time, grabbed a fire extinguisher, ran to the back of the kitchen and attempted to extinguish the blaze.
>
> However, he was forced back by the intense heat. Joined by two other patrons, Harry Waldron and Frank Lamphear, Pohl went out into the ice and started breaking a hole with a rock. Meanwhile, Fred Burke shut all the doors at the back of the building, then ran to the store and got an axe to make the hole in the ice larger. At about that time, the fire truck arrived. Soon after, assistance was requested from Blue Mountain and Inlet.
>
> Although firemen fought the blaze all afternoon and into early evening, it was of no use. The icy patches on the road between the station and the lake made it hazardous to the men pumping water from

> the lake to fight the blaze. By 5:45 p.m. most of the building was leveled and the neighboring fire assistance disbanded.

Through the night volunteer firemen from Raquette watched to prevent the fire from spreading toward the Raquette Lake Supply gas tanks a few hundred yards away.

During the night a new flame would burst forth within the remains where a spark rekindled; smoke filled the cold air rising from the dying embers. Occasionally a car would drive up and pause near the lake as though its passengers were paying their last respects to an old friend.

Just before daybreak, only the front portals were still standing. Finally they too gave up and crumpled to the ground . . . thus ending an era in the history of Raquette Lake.

After the fire, the Rogers left Raquette Lake. The Darlings remained. The Old Station was never rebuilt.

CHAPTER XII

THE CHANGING TIMES

Throughout the history of Raquette Lake many changes have come about. Some things, however, may never change.

Families residing on Long Point and other areas accessible only by water must still travel by boat during the summer months and across the ice in winter.

Tapping the maple trees in the backyard or in "sugar bush" areas will always be a spring activity. In earlier years, syrup, maple sugar candy and cookies were made and sold at some of the local camps. Today, sappin' and making syrup, Jack Wax and sugar in the yard remains a family project.

During the winter when the lake is frozen over and covered with snow, it is still necessary to shovel the snow off the ice to clear a space for a good skating area—and when the new snow falls, all too soon—a new area must be cleared. This goes on over and over each year.

Skiing equipment in earlier years, consisted of a pair of wooden skiis with toe straps and no poles. The ski slope was the Mick family's yard, as they lived on a steep hill. How high up the hill one went to ski depended upon one's skill as a skiier. To add a bit of spice, a jump was made near the bottom of the hill. There was no room for slowing down by going back and forth across the hill so one just "bombed" it. Although travel to other ski areas is much easier now, youngsters still use the local ski hill as well as the lake and wooded area for cross-country skiing.

Sledding down the back road (Mick and Whelan road) remains a winter pastime. With modern sleighs and saucers there is no need to ride down the hill on a "skip jack," but it was more fun. This conveyance was a barrel stave on which a center post with a board for a seat was mounted. To ride it, one balanced on the edge of an incline, put up one's feet trying to reach the bottom without falling off. The vehicle had to be made, as it could not be purchased.

The day the ice begins to go out remains an exciting one. The ice, all honeycombed and black in color, needs one warm day with a south wind. Weird moans and groans are heard as large slabs of ice begin to crack. More and more open water shows while the ice piles up along the shore. Residents bet on the time and day it will officially be declared "out." Some who can't wait, try to hurry things along by pushing the ice with a boat hook or breaking up areas using small motor boats. Eventually, of course, the whole lake opens up.

Raquette Lake, the once prosperous summer community, boasting large estates and wealthy landowners, took on a less ostentatious image once the railroad was gone. Train whistles are no longer heard in the distance. Not even the tracks or station remain as visible proof Raquette was once a railroad town.

A TIME TO REMEMBER

Natives who remember the railroad days enjoy sharing their memories of that period.

"People watching was a favorite pastime for old and young alike. We often watched the "sleeper" come in the morning," told Kay Garlipp, "and we rarely missed watching it go out in the evening."

"One sleeper we never missed was around the first of July when the boys and girls arrived from New York City to spend the summer at the Raquette Lake Boys and Girls Clubs. We vicariously enjoyed this excitement and had a chance to see the latest fashions. Likewise we were on hand to witness their departure Labor Day night."

To this day, arrival and departure at the childrens' camps mark the beginning and closing of the main tourist season.

"Excursion days," continued Kay, "brought in a greater influx of visitors. Natives enjoyed the garb and gab of those rushing between train and boat."

Excursion day was every Thursday during the summer. The day started early at the hotels, not only on Raquette Lake but along the route of the Raquette Lake Railway.

"We would have to rise early," recalls Freda Westfall, "picnic lunches had to be prepared for the guests to take with them. The Fulton Chain steamboat would stop at our dock about nine o'clock to pick up the passengers, and many times we had about one hundred sandwiches to make before this."

As the travelers disembarked from the train, many rushed into Griffith's station restaurant enticed by the aroma of coffee and fresh-baked bread.

"Aunt Kate, Griffith's sister, was cook," volunteered Henry Carlin, "and lived up to her reputation. Bill of fare was limited but excellent. The tables with their clean, crisp tablecloths and napkins made one feel at home. The breakfast menu offered three choices - beefsteak, chicken or ham and eggs. Price for any one was a dollar and no one went away hungry."

After breakfast, about eleven a.m., everyone would board the steamer *Adirondack*. On extra heavy days the *Tuscarora* would also be put into service. As the steamboat traveled up the lake it would stop at the various camps, dropping off or picking up passengers. At Antlers, Brightside or one of the other camps, guests carrying their picnic lunches would join the other excursionists.

As the boat steamed up the Marion River, the beauty of the clear water reflecting the emerald green trees and the bright blue sky with its white marshmallow clouds, the scent of clean, fresh mountain air, the sounds of chirping birds and croaking frogs, presented an air of peace and tranquility.

Arriving at the Carry, passengers left the steamer to board the small open-carriage train which bore them the short distance to another steamboat which would transport them across Utowana, Eagle and Blue Mountain Lakes.

Louise Porter Payne recalls the trips made on the open train were a frightening experience for her as a child. "There were no sides on the train and when I sat on those cane seats, I was too short for my feet to touch the floor. I kept sliding off and I was afraid I was going to slide right off the train."

Her sister who was taller, could brace her feet on the seat in

Courtesy Bertha Conley

Here a teamster waits for the five o'clock train to unload. Circa 1920's.

front of her, and like most passengers, enjoyed the short trip which allowed just enough time for the conductor to hurry along the running board of the train, swinging from door to door as he collected fare tickets.

The excursion was more travel than anything else. Once at Blue Mountain there was nothing to do except picnic near the water or hike the half-mile to the foot of Blue Mountain where one could then climb to the top to enjoy the magnificent view and visit the fire tower.

Later the whole trip would be reversed, "enlivened by a pair of musicians, one playing a banjo, the other an accordion, both willing to play any requested number."

"Sometimes," said Edna Colligan, "my brother and I would take the boat up the Marion River and then get out to pick blueberries. We'd come back on the late boat in the evening. We'd never pay. They never charged the local kids."

As it neared the end of the tourist season, it would be dark enough to see Antlers all lit up. The sound of laughter and chatter would carry across the lake and as the steamer drew closer to the camp, the music became louder and you could see the young couples as they danced.

"I remember," added Kay Garlipp, "a special privilege we were granted, especially in winter, was riding around the loop. After the passengers and freight were unloaded from the train, it had to be turned around so it was ready to start out the next time. For this purpose the track circled out around the village so the train could be backed into the station area in the right direction for the return trip. Provided we sat quietly on the seats we were allowed by the conductor to ride in the passenger coach while this was done. Woe to anyone who abused the privilege for it meant a long time would go by before you could ride again."

Rowena Bird recalled another treat the children enjoyed. "When the teamsters were waiting for the guests to arrive on the train, we were allowed to ride behind the four-horse team, in the buggy or sleigh, depending on the time of year, while the men exercised the horses."

"It was so cozy in the winter," she continued, "snuggled under the fur lap robes, listening to the bells on the horses jingle. The horses were always decorated, winter or summer. They had red ribbons braided into their mane and tail, and some had cockades in their bridles. They looked so handsome!"

"The passengers, wearing raccoon coats, would bundle up in the fur robes and heavy blankets," added Edna Colligan, "then the help would put hot soapstones underneath to keep them warm."

"Gone are the days," said Denny Dillon, "when we'd warm ourselves in front of the potbellied stove as we waited with old Bill Pulling watching for the trains to bring in the freight."

"When the baggage man unloaded the freight," he explained, "he slid each piece down a plank where it was distributed. Each camp or establishment had its own name or identification, which was called and the owners retrieved his freight."

"It was too long to keep calling Raquette Lake Supply, so our freight name was 'Soup.' We had to have our butter shipped in five-pound round cartons and milk in five-gallon cans from Remsen's Dairyman's League plant. This and other perishables were immediately transported to the cooler which was filled with ice, harvested the previous winter."

The spirit of that peirod of Raquette Lake history is summarized by Edna's response. "Oh! Those were the days! After the road was built from Inlet through to Blue Mountain everyone was so excited about the road and the advent of the automobile in the area, it overshadowed the passing of the railroad and steamboat."

"Looking back on it now," she said sadly, "it seems a shame. Life seemed more fun then - less complicated. All of us who remember, miss the 'good old days.'"

Several years ago Rowena Bird wrote a poem about the railroad days. It seems appropriate to close this chapter and this volume of the changing times of Raquette Lake sharing "a time to remember."

Raquette Lake was once a railroad town,
Full of bustle, trains and railroad sounds.
Departed at one for Carter and the Main Line,
Returned at 5:15—we set our clocks by the time.

The sleeper went out at 8 p.m.
While the people would wave and call.
Then quiet settled over the Lake
As the evening shadows fall.

Norton Bird, Darcy Waldron, Slim and Bert Gardner,
On the job without fail.
With their hands upon the throttle,
And their eyes upon the rail.

This all created a village scene
As the whole Town turned out for the 5:15.
First came the camp help and relatives
Stepping down from the train.
Then later Vanderbilts, Morgans, celebrities and guests
In sunshine and rain.

For thirty-four years the whistle blew,
The smoke pouring from the stack.
And sometimes we wish again
The old Railroad days were back.

—Rowena Bird

BIBLIOGRAPHY

Aber, Ted. *Adirondack Folks*. Prospect Books, 1980.

__________ and King, Stella. *The History of Hamilton County*. Great Wilderness Books, 1965.

Adirondack Arrow. November 28, 1929, May 14, 1931, June 1931, July 13, 1944.

Adirondack Echo. June 27, 1986.

Adirondack Herald. October 1, 1927.

Adirondack Museum. MS 65-14, July 23, 1956; MS 65-29, Josiah Blackwell Blossom to James Blackwell Blossom, August 8, 1886: A.F. Tait Papers; MS 65-38, Snyder Papers; MS 61-132, A.M. Callahan and MS Diary, September-October 1929.

Adirondack Private Preserves. 8th annual report of the Forest, Fish and Game Commission of New York State. Wyncoop, Hollenback & Crawford Co. (1903)

Albany Times Union. December 21, 1958.

Applegate, Howard Lewis. *The Story of Sagamore*. University College of Syracuse University.

Beetle, David H. *Up Old Forge Way*. North Country Books, 1972.

Blanchard, Earl. *History of Pine Island*.

Book of Deeds #47. August 2, 1884, pg. 422. Original abstract of Case from the State of New York to Stott dated June 10, 1884.

Book of Deeds #4. June 2, 1904, pg. 126. Quit claim deed from William K. Mead to Frank H. Stott dated October 29, 1885.

Boonville Herald. May 1976.

Brundige, Harry T. *The American Mercury - Never Never Land*.

Cadbury, Warder H. (reprint) *Murray's Adirondack in the Wilderness*. Weed, Parson and Co. 1880.

Callahan, Maurice. Diary for Raquette Lake Transportation Co. 1905-1929.

Carmichael, Rev. 100th Anniversary Report on Church of the Good Shepherd.

Colvin, Verplanck. 7th annual report of the Topographical Survey of the Adirondack Region of New York, 1874.

Cortland State College. "History of Huntington." 35th anniversary pamphlet.

DeCosta, B.F. *Lake George, Schroon Lake and the Adirondack,* 1868.

DeSormo, Maitland D. *The Heydays of the Adirondacks*. Yesteryears, Inc., 1974.

Donaldson, Alfred L. *A History of the Adirondacks* (2 vol.). The Century Co., 1921.

Fennell, Lee. Interview of Margaret (Collins) Cunningham, "Coalition to Save Camp Sagamore," 1983.

First Assistant Postmaster General. February 2 and November 1, 1889; from 1900 to 1946, Raquette Lake Post Office records.

Forest Commission of New York State. Annual reports, 1886-1895. The Argus Co. James B. Lyon et al.

Fuge, Margaret and Waldron, Beatrice. 50th Anniversary report on Raquette Lake Chapel.

Gilborn, Craig. *Durant*. North Country Books, Inc. in cooperation with Adirondack Museum, 1981.

Glens Falls Post Star, June 25, 1945.

Grady, Joseph F. *The Adirondacks, Fulton Chain - Big Moose Region*. North Country Books, Inc. 1st-1933; 2nd-1966; 3rd-1972.

Hamilton County Clerks Office. Litigation Folder #565, Complaint dated September 24, 1901.

Hamilton County News. October 1983, March 2, 1983 ("Way Things Were," Ted Aber), January 15, 1976, October 1981.

Harter, Henry A. *Fairy Tale Railroad*. North Country Books, Inc., 1979.

Headley, Joel T. *The Adirondack or Life in the Woods*. Scribner, Armstrong and Company, 1849.

Hochschild, Harold K. *Township 6*. Harold K. Hochschild, 1952.

__________. "Lumberjacks & Rivermen in the Central Adirondacks." Adirondack Museum, 1962.

__________. "Life & Leisure in the Adirondack Backwoods." Adirondack Museum, 1962.

__________. "Steamboats on Raquette and Blue Mountain Lakes." Adirondack Museum, 1962.

Hough, Dr. Benjamin Franklin. *History of St. Lawrence and Franklin Counties*. Little & Co., 1853; Regional Pub. 1970.

Hoyt, Edwin P. *The Vanderbilts and Their Fortunes*. Doubleday & Co., 1902.

Jamieson, Paul F. *The Adirondack Reader*. Adirondack Mountain Club, 1982.

Kaiser, Harvey H. *Great Camps of the Adirondacks*. David R. Godine, 1982.

Keller, Jane E. *Adirondack Wilderness*. Syracuse University Press, 1980.

Lossing, Benson J. *The Hudson*. Kennikat Press, 1972.

Morning Herald. September 12, 1899.

Murray, William H. *Adventures in the Wilderness or Camp Life in the Adirondacks*. Fields, Osgood & Co., 1869.

New York Sun Times. September 5, 1983.

New York Times. Spring 1915 (*Lusitania*), March 17, 1926.

Raquette Lake Post Office. 1889 Record Book.

Raquette Lake School. Raquette Report, December 16, 1976.

Reference Policy #51609, August 31, 1967; Joseph Uzdavinis and Richard Cohen; Title Insurance by Monroe Abstract.

Stoddard, Seneca Ray. *The Adirondacks Illustrated*. Stoddard, 1874, 1917; Adirondack Yesteryears, Inc., 1972.

Stott's Private Journal.

St. William's Catholic Church Chronicle, 1929-1933.

Tupper Lake Free Press and Herald. "Spirit of the Times." 1849.

U.S. Census Bureau Report. 1880, 1850, 1880, 1905.

Wallace, Edwin R. *Discriptive Guide to the Adirondacks*. Waverly Publishing Co., 1875; Wallace; Forest and Stream Publishing Co., 1876.

Warrensburg News. February 21, 1901, January 6, 1916, March 20, 1920, December 11, 1924.

Watertown Times. November 1962.

Wessels, William L. *Adirondack Profiles*. Adirondack Resorts Press, 1961.

White, William Chapman. *Adirondack Country*. Alfred A. Knopf, 1977.

AUTHOR'S NOTE: All family histories were verified by conversation with living relatives when possible.

INDEX

FAMILY NAMES

SUBJECT NAMES